AF262753

FRANK S. MATSURA

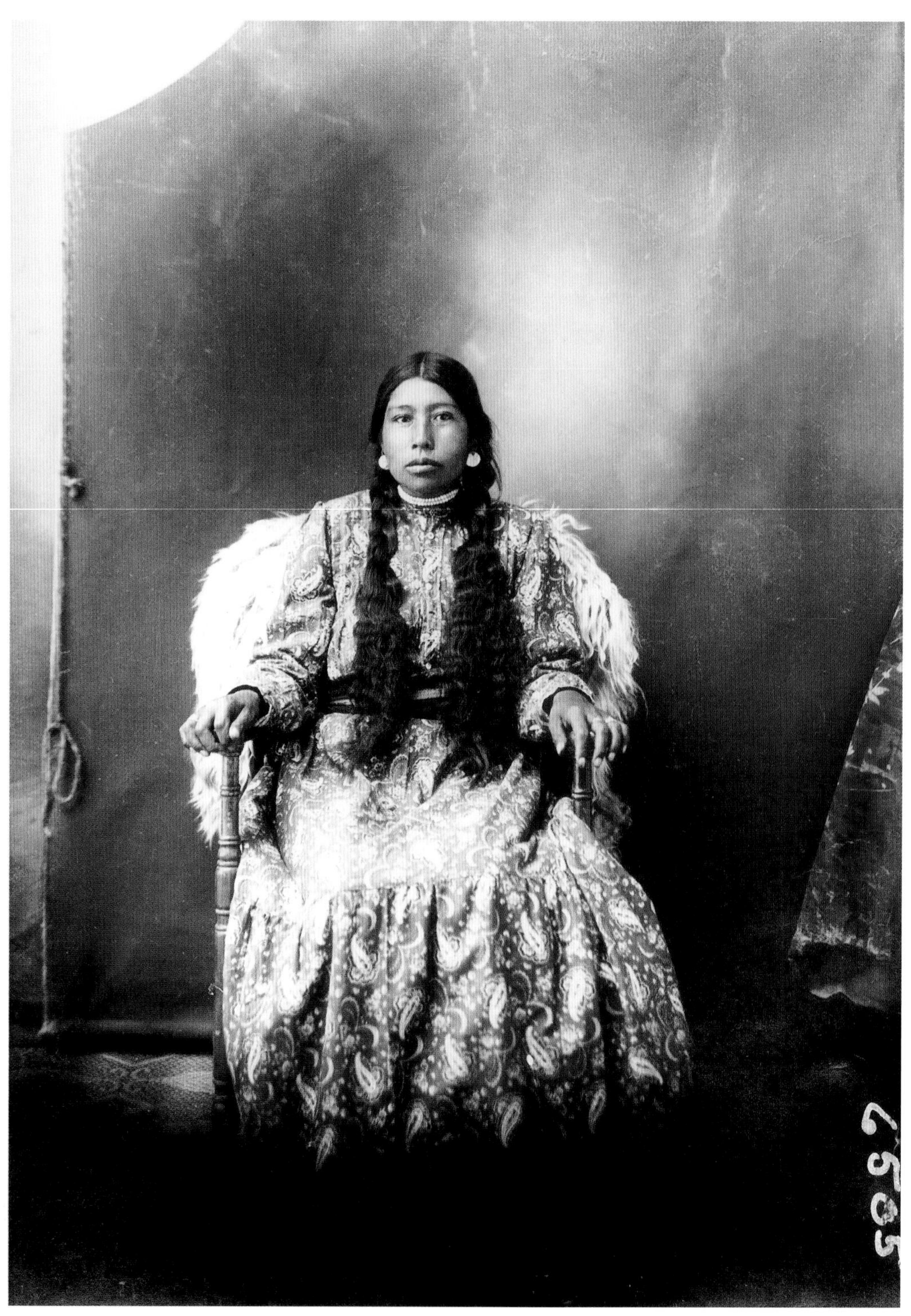

FRANK S. MATSURA

ICONOCLAST PHOTOGRAPHER
OF THE AMERICAN WEST

❖

Edited by

Michael Holloman

PA PRESS

PRINCETON ARCHITECTURAL PRESS · NEW YORK

For my two sons,
Van David and Tomoaki,
who remain my most heartfelt inspiration

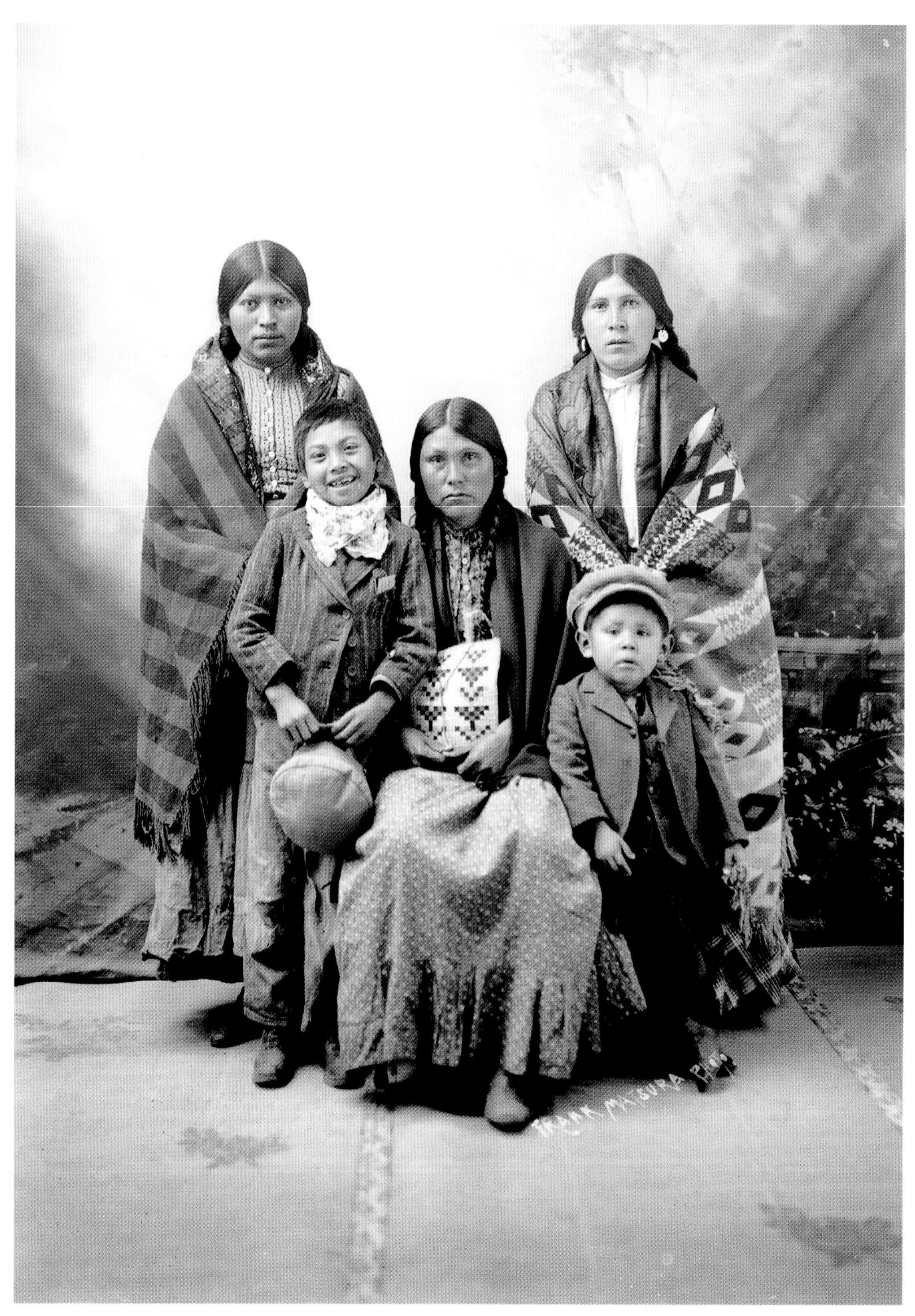

FRANK MATSURA PHOTO

CONTENTS

Introduction · 9
Michael Holloman

CHAPTER ONE · 19

INDIGENOUS HOMELANDS THROUGH
A PHOTOGRAPHER'S LENS

Laurie Arnold, PhD

CHAPTER TWO · 41

FRANK MATSURA'S COYOTE PHOTOGRAPHY:
BETWEEN SETTLER COLONIALISM
AND NATIVE SURVIVANCE

Glen Mimura, PhD

CHAPTER THREE · 83

PHOTOGRAPHY, PLAY, AND
DISSONANT SEEING

Maki Fukuoka, PhD

CHAPTER FOUR · 111

"MATSURA DID THEM RIGHT"

Beth Harrington

Selected Photographs · 135

Conclusion · 159
Michael Holloman

ACKNOWLEDGMENTS · 161
NOTES · 162
CREDITS · 165
CONTRIBUTOR BIOGRAPHIES · 166

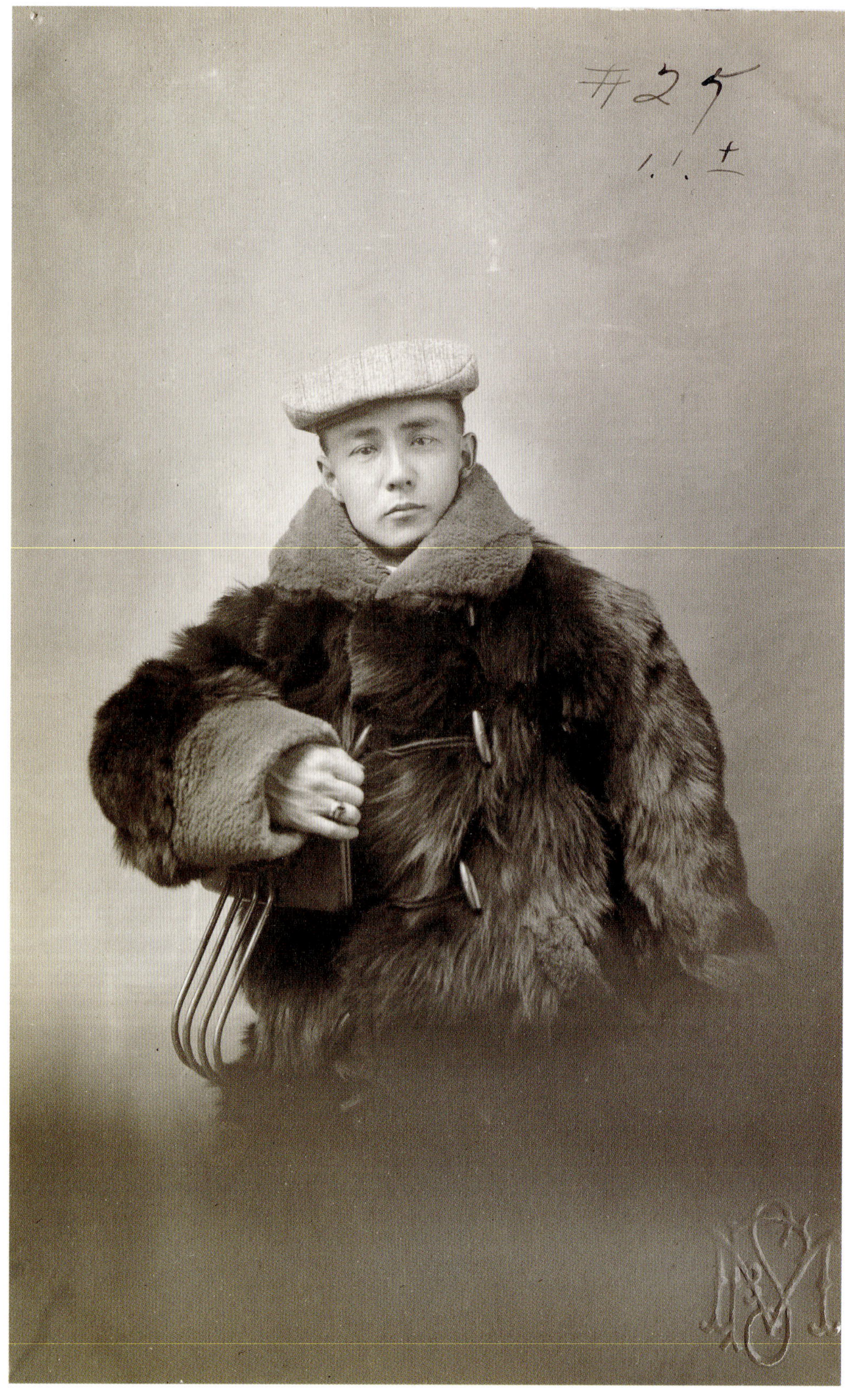
#25
1.1.±

INTRODUCTION

—

Michael Holloman

Japanese immigrant Frank Sakae Matsura (1873–1913) left an indelible photographic archive of his life in a remote pioneer community, which has captured the interest of many today. He mysteriously arrived in Seattle from Japan in 1901, then traveled north to Alaska, and in 1903 took a menial job in Washington State's Okanogan region as a hotel worker. Prior to his untimely death at thirty-nine he navigated an ebbing frontier society in transition that saw the local Indigenous population determined to maintain some agency in their homelands, all while riverboats, stagecoaches, and, later, automobiles brought new technologies and ideas to what was most recently a locale for trappers, miners, and cattlemen. He was a unique character who many identified with immediately. Matsura the photographer quickly became a popular member of the bustling community, and many flocked to his studio for personal portraitures.

Matsura's eclectic body of work was done essentially in the last ten years of his life. The hundreds of visual records he created documented local events big and small, including unique studio portraits of a variety of citizens throughout the community and some of the most poignant and potent images of Native Americans from the

OPPOSITE
Matsura in Fur Coat Self-Portrait, ca. 1910. Matsura sits for a self-portrait at his studio in Okanogan. He is wearing a thick fur coat and a cap. His right arm grasps the back of a chair turned sideways.

era. Here Matsura's photographs offer an intimate look at many Native Americans whom he had come to know on a personal basis. This intimacy defied any interest of a paternalistic gaze of photographic romanticism or nostalgia.

The 1915 Panama-Pacific International Exposition world's fair was held in San Francisco. It was attended by thousands who were amazed at the modern rebuilt municipality, which was less than a decade removed from the catastrophic 1906 earthquake. Two years prior, and nine hundred miles north in the little-known and recently incorporated town of Okanogan, Matsura was laid to rest in the local cemetery with an amazingly large group of friends and acquaintances in attendance.

Tying these two disparate events together expands upon the symbolic portrayal of San Francisco's world's fair as one of the final endnotes to the closing of the American Western frontier. The fair celebrated the new century, new technologies, and innovations, including the recent completion of the Panama Canal, the invention of the incandescent light bulb, and the accelerating future of the automobile. Of equal measure, the growing mythology of the American West was typified by the fair's artistic gold prize recipient, James Earle Fraser and his eighteen-foot-tall plaster sculpture, *End of the Trail*. This iconic image persists today, depicting the Native American warrior who sits on horseback with his head and back bowed in resignation to an unwelcoming modernity (while his nonthreatening spear is pointed to the ground). The historic transition of past to present, technology and opportunity, and diverse people and places all converge in unexpected ways and define uniquely the remarkable images that Matsura took during his short stay among the borderlands of north-central Washington State.

The story of how his artistic legacy escaped obscurity and found favor is quite remarkable. By no means was Matsura the first photographer to document the American West and its regional tribes. Nor was he the only Japanese photographer to travel with a camera during this period of American history. He didn't have a monopoly on the medium, either, as he was one of two photographers working in the local communities along the Okanogan River, while another photographer was working at the Colville Agency of the Bureau of Indian Affairs forty miles east in the Nespelem Valley. However, his singular distinction has risen due to fortuitous circumstances, committed community members, and an unexpected contemporary recognition of his artistic accomplishments that has gained favor while others have been lost to time in comparison.

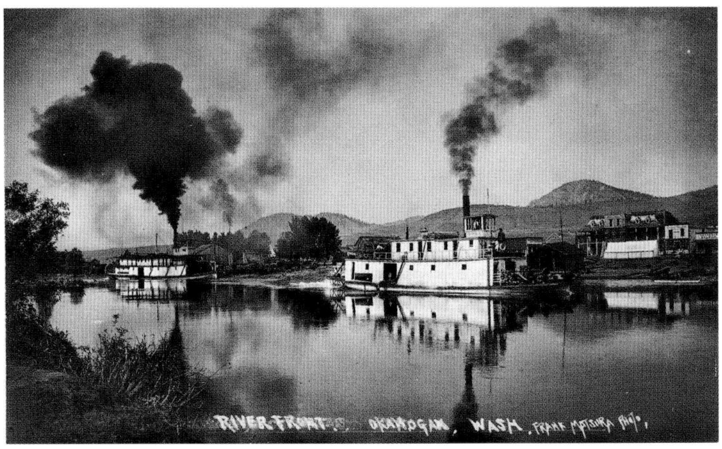

The North Star *and* Enterprise *on the Okanogan River*, ca. 1907. *Okanogan Independent*, July 19, 1907, article: "Frank Matsura, the photographer, has been taking some excellent pictures of views in and about Okanogan. Among others are some scenes along the river front [*sic*] while steamboats were at landing."

When author JoAnn Roe published her 1981 book, *Frank Matsura: Frontier Photographer,* she was intent on bringing a local legend's story to a larger public for the first time.[1] Three years later TV Asahi in Japan presented a two-hour docudrama on Matsura. A decade later author Tatsuo Kurihara traveled from Japan to the Okanogan Valley to expand the scholarship for Japanese audiences. All were essentially historic narratives. American curator Rayna Green led the way for recent academic interest, which has bolstered his stature as an early player in the cultural and political dynamics of race, immigration, diaspora, and gender studies.[2]

Discussing Matsura and his artistic capabilities is often secondary to his personal identity and background. It is easy to note that he was a professional photographer, but there is no evidence of this experience before arriving in America. He purchased an expensive camera with borrowed money while mired in a menial job at the Elliot Hotel in Conconully a number of years before his move to the nearby river town of Okanogan. He spoke English confidently, he was clever and industrious, and he was able to purchase a studio and later a home. Academics, collectors, and locals who all share a common interest simply refer to him as Frank. Curiosity and inspired speculation about his life before coming to America continue regarding his artistic intentions and personal experiences when he wasn't staying employed with his camera. The blank spots are the allure, because so many of his images are visually inviting. What exists are comments and references about Matsura that showed up in local news articles of the day and familial stories passed on that still exist throughout the local communities.

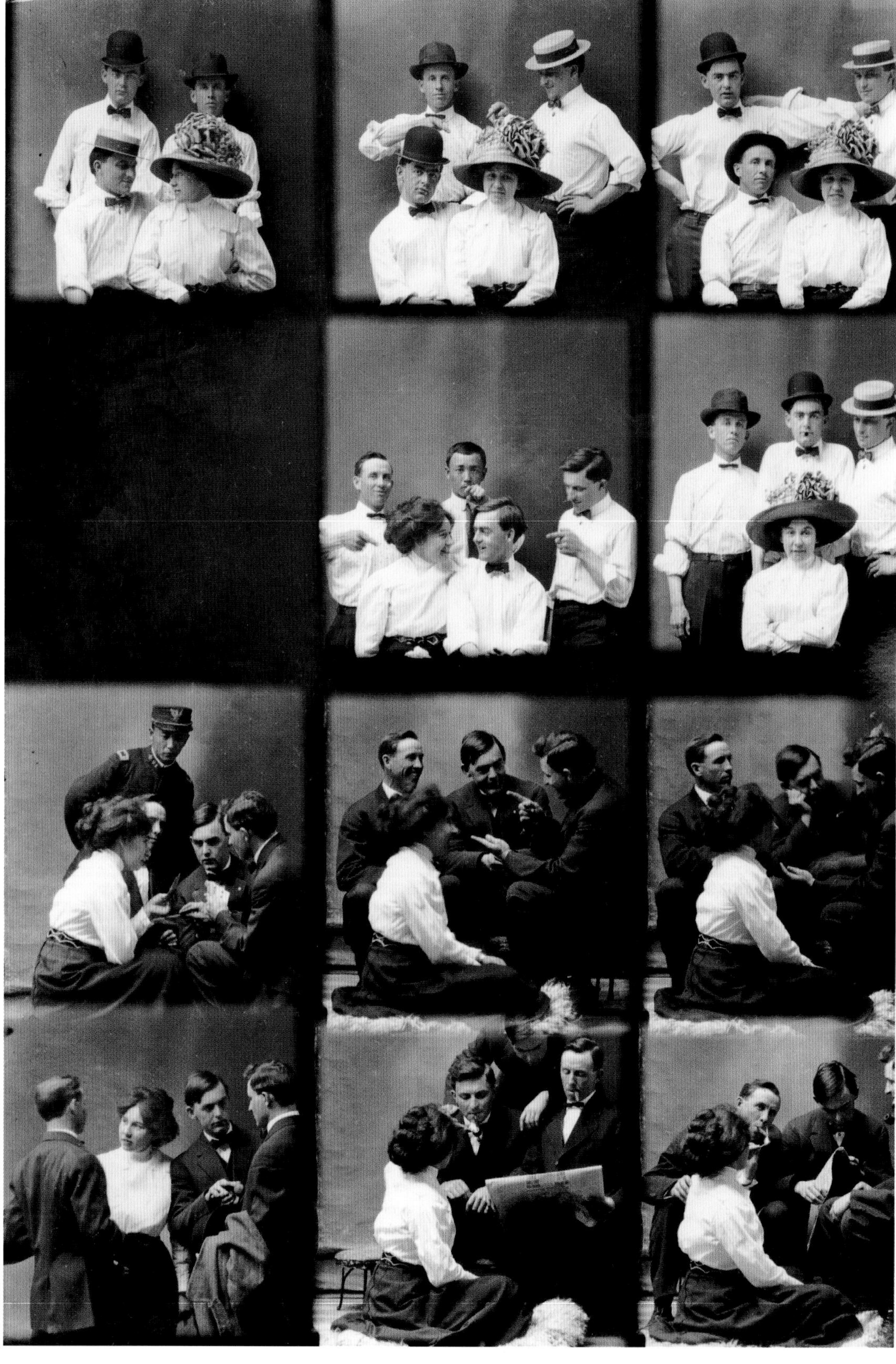

When considering critical, sound artistic choices, one could identify many examples in the work of Matsura. An analysis of his studio portraits reflects how the basic principles of design are competently resolved, allowing the viewer to venture deeper on an intellectual, emotional, and/or imaginative level without distraction. Like so many renowned artists, Matsura's competent technical skills opened the door for some creative decisions that produced so many memorable images that have outlived him. Whether Matsura initially relied on intuitive, innate design skills to accomplish this or if he had previous art training one might never know. Most of Matsura's images are labeled with a date range of circa 1903 to 1913. There are some that have an actual date inscribed. It is therefore a challenge to document his artistic evolution accurately. Still, many of his photographs move quickly beyond mere documentation into the realm of both imaginative and conceptual art.

Decades ago, when people had to send their photographs to a lab to be developed, one out of a hundred pictures taken by an ordinary individual might yield an image that could be considered artistically good. Professional photographers might get twelve to fifteen. The context here is regarding the difference between the need to document a personal moment (and getting lucky with some visually potent design elements) and the formal artistic choices made by a trained photographer. The public is just looking through the camera lens seeing a person, place, and event to memorialize, whereas a photographer like Matsura is deeply considering the aesthetic possibilities of the image. This example typifies the concept of artistic intention, while knowing that a good quality image can better pay the bills.

Photography reflects the breadth of technological advancement maybe as well as any medium. Taking pictures on a cell phone is a daily habit for most today, including posting them on social media for others to see. Of course, it was not always like this. Some of the multiplying camera photographs that Matsura took of people in his studio predate this social documentation. These reaffirm that photography is also a performative medium. He balanced these dynamic and intimate photographs with the professional need to keep his business afloat. His oeuvre reflects this diversity of activity while managing a professional skill set.

The typical stoic and staid images of the era have as much to do with the

OPPOSITE
Mathilda Schaller and Three Male Friends at Matsura's Studio, ca. 1909. Mathilda Schaller and friends sit in various comical poses for the camera. The man standing in the derby hat in the first image might be her brother, John Schaller, owner of the Schaller Bakery. The Schallers came to Okanogan in 1908, from La Crosse, Wisconsin.

complexities of the technology that required the sitter to stay still during a time-consuming photographic process. A typical 5 × 7 box camera (which Matsura predominantly used) required the photographer to adjust the focus on the subject, which was seen upside down through the lens, then to insert the emulsified glass plate into place, wherein the photographer could no longer see the subject, click the shutter, and thus expose the image onto the plate that could be used for printing. Beyond time-consuming, the process required a competent photographer to be able to visualize in advance what the image could be and then later develop the images to ascertain if they were successful.

> A portrait is not a likeness. The moment an emotion or fact is transformed into a photograph it is no longer a fact but an opinion. There is no such thing as inaccuracy in a photograph. All photographs are accurate. None of them is the truth.
> —Richard Avedon (*In the American West*)[3]

Richard Avedon's philosophical perspective on the artist's intention and production reflected a zenith of postmodern considerations that were inspired by Walter Benjamin's "The Work of Art in the Age of Mechanical Reproduction" essay from 1936.[4] This treatise was monumental in the later movements of cultural criticism and the literary and artistic deconstruction of authoritative political and cultural hierarchies. Meanwhile, Minnesota Chippewa scholar Gerald Vizenor was one of the first published critics of American photographer Edward S. Curtis's constructed images of Native Americans. Other Western photographers such as John K. Hillers dressed Native Americans in fake headdresses as early as 1873.[5] However, Curtis led the charge in the "truth telling" of what authentic Native Americans were supposed to look like for generations to come. Vizenor lamented, "Curtis retouched tribal images, he, or his darkroom assistants, removed hats, labels, suspenders, parasols, from photographic prints."[6] It was the removal of a clock in Curtis's 1910 photograph *In a Piegan Lodge* that Vizenor focused on as a symbolic testament to visual oppression and a denial of Native American cultural agency. Curtis painstakingly removed the clock (a symbol of present time) from his original image, effectively keeping his Native subjects in a romanticized past and not allowed to navigate and contribute to modernity like other Americans.

In contrast, Matsura's portraits convey a nuanced version of regional Indigenous identity. Participants present evidence of converging cultures and the lived experience of Native peoples during a time of mass transition. Their personal

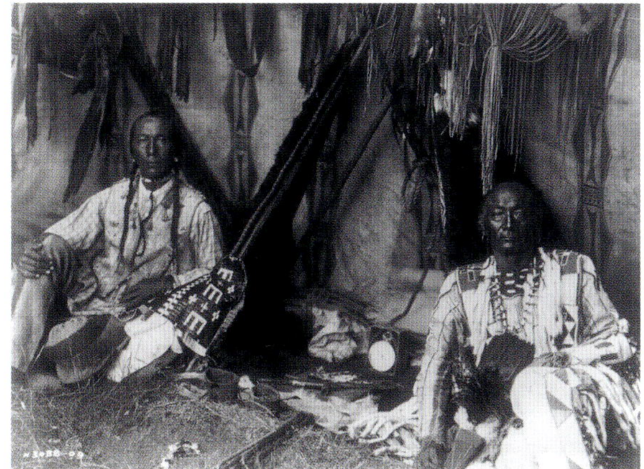
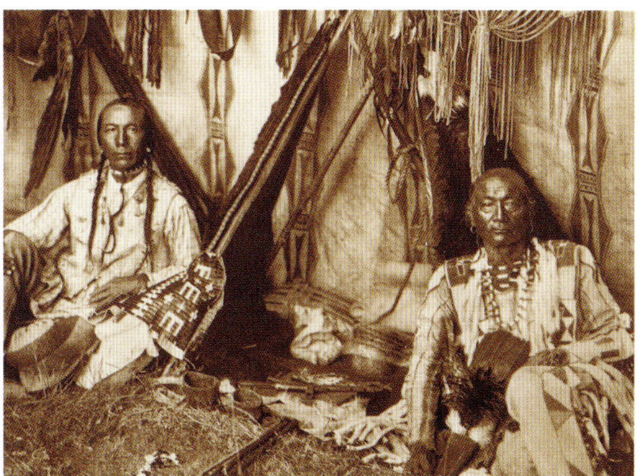

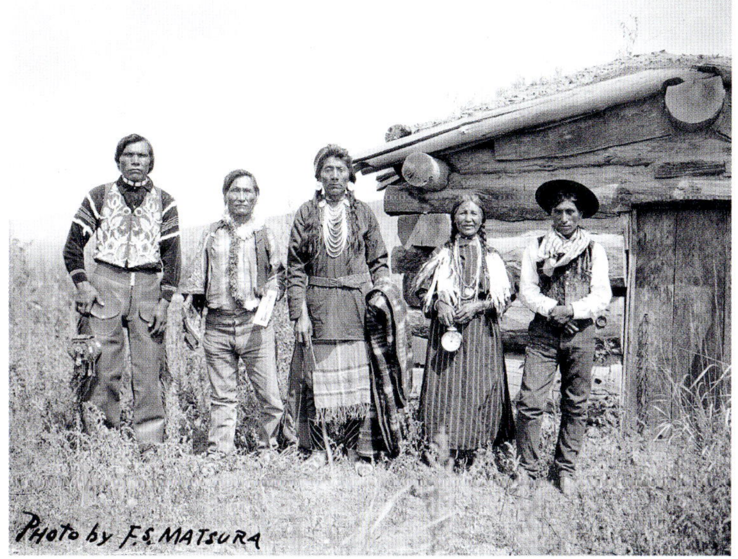

TOP, LEFT
Edward S. Curtis, *In a Piegan Lodge*, photographic print, 1910. Little Plume and his son Yellow Kidney are seated on the ground inside the lodge, a pipe between them.

TOP, RIGHT
Edward S. Curtis, *In a Piegan Lodge*, sepia-toned photogravure, 1910. The round clock seen in the adjacent image was removed by Curtis in this rendition.

BOTTOM
Okanogan Indians Twit-mich, unknown, Charley Leo, Suzanne Leo, and Joe Leo, ca. 1910. A group of Okanogan Indians pose for a portrait. The man on the left is Twit-mich, or "Big Jim." The next man is unidentified. To his right is Charley Leo, a local rancher. Holding a clock beside him is Suzanne Leo, a member of his family, not his wife. She was a medicine woman. Beside her is her son, Joe, or "Little Joe."

styles, influenced as much by their dual roles as ranchers or cattlemen as by ancestral practices, point to a complex cycle of ongoing reinvention. Contemporary clothing and accessories blend fluidly with "trade blankets," glass beads, and natural materials. Instead of nostalgia, Matsura's portraits of the Native peoples in his community reflect a living culture that defied a colonial definition of being solely authentic or traditional.

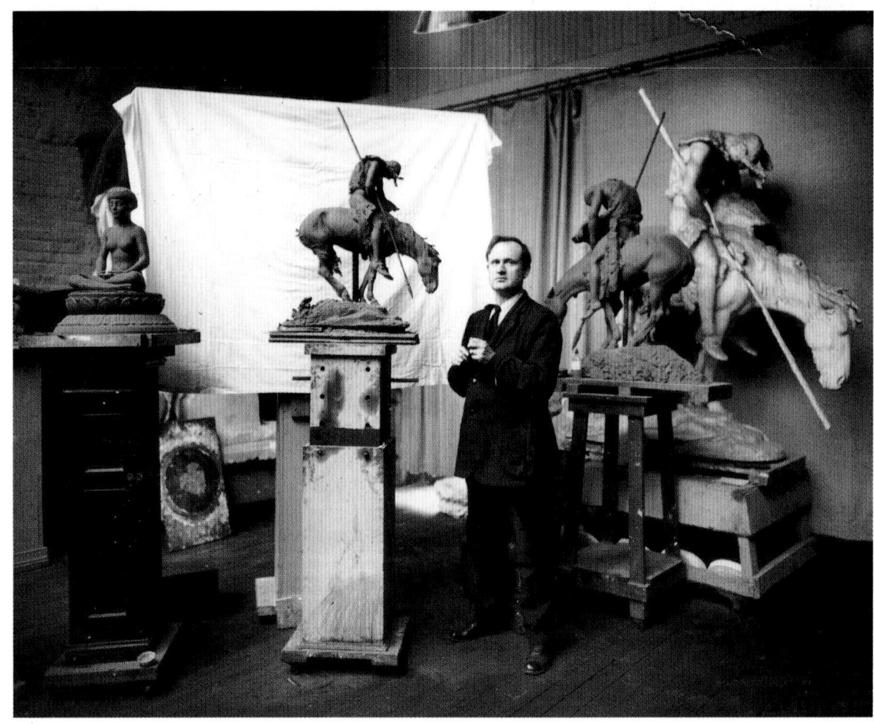

James Earle Fraser in His Studio with Clay Maquette of the End of the Trail *Sculpture*, ca. 1910

Charley Leo and Wife, ca. 1911

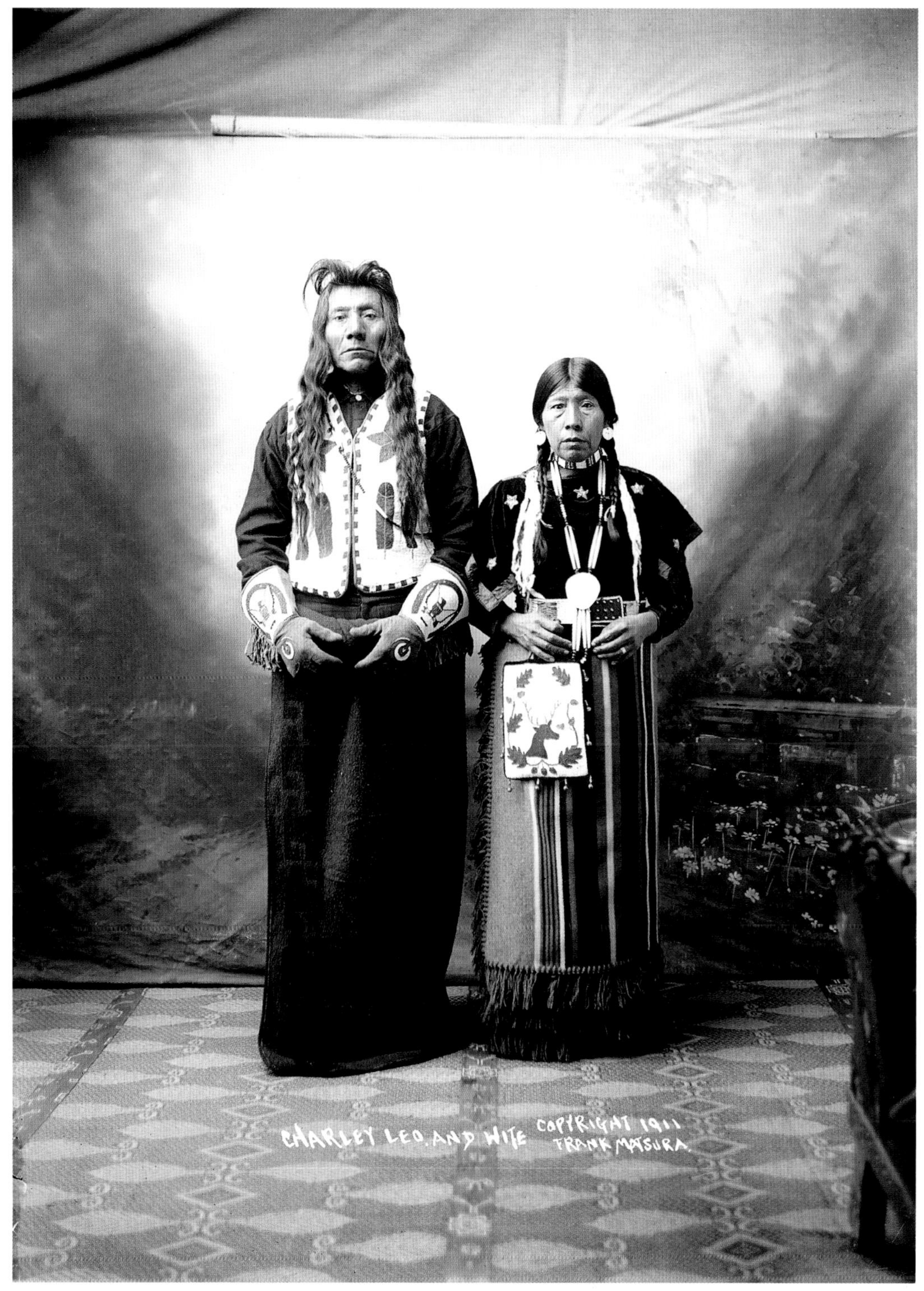
CHARLEY LEO. AND WIFE COPYRIGHT 1911
FRANK MATSURA.

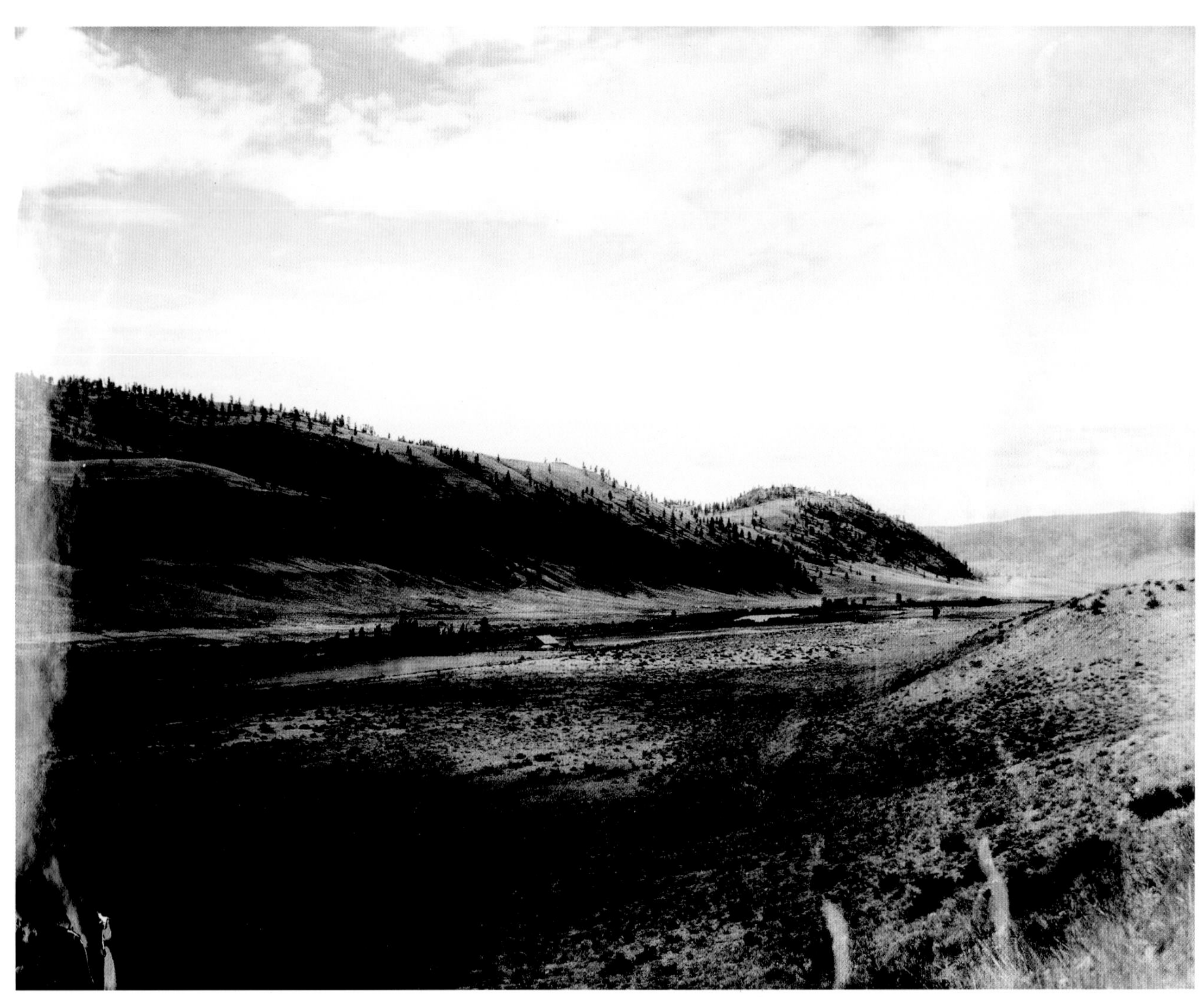

Okanogan Landscape, ca. 1910. Low, rambling hills and a large expanse of flatland running along a creek are the focus of this Matsura photograph. A home next to the water is visible in the center of the photograph.

CHAPTER ONE

INDIGENOUS HOMELANDS THROUGH A PHOTOGRAPHER'S LENS

—

Laurie Arnold, PhD

When Creator put the human people who are now known as "Colville" in their homelands along the Swanetkqha, the Columbia River, he knew they would be pitiful and helpless compared to the animal people, so he called on the animal people for help. Salmon responded first and said, "The people can eat my body."[1] This offer was one of caretaking, sacrifice, nourishment, and reciprocity. Salmon fed the people and the people honored salmon with ceremonies and with careful stewardship of the river human and animal people call home. These have always been Indigenous homelands. Swanetkqha begins in British Columbia and flows nearly 1,250 miles to the Pacific Ocean. Less than a century ago, and during Frank Sakae Matsura's life in the Okanogan, it still followed its self-selected channels.

When the Ancient One was disinterred from his rest along the Swanetkqha in Kennewick, Washington, in 1996, scientists imagined that he traveled across the ocean to end up there. They didn't listen to stories Plateau people shared about Creator and how long they had been living on this land. For scientists, believing a person had traveled thousands of miles was less fantastical than acknowledging Plateau people had been in this place for millennia. Ultimately, science debunked its own initial conclusion when DNA results (from samples taken from the Ancient One under strenuous protest from Plateau tribes) proved

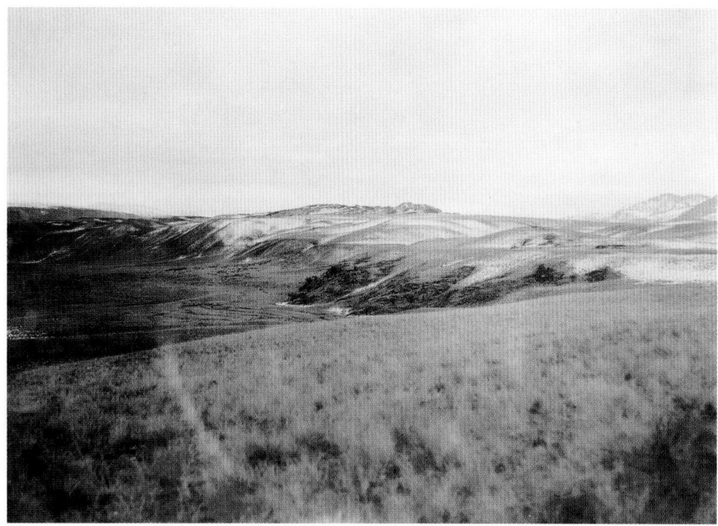

Snow on the Plateau, ca. 1910.
A range of snow-dusted flats are the
focus of this landscape photograph
taken by Matsura. In the foreground
is a patch of scrubland.

that today's Plateau peoples are direct descendants of an ancestor who lived in these homelands nearly nine thousand years ago.[2] In the twenty-first century, science confirmed what Plateau peoples know: these have always been Indigenous homelands.

Europeans, Canadians, and Americans ventured into the Okanogan region beginning in the 1810s, seeking their fortunes, whether animal (fur) or mineral (gold). By the time Frank Sakae Matsura arrived on the Columbia Plateau, a great deal had changed but one constant remained true: these were still Indigenous homelands. I call this place the Indigenous Plateau because it was and remains an Indigenous homeland and because the man after whom it was named never ventured to it. Rather than erase its own people, we can decolonize that name and restore them. The people of this place have resided on these lands together since Europe was in its Mesolithic epoch. Imagine that for a moment—our ancestors recognized each other then in ways we recognize each other now. Plateau peoples were interdependent. They typically lived in small groups or village formations, joining other villages sometimes, separating into smaller groups at others. They practiced the seasonal round of food gathering and harvesting, a lifeway built from place-based knowledge of foods, animal migrations, and seasons. They were not nomadic, as scholars and popular culture have previously characterized many Native and Indigenous groups, but practiced an informed cyclical migration that derived meaning from ancestral knowledge passed through generations. Interdependence allowed them to thrive in good years and survive in lean years, while

Mouth of the Okanogan River, Near Present-Day Brewster, Washington, 1911

trade and kinship with partners and families across mountains, plains, and rivers connected this place to much of what is now the American West.[3]

In 1846, the United States and Canada settled on the 49th parallel as the boundary between their nations, a boundary that bisected the Columbia River and Plateau, but even decades later, the Plateau felt more like its own distinct place rather than a site of American settlement. In the decades prior to the boundary, the United States and Great Britain jointly occupied what is currently the Pacific Northwest and British Columbia; neither empire was fully committed to this place but neither wanted to relinquish the territory, either. Plateau people remained constant despite waves of disruption that began with the fur trade and continued through missionaries, mining, commerce, immigration, and displacement as a result of US federal Indian policy. This chapter will discuss some of these disruptions and will highlight some of the many ways Plateau people adapted in order to ensure their presence and fulfill their commitments to these Indigenous homelands. This is the world Matsura entered.

The reservation was established by an executive order from President Ulysses S. Grant in 1872, the government's attempt at an efficient solution for dealing with the bands of nontreaty Indians the reservation initially included: Colville, Arrow Lakes (or Lakes), San Poil, Nespelem, Okanogan, Methow, Calispel, Spokane, and Coeur d'Alene. Ultimately, the Calispel (Kalispel), Spokane, and Coeur d'Alene tribes would receive their own reservations. The United States ended treaty making in 1871. All reservations created after this date were made via executive order. The first Colville reservation was created in April 1872 and spanned roughly three-and-a-half million acres on both sides of the Columbia River, almost reaching the northeasternmost corner of Washington. The original reservation included white settlement areas near Kettle Falls and Colville, Washington. Non-Indian mill operators, shopkeepers, and settlers who had arrived in the area not long before cried foul at the prospect of residing on the reservation. President Grant heeded their dismay and reduced the reservation by more than 10 percent in July 1872. The new reservation encompassed 3.1 million acres, from the Canadian border to the north and following the Columbia River for its eastern and southern boundaries. Matsura ultimately settled in one of the towns along the western edge of the reservation, Okanogan.

The United States also granted Chief Moses an executive order reservation in 1879. It became known as the Columbia Reservation, and the Chelan, Entiat, and Wenatchi bands joined Moses on that reservation. By the mid-1880s, these bands moved to the Colville reservation (now known as the Colville Indian Reservation), as did Chief Joseph's band of Nez Percé Indians. The current reservation includes twelve bands: Colville, Lakes, San Poil, Nespelem, Okanogan, Methow, Moses-Columbia, Chelan, Entiat, Wenatchi, Nez Perce, and Palús.[4]

The reservation was reduced twice more, in 1891 and again in 1906, neither time with approval of the Colville people or leadership. In 1891, Congress reduced the reservation by half, taking from reservation status the northern half of the reservation, a land base that directly connected the tribe to Canada. In 1906, Congress deemed a great swath of land on the southern half of the reservation as "surplus," and determined those lands should be open for purchase and settlement by non-Native people. The United States made these land "deals" possible when Congress passed the Dawes General Allotment Act in 1887. Named for its author, Senator Henry Dawes of Massachusetts, the legislation aimed to break up reservations by granting Native people individually held allotments of land that they owned as private property instead of sharing land in common. Congress made this policy without input from tribal nations, and supporters of allotment believed private ownership would finally assimilate Native people fully into American cultural values.

Dividing land into plots required surveyors. Colville people were used to surveyors by this time, having watched them work along the 49th parallel, then with the railroads, then to measure other privately held land. Crews like this one traversed ancient Indigenous trails and put them to new use in the nineteenth

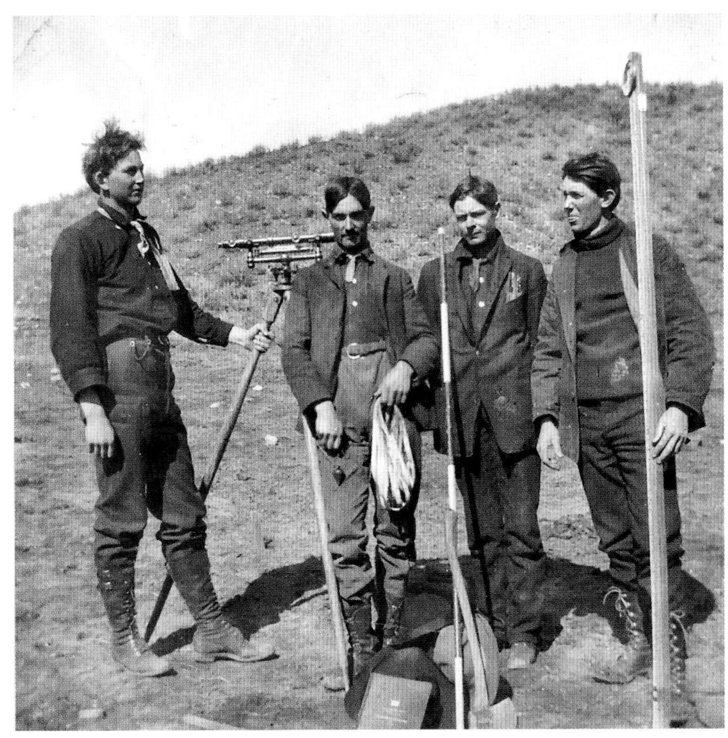

Surveyors on the Indigenous Plateau, ca. 1903–1913. From left: Chelsea C. Woodward, Harry W. George, and two unidentified men. Pouge Frey scrapbook.

century: traders, missionaries, miners, and government officials making way for commercial and residential development of lands mischaracterized as "free and open." Regardless of measurements, regardless of purpose, these lands remained Indigenous homelands, known best to Colville people.

Outsiders and their extractive and agricultural industries wrought massive changes on Plateau homelands, disrupting sacred sites and decimating traditional food sources that had nourished generations. Colville people witnessed these changes, adapting land use practices when possible and participating in the associated wage economies when necessary. Colville author Christine Quintasket began to chronicle these changes as a practice grounded in historical and cultural preservation. She feared the landscapes would become unrecognizable and that younger people were losing sight of cultural traditions and teachings as the twentieth century dawned. She also engaged in wage labor across the region, which gave her an insider view of the commercial enterprises newly operating on the Plateau.

Quintasket published as Mourning Dove, and we recognize her as a novelist, an ethnographer, and an activist. Today we would also characterize her as a public intellectual for the extensive public-facing work she undertook to teach non-Native communities and institutions about Native peoples and Native lives. Quintasket was raised with ancestral traditions and Salish was her first language, but her mother was also intent that she obtain a formal Western education and Catholic religious training. Born in the 1880s, Quintasket was among the first generation of Colville people who had to live in an increasingly modern and American world but who also retained the values and practiced the lifeways of earlier generations of Colville people. In the 1920s, Quintasket spent more than a decade transcribing and translating Coyote stories from family members and friends in order to publish them for the posterity of future generations. Neither animal nor human, the Coyote of these stories is something greater than both, possessing a spirit power, *squ-stenk*, which he can use for good or for mischief. Neither good nor evil, he is a trickster. In the Nselxcin dialect of Salish, he is *snkalip*, which Quintasket translated as "imitator."[5] These stories were a central component of the oral tradition, shared among and between families during winter months when the seasonal round turned to the culture work of storytelling and social and spiritual training.

In one story, Coyote and Beaver train their sons to be strong future warriors. Each assert that his sons are the best, fastest, most skilled. One day, a piece of the sun broke off and fell to earth. Mourning Dove transcribed this piece as a "roller," and in the story, people traveled from near and far to see it. Both Coyote and Beaver coveted the roller, and they each sent their sons to retrieve it from the encampment where it had fallen. Coyote's sons perished one by one, due to their insufficient training, and Beaver's sons returned triumphant, bringing the roller to their father. Coyote mourned his sons and eventually sought vengeance against Beaver for his family's success. Coyote stole the roller from Beaver, broke it into many pieces, and scattered them widely across the earth. He proclaimed, "You will be for the future generations; for the new people who are to come. They will prize you as a shining sun-rock. For you, men will slay one another as my sons were killed by the warriors of the enemy people. You will be found among the rocks of the mountains and the streams. Through hardships you will be found."[6]

In this story we see a cautionary tale about greed. It also offered an explanation about how minerals came to be hidden throughout the Plateau and insight about what it would cost to retrieve them. The story refers to the roller as both copper and gold, and in the mid-nineteenth century, miners charged into the Okanogan desperately seeking their fortunes in the hills and streams where

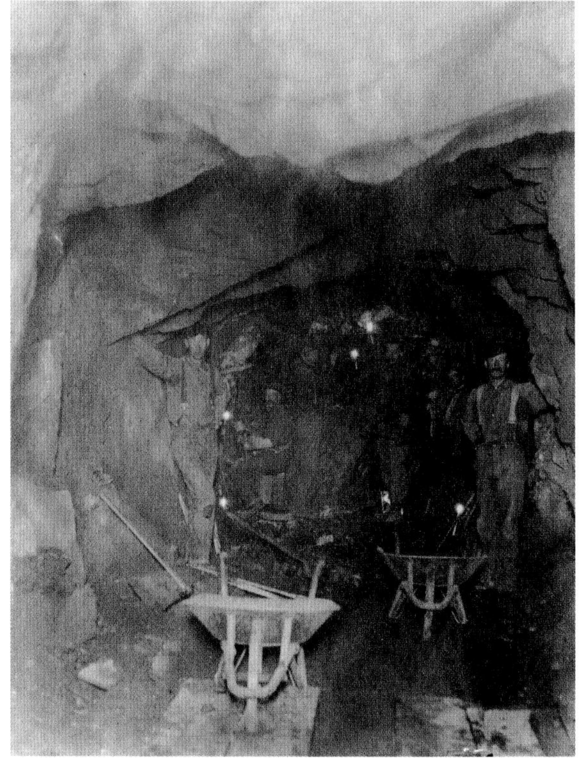

LEFT

Miners in a Mine Shaft Dug Deep into a Hill near Conconully, ca. 1909. Many mines like this one closed without repairing any damage mine owners caused to the geography or the environment.

BELOW

A Flume Brings Water to a Placer Mine, ca. 1910. Placer mining causes environmental damage through moving stream channels, which can impact aquatic life. Owners typically did not repair environmental damage caused by placer mining.

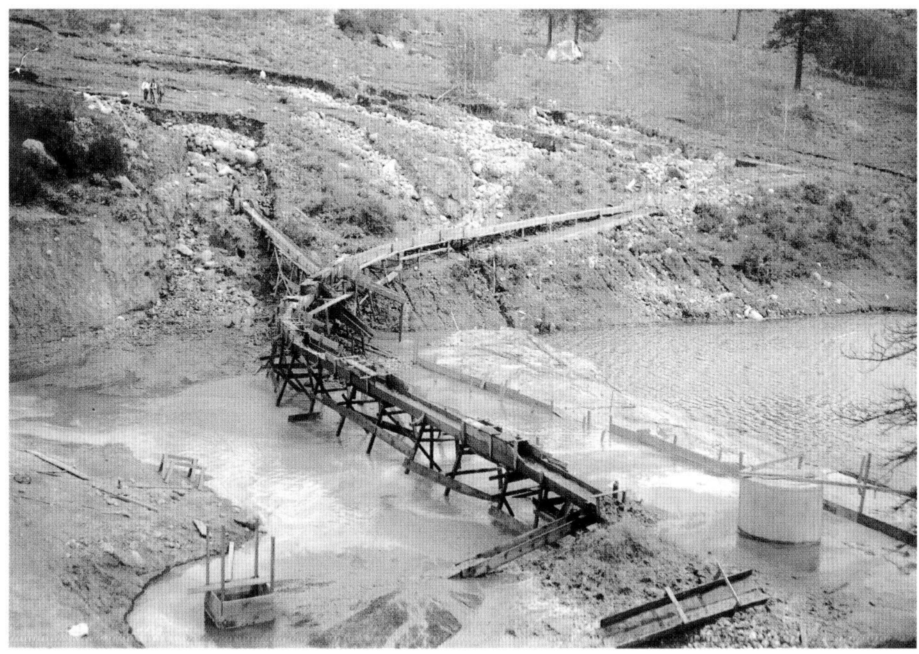

Coyote might have scattered the sun-rock minerals. They came across Indigenous homelands, displacing Native people, often through violence, in pursuit of the gold, silver, and copper they believed lay buried just beyond their reach. The United States was not prepared to stop these incursions, having claimed the land from the tribes for settlement by Americans. Miners gave little thought to Native people or their rights, and they certainly didn't consider the environmental impacts mining would wreak on tribal homelands. Decades after the initial rush, Matsura photographed some of the working mines, capturing ways mining damaged landscapes, ruining them for the foods that had traditionally thrived there as well as for cultivation of foods that might support Plateau life.

Christine Quintasket was a published author and a speaker in great demand throughout the region, but she did not earn enough to live on those professions alone. Like many Plateau people, she worked as a migrant agricultural laborer, working the seasons from hops to apples, and apple season could last the entire fall some years. At the end of November 1918, Quintasket wrote to her friend and literary partner Lucullus McWhorter that she was relieved about the cushion her income would provide: "My bonus is over twenty-five dollars now. I have packed over four thousand boxes of apples this season....I still have about two or three weeks work in the shed."[7] In the off-season, Quintasket spoke at guilds and clubs and schools, but during the harvest months she worked side by side with others in the orchards or the hop fields, seeing herself as no different from "the rest of the Indians there working."[8]

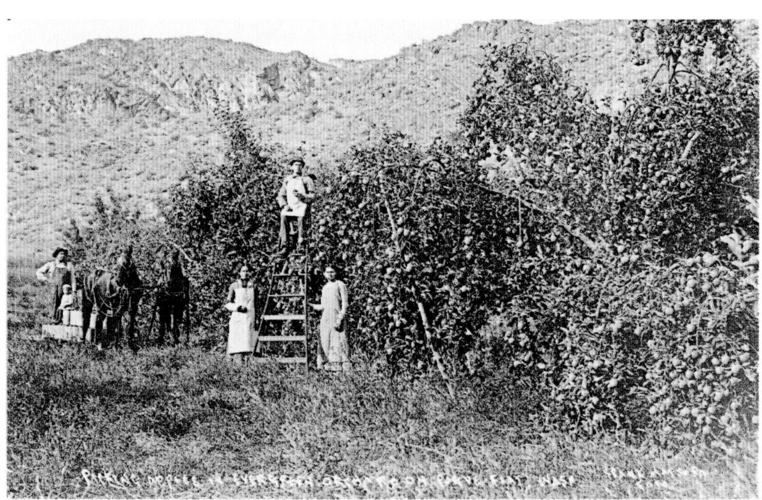

Apple Harvest at Evergreen Orchard, ca. 1912. These are non-Native people, but the photo is representative of labor that workers like Mourning Dove performed.

Quintasket moved back to the Plateau permanently by 1914, after roughly a decade of living in Montana and Oregon. Given the timing of her return, it is unlikely that she knew Matsura, but we can understand her experiences as a laborer, culture keeper, and Plateau person as generally representative of the lifestyles of Colville people in this era. The processes of adaptation did not erase tradition and culture; instead, Native people infused these experiences with their own sensibilities and priorities.

The breadth of Matsura's photographs demonstrates his close relationships in the community, including with Native people. His collection of serious portraits and playful candids reflects a high level of ease with each other, a result of mutual respect and trust. Matsura photographed many instances of tradition meeting modernity, whether in the studio or in work or play. Tlingit/Nisga'a photographer Larry McNeil has observed that photography was a medium Indians and non-Indians discovered concurrently because both groups witnessed the invention of the camera and participated in its widespread adoption. Matsura's photos often captured moments that seem to illustrate both change and continuity; Plateau permanence pervades any subject of the photographer's lens. It is also clear that Plateau people wanted to be photographed—they wanted records of their lives, their families, their fashions, their dogs, and their horses. Oh, their horses. Matsura photographed horses in regalia, horses doing tricks with their riders, and horses racing for the win. He understood that recording these relationships would both preserve beloved kin and tell important stories from an era witnessing the arrival of the automobile.

The horse arrived on the Plateau by the eighteenth century, and Plateau people quickly developed an affinity for the horse. The National Museum of the American Indian has characterized Native/horse relationships as two beings with a common destiny.[9] In the twentieth century, sometimes that destiny was work but often it was sport, and few sports were more exciting than horse races. Racing could occur anywhere, on a flat plain, across riverbeds (dry or full), through towns, at celebrations and gatherings, even in fields while horses were attached to plows, an event that combined work and play in a quintessentially Native way. The action shots included here don't allow us to see riders' faces but Matsura captured the energy and joy of the races. Racing was also exciting for spectators, as demonstrated in a photo from July 4, 1911 (see similar photograph on page 126)—people watched from balconies and climbed rooftops to get the best look at the action (see a similar photograph on page 126). This photo also

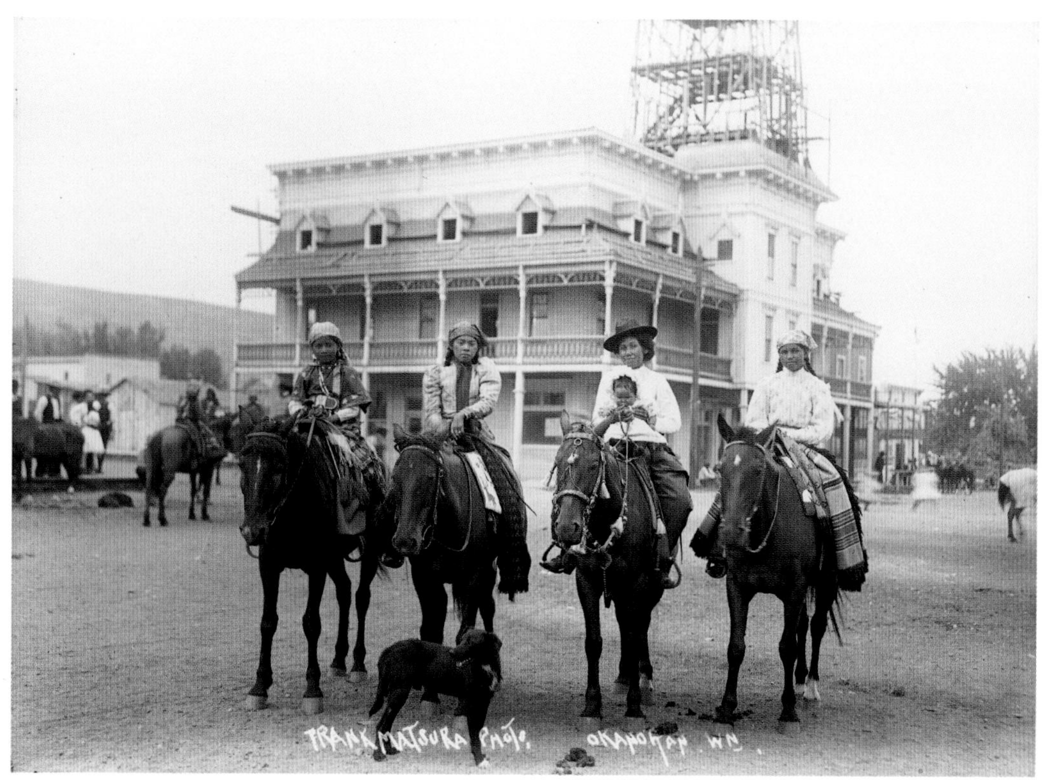

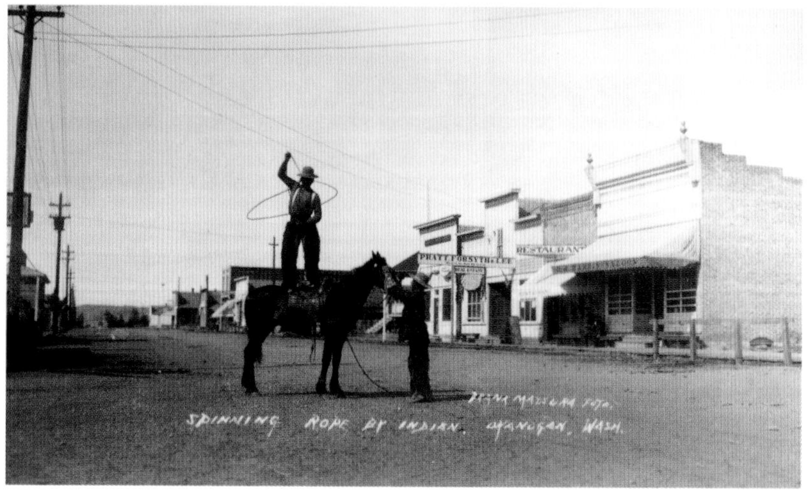

TOP

Josephine Carden and Camille Marchand with Two Other Colville Women in Okanogan, ca. 1903–1913

BOTTOM

Colville Indian Man Trick Roping atop His Horse, ca. 1903–1913

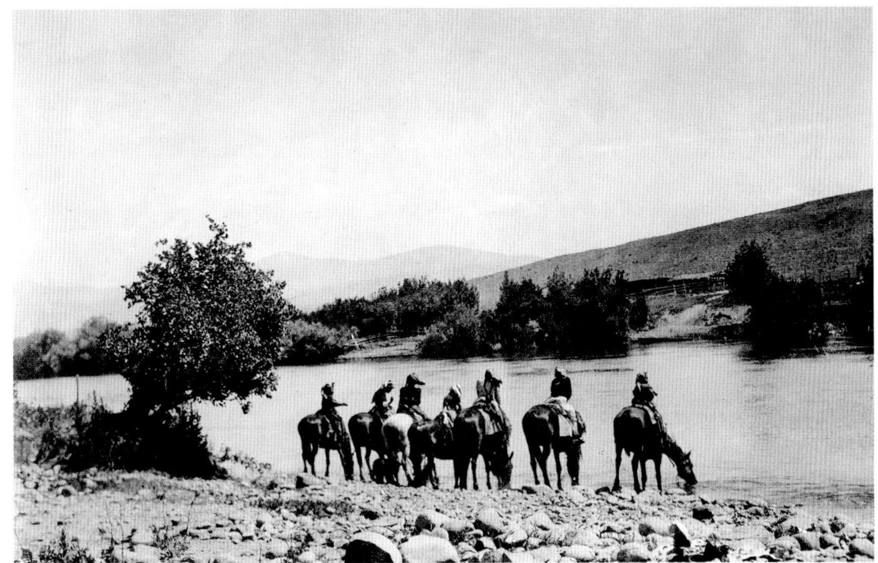

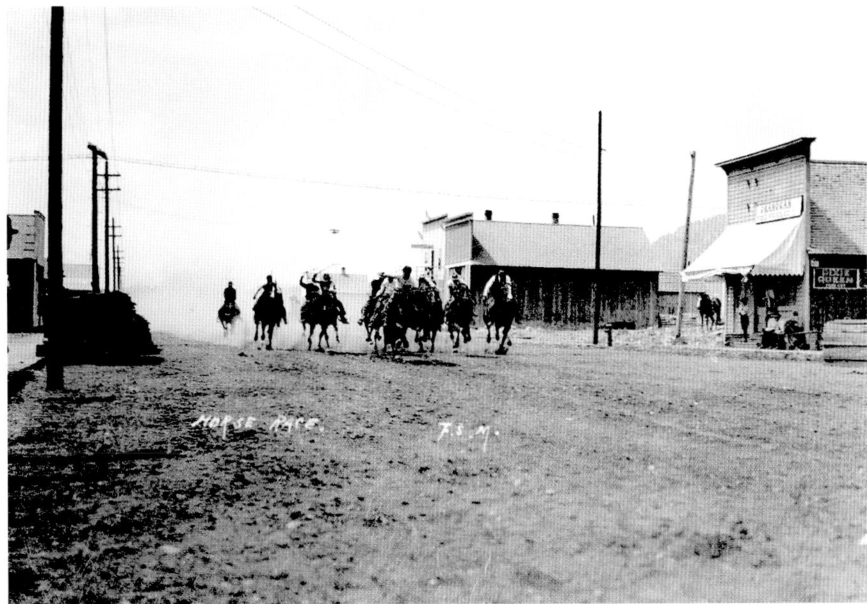

BOTTOM
Horse Race on Second Avenue in Okanogan, ca. 1910.
This scene suggests that this race may have taken place on
the first Fiesta Day holiday on May 21, 1910. Townspeople
set this day aside for a relaxing community afternoon of
baseball, horse racing, and music.

TOP
*Colville Cowboys Water Their Horses at the Okanogan
River*, ca. 1910. This might be a group of Native American
women at the Okanogan River.

features viewers on horseback, perhaps getting ready for their turn on the course. The other image recorded a race in May 1910, during Fiesta Day, a town holiday established specifically for a relaxing community afternoon of baseball, horse racing, and music. The catalog entry for this image notes "Native Americans living in the South Half of the Colville Indian Reservation often attended Fiesta Day and were usually favored to win [the races]."[10]

Horsemanship, spectacle, and pleasing crowds in the Okanogan inspired a non-Indian to create the Suicide Race as a marketing gambit for the Omak Stampede rodeo in 1935. The race was designed as a high-speed run down a steep dirt hillside into the Okanogan River, and the course has remained largely the same. Colville riders and their horses have ruled it from the outset. Many have noted that, in this race especially, the rider must become one with the horse. Today, the race is not without controversy—animal rights groups consistently protest the event—but Native riders have grounded it in culture, erasing its origin as a marketing ploy and remaking the race into something meaningful for Colville people. The riders celebrate their horses, and perhaps each reminds the other that victory is their common destiny.

As with all cultural practices, one connects to another; where there's racing, there's gambling—not gambling that we see in contemporary casinos, but types of wagering that reinforced community and social values, reciprocity, and spirituality. Gambling could reflect the strength of one's spirit power, meaning something more significant than luck or skill was engaged in a player's success. Gambling was also a method for redistribution of wealth, an avenue that was not trade or charity, but which signified shared community responsibilities. One anthropologist has observed, "Gaming is a supremely sacred activity, tied up with narratives of social behavior and competitive interaction between tribes. The luck involved in winning and losing is very much linked to ideas of morality, sanctity, and the will of supreme deities or gods."[11] Plateau people acquired spirit powers through vision quests or meaningful deeds. The spirit power, perhaps an animal or even the wind, chose the person, not the other way around, and because this was a reciprocal relationship, the spirit power aided the person so long as the person continued to behave correctly. Individuals could honor their spirit powers in a variety of ways, and during gambling play, spirit singing was central to the game, as players called on their guardians to bring them success.

Stick game is played by two opposing teams, typically with one polished bone and ten sticks on each side. Traditionally, players would kneel facing each

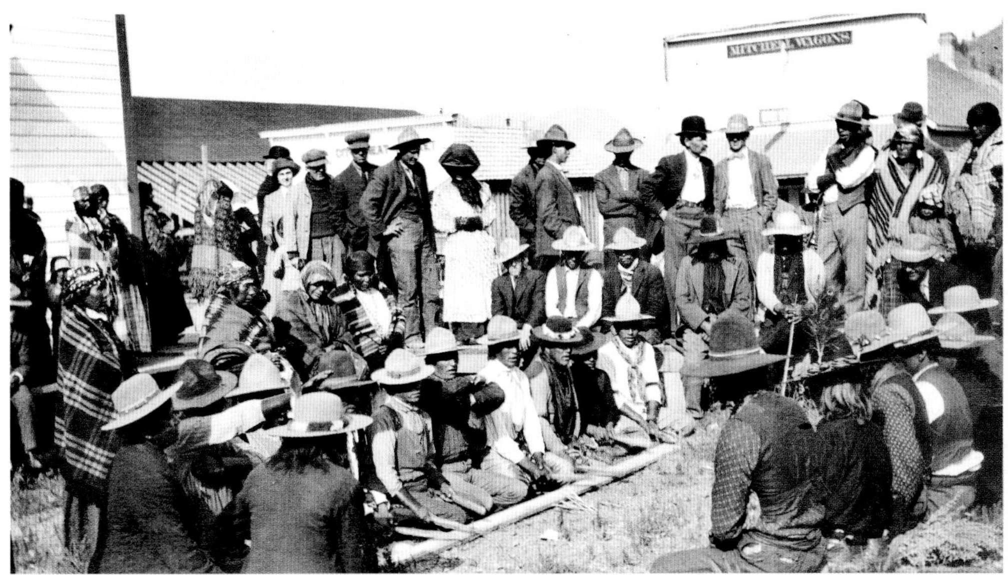

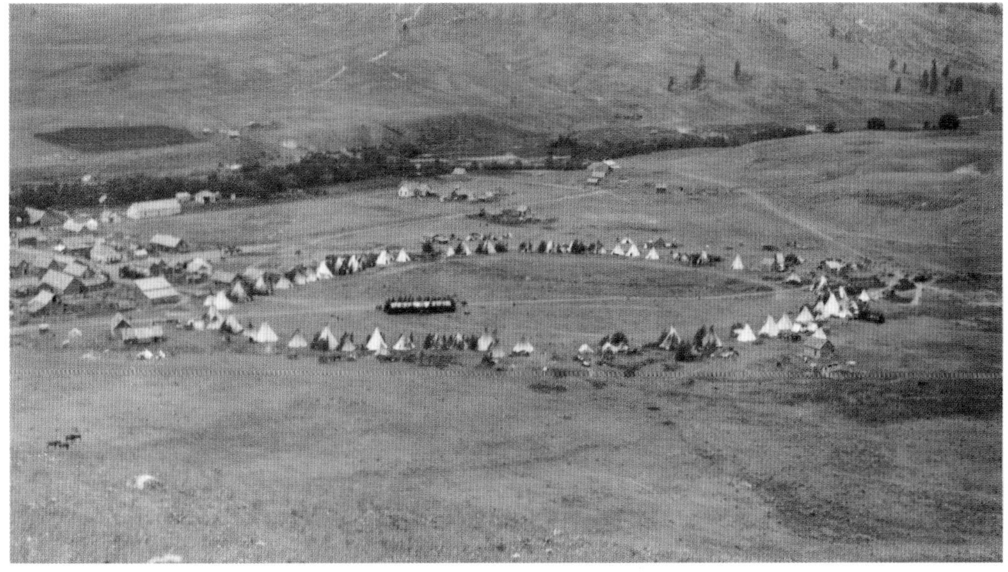

TOP
Colville People Playing Stick Game, ca. 1907–1908.
Probably at Riverside Fair in 1907 or 1908.

BOTTOM
Fourth of July Encampment, Nespelem, Washington,
ca. 1903–1913. Native American gathering at the Indian
Agency at Nespelem.

other over a log or long piece of wood, separated by a few feet, allowing space for items to be placed in a pot. Each team beat on the log during their turn to keep time with singing. During play, one person held the bone in one hand, seeking always to confuse opposing players and prevent correct guessing. An opposing player would make a guess and the player holding the bone would open their hand to reveal either the bone or an empty palm. If the guess was incorrect, the guessing team had to surrender a stick. If correct, the other player ended their turn and gave a stick to the opposing team. All the sticks had to be on one side to finish the game. Games could last for days or a week or more and there would not always be a winner. This game is serious fun, deeply rooted in culture and tradition. The game is a standard feature of any celebration, including the Nespelem Fourth of July Encampment, which still occurs each year. The same teams play together for decades, singing the songs that connect them to the game and each other.

Plateau people avidly played all types of games and sports. Matsura photographed baseball, football, basketball—typical "American" games—as well as racing. Choctaw writer LeAnne Howe describes baseball as inherently connected to Native cultural practices. Base-and-ball games were pervasive across Native communities centuries before Abner Doubleday was credited with inventing baseball and before colonists played the English game of rounders in North America. In Howe's novel *Miko Kings*, a Choctaw character described base-and-ball as "a game played in every ancient square in North and South America," and further noted that it advanced diplomacy between tribes. "*Our game* [emphasis in original] was created so we could include everyone. We played the game to collaborate with other tribes, the stars, and with the great mystery." The character also wonders why people believe Americans, always tied to a clock, could create a game where bases are run counterclockwise in a game without timed innings.[12]

Beyond the cultural connections, Native players succeeded in baseball because coaches sought to teach them. At Carlisle Indian Industrial School in Carlisle, Pennsylvania, baseball was part of the formal curriculum. At least seven Carlisle alumni played major league baseball, the most famous being Jim Thorpe, a member of the Sac and Fox Nation and widely regarded as one of the finest athletes of the twentieth century.[13] Closer to home, a young Colville player living just outside the reservation was a rising baseball star at Gonzaga College in Spokane and on a semiprofessional team in Chewelah. David Skeels was a teenager when he caught the attention of larger ball clubs and, at eighteen, he pitched his first game as a Detroit Tiger. This move into the major league drew comparisons with Charles Bender, an Ojibwe pitcher for Philadelphia when they were still the Athletics. Skeels's major league career was short-lived, but he continued to play baseball in the Plateau region, and he earned a place in sports history for his prowess as a pitcher.[14]

In this photo, Matsura may have thought he was capturing a quintessentially American moment—two teams participating in the American pastime. Instead, when we reframe our comprehension of Native peoples and their lived experiences, we can understand this game as an act of diplomacy for the Native players while it was also a public sporting event. By this time, Colville people had been sharing their homelands with outsiders for more than a century. Matsura's candid photos taken in town or in other community settings do not often illustrate one

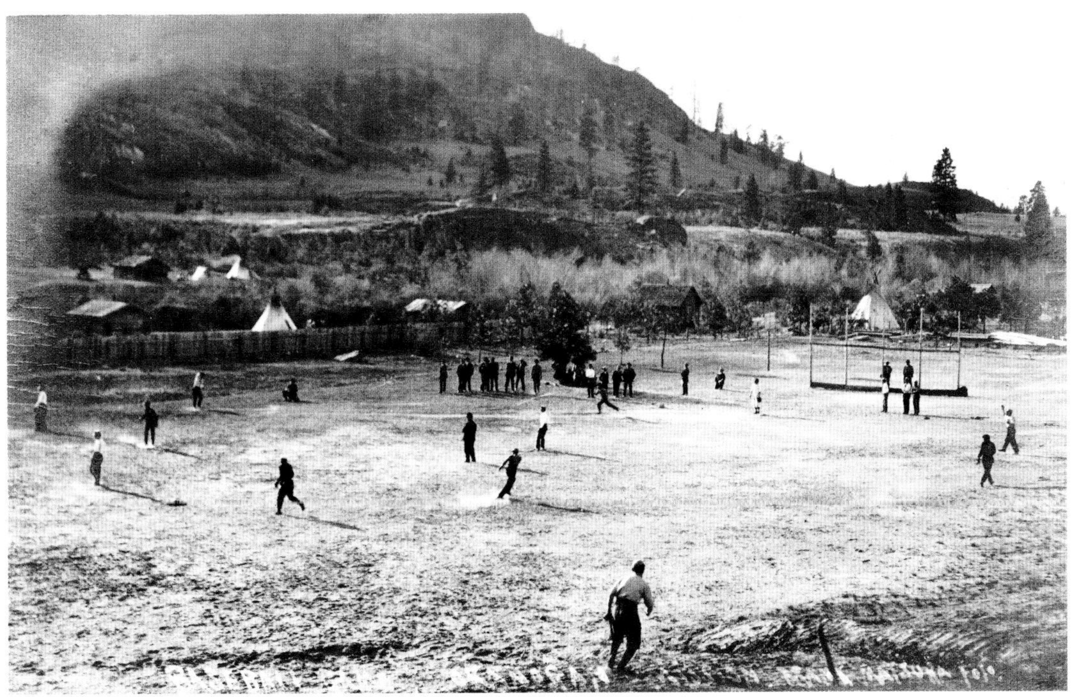

Baseball Game at St. Mary's Mission, ca. 1903–1913.
Catholic priest Father DeRouge built a chapel at the north
end of Omak Lake in 1886, east of the Okanogan River on
the Colville Indian Reservation. This later became
St. Mary's Mission and boarding school.

group objectifying the other, and in many images people are simply going about their business. Most people who had settled in the region no longer regarded Colville people as spectacles, but it is important to remember that the balance of power had shifted away from Colville people toward the settlers. The familiarity captured in images speaks to longtime co-occupation of Plateau homelands but, even though it remained an Indigenous homeland, settlers exerted control over land, resources, labor, and wealth.

When Jesuit missionaries arrived on the Plateau in the 1840s, they did not seek control over land or resources, but of Colville people and their spirituality. The Jesuits who arrived in this region were from various European countries. They were not American, so were generally unconcerned with US assimilation goals. Their aim was conversion to Catholicism, to save Native people from spirituality the Jesuits considered pagan. As Europeans, most priests were multilingual, and this openness to language learning helped Jesuits establish relationships. They learned several Salish dialects and could differentiate between them. As Jesuits offered instruction to Native people, they taught Latin alongside English. Priests quickly realized the importance of song as a form of prayer for Plateau people, and they eagerly set out to translate hymns into Salish dialects as an entry point for conversion of Plateau people. Ethnomusicologist Chad Hamill, PhD (Spokan), applied his own family's spiritual traditions to consider how song maintained Indigenous spiritual power even as Christian missionaries changed some approaches to prayer. *Songs of Power and Prayer in the Columbia Plateau* also describes how, during processes of transforming Plateau spiritualities, the priests themselves were changed, thus highlighting the mutual nature of knowledge exchange on the Plateau.[15]

As the nineteenth century progressed, Jesuits became more embedded on the Plateau, and they opened schools adjacent to missions so Native children could be instructed in the three R's and vocational trades as well as Christianity. St. Mary's Mission in Omak was one of the first Jesuit schools in the region and Matsura made many photos of the church, the school campus, and sometimes the students. The United States initiated its own program of educating Native children when it opened the Carlisle Indian Industrial School in Carlisle, Pennsylvania, in 1879. The school's founder, Richard Henry Pratt, sought to "kill the Indian and save the man," considering education and vocational training the only path for full assimilation of Native people into American society. Some have described the first Jesuit schools as kinder than schools that would follow—both mission and federal—but children were always prohibited from and disciplined for speaking Indigenous languages and practicing their cultures. Native communities highly prized children, and corporal punishment was a rarity. Children attending schools were shocked and confused that adults would strike them, having never witnessed or experienced that kind of discipline at home. Children were often threatened with greater consequences if they told their parents about the abuse. Today we know far more about the violence that went hand in hand with the "civilizing" process schools sought to undertake. Firsthand accounts of boarding school survivors reveal many forms of abuse and violence committed by the priests and nuns who were supposed to care for and uplift Native children, including narratives from former students at St. Mary's. In the midst of this abuse, Native children built new forms of kinship that expressed survivance—survival and resistance—as they supported each other. Former students have noted that activities such as sports and music provided a way to move beyond the usual constraints of their schedules and participate in forms of play that recalled traditional practices.[16]

Reformers and school officials pointed to Native students' aptitude for music as an example of successful assimilation into American life. While it is true that students may not have played (or perhaps seen) a tuba prior to their Western educations, music and song were central to all Native cultures. As Native students, usually boys, became better musicians, schools would have the bands perform in public. School leaders viewed these performances as opportunities to demonstrate the effectiveness of education as assimilation and as ideal formats for fundraising. Student performers experienced moments of liberty during travel to and from shows and got to very publicly engage in musical forms that, while different, connected them to their own communities.

Matsura captured the St. Mary's band performing at commencement in 1907. Larger schools had larger bands that often took the form of marching bands in keeping with federal boarding schools' military sensibilities. This group was perhaps too small for that kind of endeavor, but it is likely that they performed around the region. Their repertoire certainly would have included patriotic songs but because St. Mary's was a Catholic school, not a federal school, the band may have had access to a larger songbook, especially since they were one of the few bands in the region at this time. Historian John Troutman has discussed ways students used music instruction and training for their own ends and how, after graduation, boarding school alumni often formed their own bands and traveled the United States performing. Music and performance gave the bands access to American

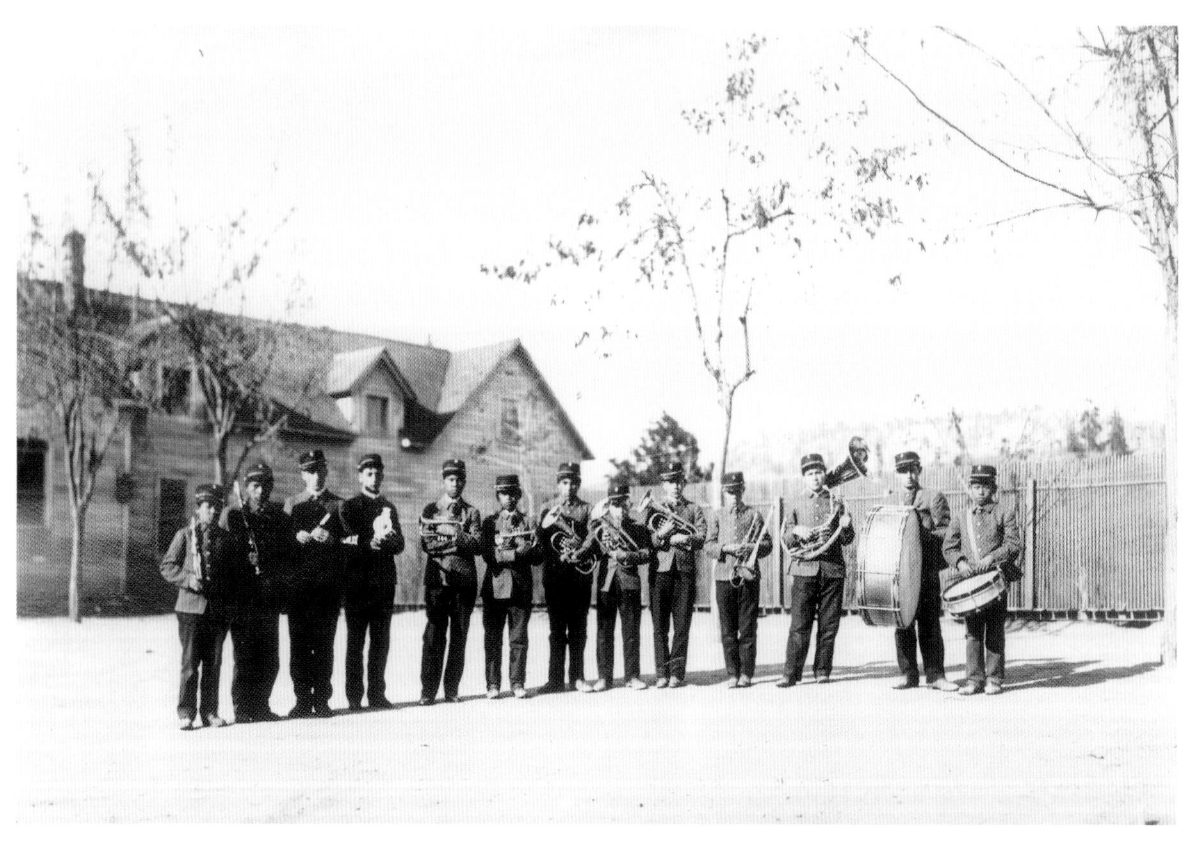

*Native American Students in the
St. Mary's Mission Band at
Commencement in 1907*, ca. 1907

society in ways they might not have had otherwise, which allowed them degrees of autonomy from federal Indian policies that sought to control Native people. In one more example of ways musical training gave Native people access to American society on their own terms, archivist Erin Fehr (Yup'ik) has brought new insight to discussions of Native service in the US military in World War I—many school band alumni enlisted as military musicians, playing in army bands, navy bands, and orchestras. "Musician" was and is a rank in the US military.[17]

St. Mary's had a significant impact on Colville children, families, and family lives. One student, Frank Wapato, credited the education he received there with making his subsequent educational opportunities possible. Wapato's Indian name was Quas-quay, Blue Jay, but during his time at St. Mary's, he took the name Paschal Sherman. A priest at the school asserted the importance of appearance and felt the boy would have greater access to the white world with a more commonly heard name. In ancient Plateau Salish tradition, the blue jay travels to distant places, seeing different peoples and cultures, and, upon his return, weaves a tale of those experiences so his own people may know them. As a boy, Sherman learned to care for his homeland and for his people and their traditions, but he was curious about the wider world. He carried the cultural teachings of his Chelan/Wenatchi heritage *and* his education with the Jesuits with him the rest of his life, and both traditions influenced his values and perspectives. From St. Mary's, Sherman advanced to St. Martin's College in western Washington State, where he completed a bachelor's degree. He then moved east to Catholic University in Washington, DC, for his graduate work. Sherman completed a PhD in constitutional history—his dissertation was entitled "Our Indian Land Law: Its Origins and Development"—as well as an LLB and a master of law in patent law. He became the first citizen of the Colville Tribes to achieve a PhD and the first to earn a law degree.

Sherman spent his professional career in Washington, DC, working for the US Department of Veterans Affairs. On his frequent visits back to the reservation, he would join his mother on her summer outings to see friends and join the seasonal round. Perched atop her horse-drawn carriage, imagining the camas and huckleberries she would procure during her travels, she became a famous sight, and Sherman loved to be in her company. Sherman was a diplomat, a connector between rural and urban, Native and white, tribal and federal governments. Letters and postcards poured into the family homes and the community upon his passing in 1970, each remarking upon his commitment to Native people and his humanity. In 1974, St. Mary's Mission transferred control of their school to the Colville Tribe. The tribe renamed the school in honor of its most prominent student, and the Paschal Sherman Indian School still operates near Omak, serving preschool through ninth grade students.[18]

Given Sherman's age—he was born in 1895—it is likely that he and Matsura were acquainted, even if only superficially. Sherman was very involved in his community and at St. Mary's, so while he does not seem to have had a portrait made, it is entirely possible he is in the background in one of the many events Matsura photographed.

Dynamism and inclusivity are two hallmarks of Matsura's photos; he was an outsider invited into these communities, and he returned the favor by inviting Plateau people and others into his frame. He seemed to have looked beyond the commercial promise of the Okanogan—something few settlers could do—and see the place for what it was: Indigenous homelands made by the Creator for Colville people. Making records of this homeland and its people are among Frank Matsura's most significant legacies.

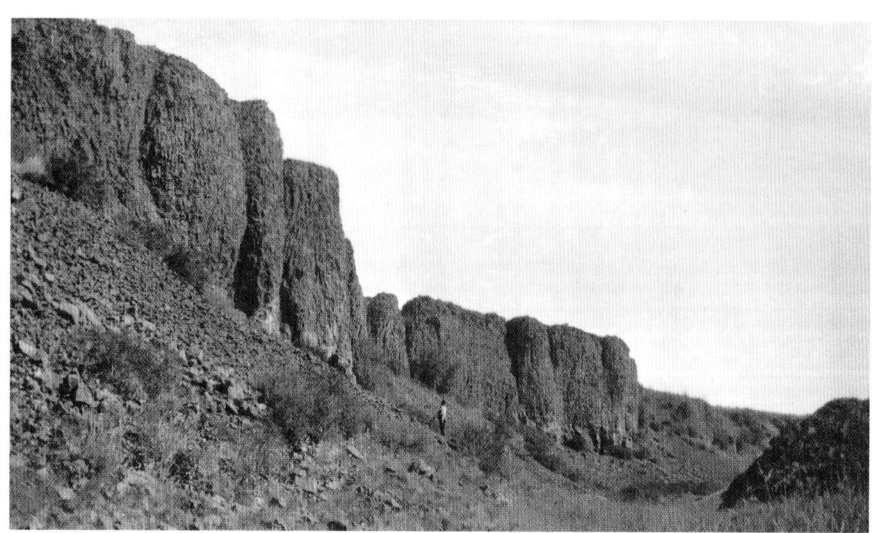

Basalt Cliffs, Colville Indian Reservation, ca. 1903–1913

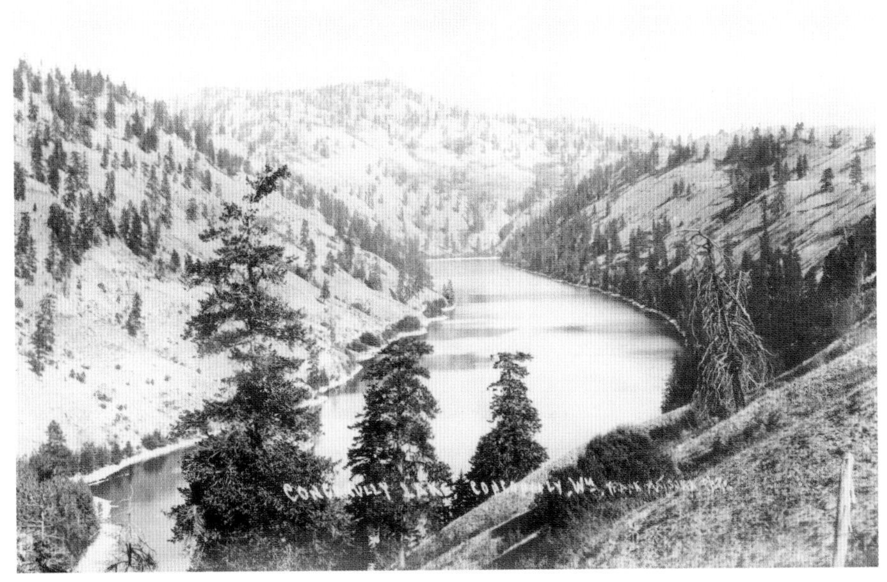

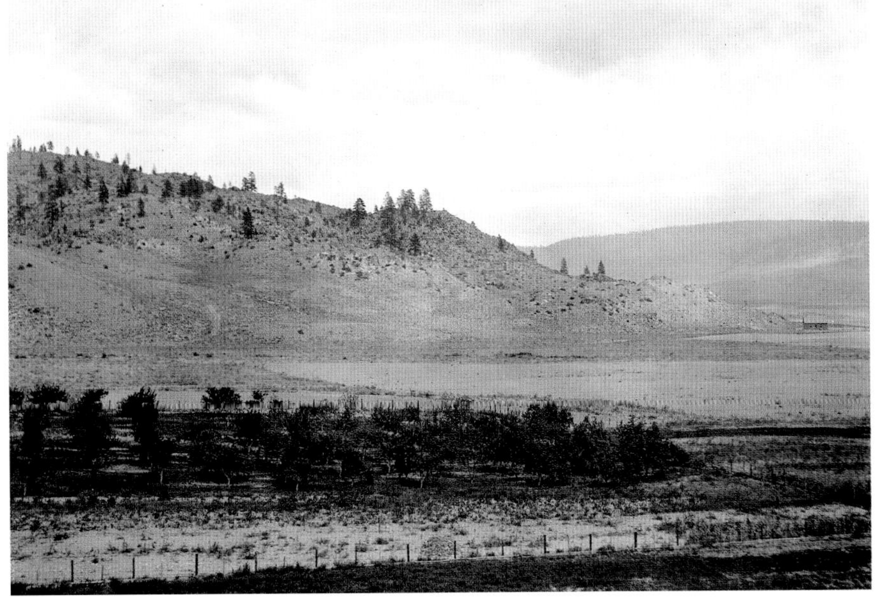

TOP
Upper Conconully Lake, ca. 1903–1913.
On the back of the photo: "This is where the wagon
road winds along so close to the lake."

BOTTOM
*Apple Orchard Amidst Plateau Landscape,
Okanogan*, ca. 1910

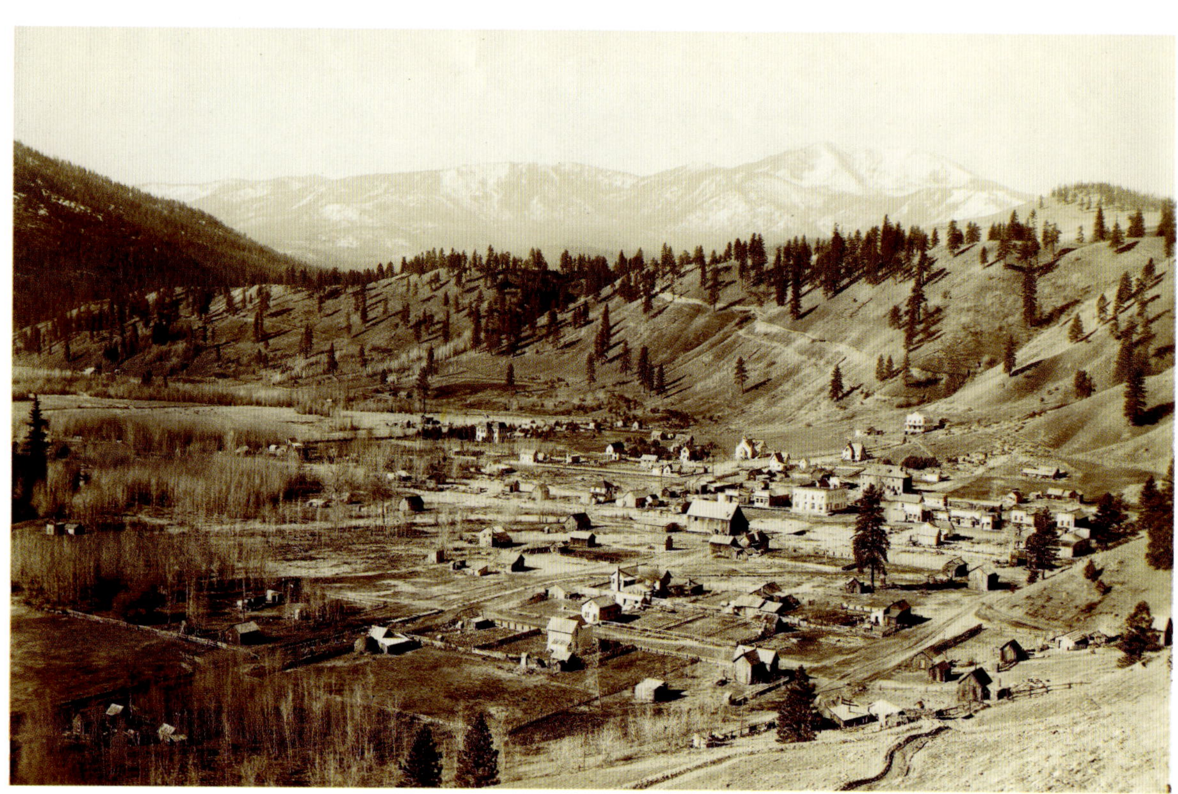

"Deserted Village" Landscape of Conconully, ca. 1906

FRANK MATSURA'S COYOTE PHOTOGRAPHY: BETWEEN SETTLER COLONIALISM AND NATIVE SURVIVANCE

Glen Mimura, PhD

This story is well-worn local lore, yet still little known beyond the territories of present-day north-central Washington State. But the story bears significance well beyond the remoteness and seeming inconsequence of its place: as a long over-due contribution to the history of photography, certainly, and at least equally for what it illuminates about the history of US settler colonialism at the micro-level of its regional transformations and interpersonal relations. Indeed, the region's uneven, overlapping histories resonate with that larger settler colonial narrative, which remains conspicuous in its geography: comprised of the Colville Indian Reservation and its twelve confederated tribes; the southern ancestral lands of the Syilx Okanagan Nation;[1] and the settler towns of Okanogan, Omak, Conconully, and dozens of others—all part of the world of the Indigenous (Columbia) Plateau and the Native peoples who have lived on its lands and cared for them since time immemorial. Immersed in this history, this story begins with the arrival of a stranger thirty years after the forced establishment of the Colville reservation in 1872.

In 1903, a Japanese immigrant named Frank Sakae Matsura moved from Seattle to Conconully, then to newly built Okanogan, from a cosmopolitan city steadily growing as a major trade and shipping center to what would have appeared to most city dwellers as the middle of nowhere. A handsome, impish extrovert, good old Frank quickly befriended seemingly everyone in the local communities. He also hauled quite of bit of photographic hardware to this apparent middle-of-nowhere; set up a photography studio and gift shop; and, as a beloved resident, proceeded to take thousands of photographs of its people, places, and events until his untimely, unexpected death caused by tuberculosis in 1913.

Matsura's photographs were prized by the locals to whom he sold and gifted his work, and they gained limited recognition and circulation beyond: magazine illustrations used to entice potential homesteaders back east; celebrated submissions to the 1909 Alaska-Yukon-Pacific Exposition in Seattle; scenes of industry and agriculture used in a 1911 Great Northern Railway advertising campaign; and the thousands of postcards sent by locals to family, friends, and others elsewhere. After Matsura's death, a substantial collection of his photographs, bequeathed to his friend Judge William Compton Brown, was donated as part of Brown's estate to the Washington State University archives. However, thousands of fragile gelatin dry glass plates on which his photographs were recorded remained stored in a garage in Okanogan, undiscovered until the mid-1970s; the late historian JoAnn Roe selected and introduced some 140 of these photographs in an elegant, small-press book, *Frank Matsura: Frontier Photographer*, that was published in 1981. Although it soon went out of print, the volume garnered sporadic attention for Matsura's work over the next three decades. Since the 2010s, however, his photographs have started to appear with greater frequency and impact in small exhibitions throughout the Pacific Northwest, earning Matsura an ever-widening circle of admiration and appreciation.

Settler Authenticity as Fiction, Coyote Fiction as Native Authenticity

Over the span of a near decade from 1903 to 1913, with unflagging enthusiasm and dedication, Matsura visited seemingly everyone and everywhere with his "magic box" and tripod in hand—sometimes with at least two, since several photographs portray Matsura posing with one of his cherished cameras. Hence, his photographic archive provides a comprehensive visual record of the region's colonial settlement: infrastructural development including the founding of his adopted hometown, Okanogan, construction of Conconully Dam, installation of electricity and waterworks, planting of orchards, extension of the railroads, and arrival of automobiles. And he produced portraits—serious and playful, formal

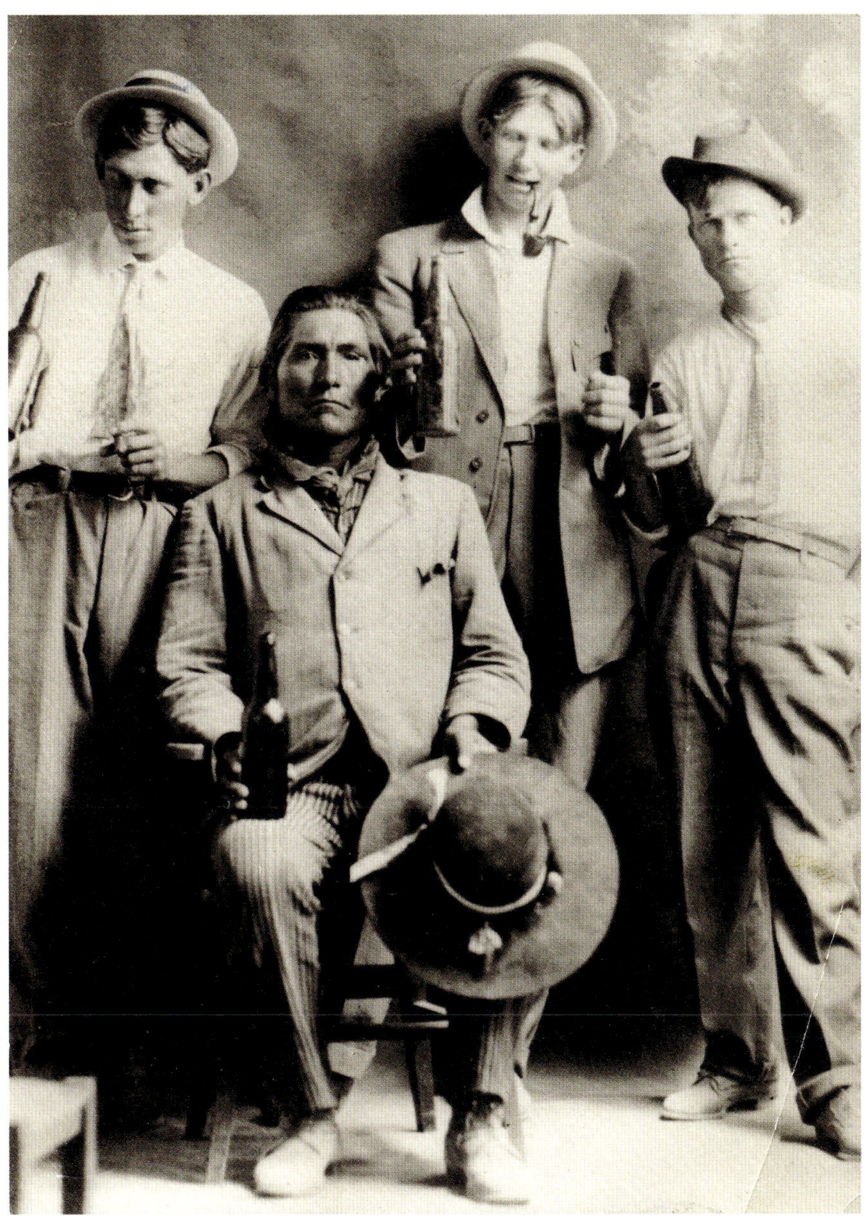

Untitled, Frank Matsura photograph, ca. 1903–1913.
Four men with alcohol bottles: Wade Troutman standing
in the center with a tobacco pipe; Mathew Barkley
at left and his cousin Roy S. Smith on the right; and
Chief Long Jim, seated.

and casual—of Native peoples and settlers alike, adapting to the modernization of the Indigenous Plateau.

The most remarkable quality of this body of work, however, is the manner in which it unsettles and departs from the perspectives and conventions of canonical American West photography and studio portraiture.[2] This radical difference is most evident in his portraits of the region's Native peoples, which art historian ShiPu Wang felicitously characterizes as "imagery of the Other by the Other": a counterarchive of American Indian representation produced by an eccentric, educated Japanese immigrant, whose motives for relocating to Okanogan remain undetermined.[3] The canonical work of Edward Curtis established the tragic view and elegiac rhetoric of Native people as noble savages unassimilable to Progress and hence destined for cultural, if not biological, extinction.[4] Even the preceding work of distinguished white male photographers like William Henry Jackson and Lee Moorhouse participated in this romanticizing project. Jackson, celebrated for his iconic landscapes of "untouched" Western landmarks, documented the tribes that his Union Pacific and US Geological Survey expeditions encountered not for themselves, but as features of the unincorporated territories to be transformed by the inexorable force of westward expansion. Moorhouse, like Matsura and unlike Curtis or Jackson, was a resident of the Pacific Northwest (and additionally a federal Indian agent) who had long-standing relationships with the tribes of the Umatilla Indian Reservation. Yet he, too, adopted and produced a romanticizing view of his Indian subjects: like Curtis, Moorhouse staged his portraits to better conform to *his* ideal of melancholic authenticity, costuming Indians with clothing and artifacts from his extensive Native wardrobe and posing them stoically, to exemplify the Indian way of life that he believed would disappear as a fatalistic corollary of Manifest Destiny.

Arguably, the single image most responsible for codifying this trope is Edward Curtis's 1904 masterpiece, *The Vanishing Race*: a group of Navajo on horseback slowly riding into the perspectival distance of the photograph—vanishing, metaphorically, into the past. The image was so vivid and memorable that it appears to have served as the template for the closing passage of Zane Grey's popular, if controversial, 1925 novel, *The Vanishing American*: against a "magnificent, far-flung sunset...the Indians were riding away." Grey continues:

> It was an austere and sad pageant....Far to the fore the dark forms, silhouetted against the pure gold of the horizon, began to vanish, as if indeed they had

ridden into that beautiful prophetic sky.…At last only one Indian was left on the darkening horizon—the solitary Shoie—bent in his saddle, a melancholy figure, unreal and strange against that dying sunset—moving on, diminishing, fading, vanishing—vanishing.[5]

To be sure, Grey's novel is a literary protest against the mistreatment of American Indians by the federal government and Christian missionaries, and his original denouement is a little more complicated. In it, Nophaie, the novel's Indian male protagonist, and Marian, his white female companion, plan to marry and live on the reservation as they watch the survivors of Nophaie's tribe "vanishing" into the sunset. The press, however—fearing backlash to its positive depiction of interracial romance—rewrote the conclusion without Grey's knowledge or consent, killing off Nophaie and the offending prospect of miscegenation. Grey's son, Loren Grey, restored his father's original ending in the novel's 1982 Pocket Books reprint, but the vanishing mythos remains intact, with the last of the tribe wistfully following Curtis's Navajo into the temporal graveyard of the past.

Matsura's photographs stand in sharp contrast to this powerful, prevailing myth. Unlike his more prestigious white male counterparts, Matsura did not impose any particular interpretive frame onto his subjects and certainly not a dominant cultural belief or perspective with which he may or may not have been familiar. (And if he knew about it through reading or his visits to Seattle, evidently he didn't buy it.) Instead, his photographs are distinguished by, as Colville tribal artist and curator Michael Holloman puts it, "conceptually sophisticated and collaborative portraits of individuals and families with whom Matsura maintained trusting relationships."[6] He did not ventriloquize through his subjects; he enabled them all, settlers and Natives alike, to present themselves to themselves and others, on their own terms. Hence, contrary to the melancholic archive of vanishing Indians inexorably dying off to make way for settler colonial modernity, Matsura's work instead illuminates what Anishinaabe writer Gerald Vizenor calls "survivance": "renunciations of dominance, tragedy and victimry" and the "active sense of presence, the continuance of native stories, not a mere reaction, or a survivable name."[7] This "active sense of presence" is seen and felt in Matsura's just-visiting portrait of his friend Chiliwhist Jim, Methow medicine man: we don't know why he's in town, but he rides and carries himself with purpose. Front and center frame, Chiliwhist Jim presides over the scene, and the camera, while the white men and their dog sit or stand idly, receding into the perspectival distance

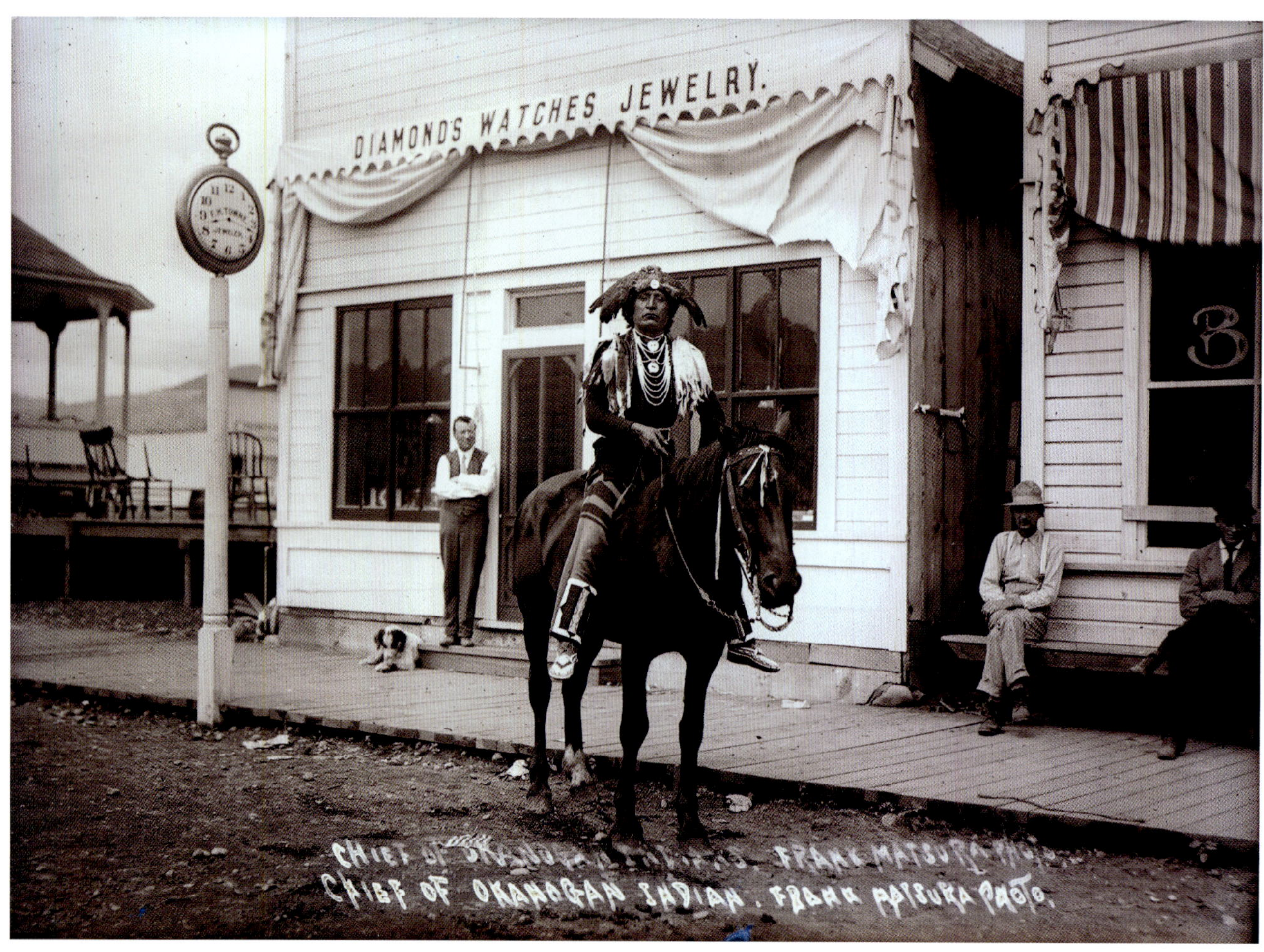

Chief of Okanogan Indians, ca. 1903–1913. Chiliwhist Jim in front of Townes Jewelry Store in Okanogan. Chiliwhist Jim is wearing Native attire, including a feather headdress.

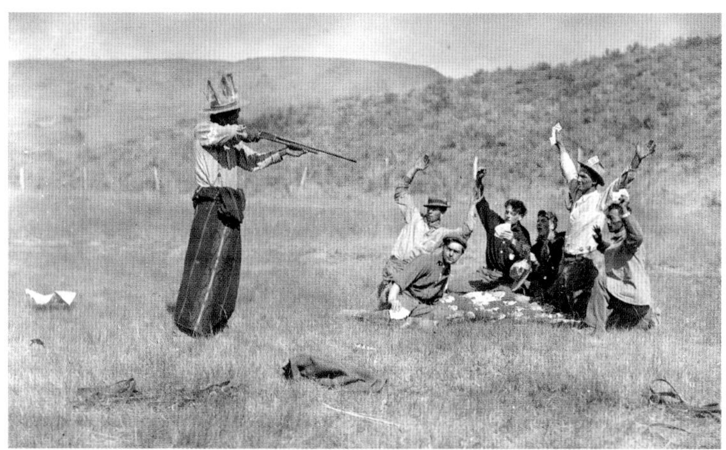

Untitled, Frank Matsura photograph, ca. 1903–1913. A staged scene of a Native American man with feathers in his hatband and blanket wrapped around his waist using a rifle to stop a card game among six men; Matsura is on the far right.

behind him. Ironically, although this photograph in itself does not reveal it, the clock is broken with its arms forever frozen at 8:17, the same time as it appears in other photographs. In any event, Chiliwhist Jim has business to attend to and is not here to wait for his extinction or ride off into the past.

More broadly, what kinds of stories of survivance do these photographs enable, support, and continue? At the Northwest Museum of Arts and Culture in Spokane, Washington, at a panel event commemorating its extraordinary exhibition of Matsura's photographs, curator Holloman intriguingly remarked that "Frank was a coyote."[8] Of course, shape-shifting Coyote ranks among the most venerated Animal People throughout Indian country, who "amused himself by getting into mischief and stirring up trouble," according to Mourning Dove, esteemed Okanogan and Colville writer of the 1920s and 1930s. Further, Coyote "delighted in mocking and imitating others, or in trying to, and, as he was a great one to play tricks, sometimes he is spoken of as 'Trick Person.'"[9] This is not to suggest that Matsura was Coyote personified; rather, that Matsura's persona and perspective manifested trickster qualities inscribed in and expressed through his photography.

Contrary to his canonical white counterparts, who passed off their fictionalizing display of Indians as authentic and true, Matsura's photographs often mirthfully reveal their ruse—like Belgian surrealist René Magritte's 1929 painting *The Treachery of Images*, baldly divulging, "This is not a pipe." Take, for example, an outdoor scene that the Okanogan County Historical Society captions thus: "A staged scene of a Native American man with feathers in hat band and blanket using a rifle to stop a card game among six men on a blanket." Whose idea was

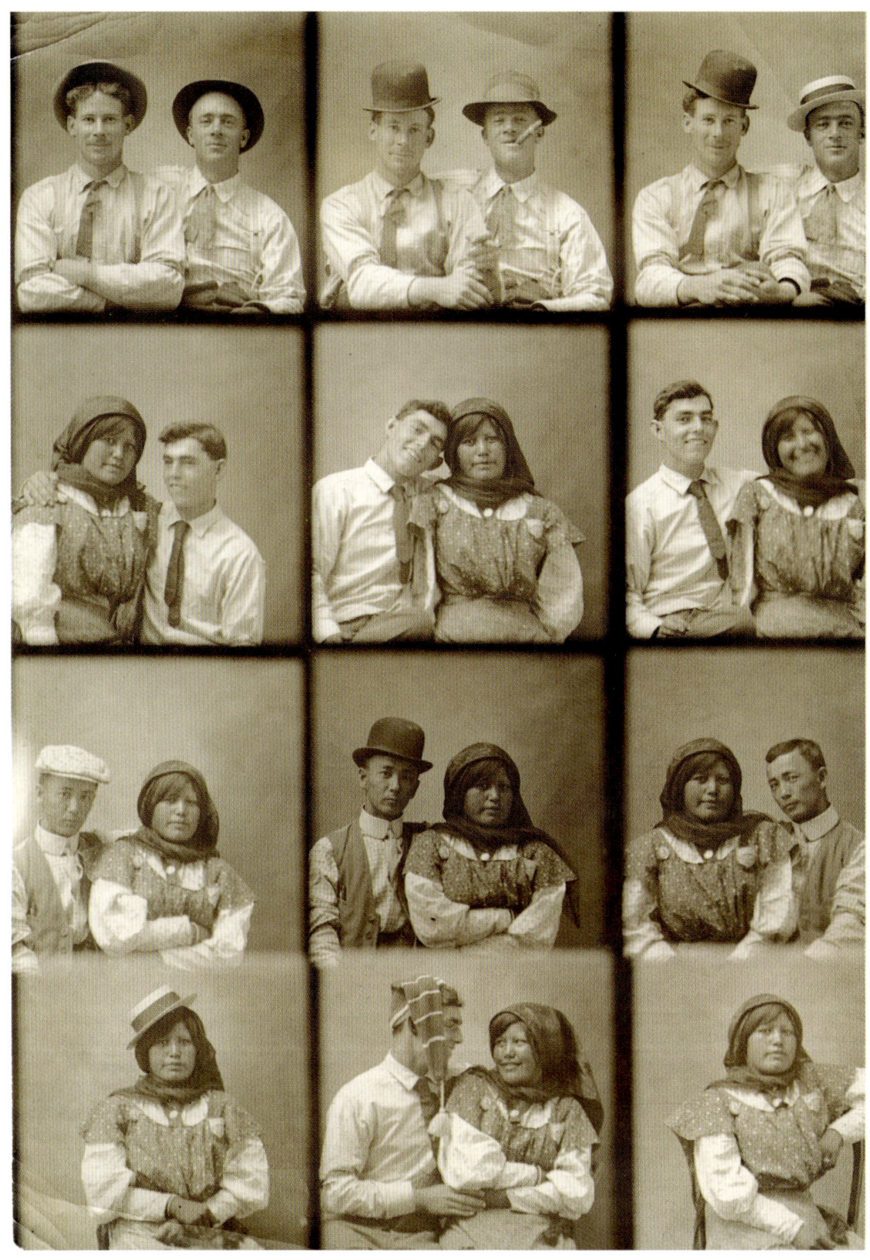

Untitled, Frank Matsura photograph, ca. 1910.
Matsura, Cecil Jim, and young men pose for portraits
at Matsura's studio.

this, and what kinds of settler-colonial relations does this mock holdup invert? The joke is evident in the photograph itself. Presumably, everyone is in on it; but who is the joke on, and for whom? The answers may well depend not only on whether we ask these questions in 1910 or today but on which side of the Okanogan River—settler towns or Colville reservation—we pose them. Likewise, reflect on a series of twelve portraits in which three young white men, Matsura, and his friend Cecil Jim (niece of the imposing Chiliwhist Jim) assume different pairings and playfully switch hats.

What do we make of this cross-racial chumminess between the sexes in 1910 Okanogan, on the settler side of the river? In photographs taken outside the studio, we see no such casual sociability, and certainly not flirtiness, across race and sex and perhaps class, as well. Indeed, Matsura's work, as Colville (Entiat) engineer and writer Wendell George says of Coyote, "made you realize that things were not always the way they seemed to be."[10] Throughout his archive of Coyote photography, colonial settlement of the Indigenous Plateau—landscapes—and the fate of its first peoples—portraiture—are not what they, in the canonical record, seem to be.

Portraiture as "Photographic Miscegenation"

No doubt Matsura's portraiture, both studio and outdoor, is the most immediately distinct aspect of his work. Perhaps part of the scholarly inattention to his work is because it does not readily square with his American contemporaries seeking to define photography as something grand or edifying. Insofar as Matsura can be said to have a discernible style or approach, his work did not partake in the movement of photography as art or artistic personal expression advocated by Alfred Stieglitz and promulgated by pictorialism, as well as the various city camera clubs that proliferated in the era. Nor was he a documentarian in the burgeoning tradition of Jacob Riis or Lewis Hine, seeking to bring attention to social ills. Matsura's style is neither aesthetically nor socially didactic; rather, it may share an affinity with the studied curiosity, if not eroticism, of E. J. Bellocq, whose archive is likewise composed of conventional professional photographs and those more idiosyncratic and personal, if not private. Matsura's work is also, arguably, a precursor to the evocative realism of Walker Evans, for whom the purpose of the photograph was to dignify its vernacular subject—ordinary people in ordinary places—rather than call attention to the photographer's skill or vision per se. To be sure, Matsura occasionally dabbled in compositional sleights of hand like the use of multiple exposures (see, for example, those examined by Maki Fukuoka in her contribution to this volume). But he was less interested in manipulation in the production process and more engaged in theatricality and performance in front of the camera lens. Sharing the best spirit of the American documentary tradition, Matsura humanizes his ordinary subjects by dignifying them; but unlike Hine, Riis, or, later, Evans, Matsura's portraits also often display a humanizing irreverence that is participatory and collaborative between himself and his subjects.

Frequently, he was enthusiastically, and simultaneously, both photographer and subject. These photographs in particular express what art historian ShiPu Wang astutely calls "photographic miscegenation," exemplified by the series noted earlier with Matsura, Cecil Jim, and the three white men.[11] The format of the serial photographs, with their juxtapositions and progressions, lends itself to such theatricality and carnivalesque. Some are notable for the degree of camaraderie and homosocial intimacy they display between Japanese immigrant Matsura and the white men he is horsing around with, for example, a later comical series of forty-two stamp photos titled *Matsura, Charles Herrmann, and Two Other Friends*, circa 1912, in which the four men goof off with a straw hat and a popped-out hat, mug in various profiles, and drift around in the photographic frame, with two of them even bending over and showing their asses to the camera.[12] But the most extraordinary displays of photographic miscegenation, as Wang notes, are those in which Matsura pairs himself with white or Native women: suggestively transgressive stagings of interracial intimacy in a period of anti-Indian and anti-Asian racism, antimiscegenation policy and sentiment, and aggressive efforts to assimilate and culturally "exterminate" Native people. In a curious and interesting turn of Washington State history, in 1868, the then territory rolled back its ban on interracial marriage. However, the state effectively restricted interracial marriage until at least the mid-twentieth century through racist anxieties and sentiment in step with neighboring states like Oregon and Idaho. Racist restrictions on the issuance of marriage licenses served as an additional gatekeeping measure.

Certainly, many of Matsura's images are typical of professional studio photography: solo portraits, couples, families, friends, organizations, sports teams, and the like; but the poses, fashions, and decorum of Matsura's photographic miscegenation often depart strikingly from those modeled on the conventions of portrait paintings. In his award-winning book *The*

OPPOSITE
Matsura, Charles Herrmann, and Two Other Friends, Frank Matsura photograph, ca. 1912

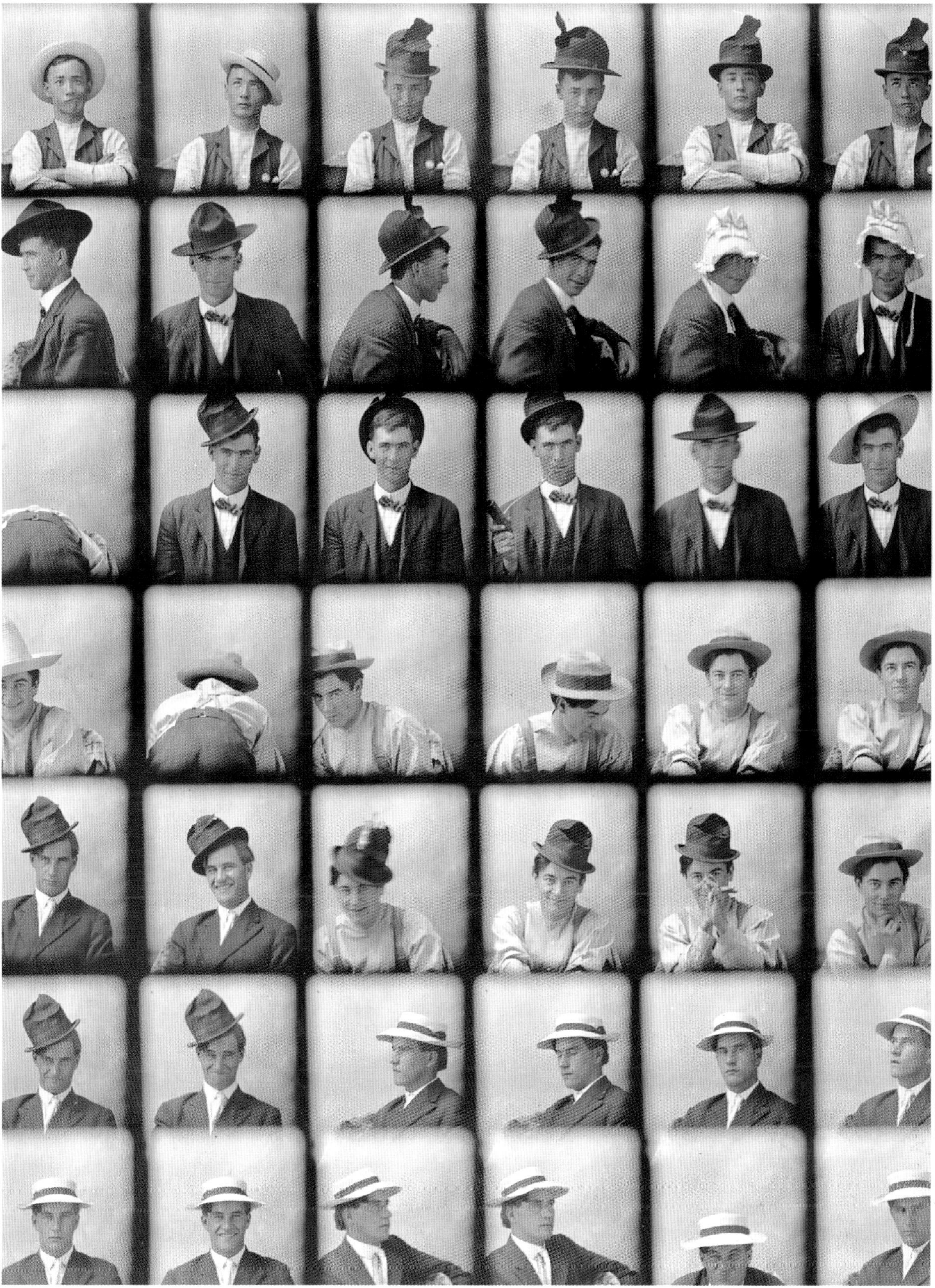

Other American Moderns, Wang centers his analysis of Matsura's studio portraiture writ large through a careful reading of a particular photograph, *Matsura and Susan Timento Pose at Studio*, circa 1912.

He insightfully elaborates on Matsura's contemplative performance of "going Native," not in a manner that repeats redface stereotyping but that draws attention to his racialized similarity with Susan Timento: phenotypically, they share features that mark them both as nonwhite and therefore subordinate in the settler colonial world outside the photographic frame. Yet he also performs a difference legible at least for Native viewers of the image, passing himself off not authentically as Indian but ironically as "Indian"—which is to say, as someone self-consciously playing Indian. Wang deftly unpacks the significance of the American-made "Indian blanket" in which Matsura adorns himself: mass-produced with generic Indian patterns and colors and distributed by federal Indian agents throughout the reservations, the blankets were appropriated by Native people who appreciated their durability and resignified them as everyday symbols of pan-Indian identity. In the popular American imagination, however, the blanket-shrouded Indian became a symbol of the lazy, unassimilable Native, and forsaking the blanket was taken to signal a Native's willful abandonment of Indian ways and acceptance of white American civility. Hence, by wrapping himself in the blanket and posing solemnly with Timento, wife of medicine man Chiliwhist Jim, Matsura both ironizes his Indian self-fashioning and expresses Native peoples' refusal both of racist stereotyping and assimilation.

Two other serial photographs with Indian women bear notice. First, given the context richly opened up by Wang, even a seemingly conventional rendering like a circa 1909 four-portrait series of two young Native women with Matsura takes on greater significance.

In turns, they sit solemnly with their photographer, presenting to the camera in the same way as Timento. The two other portraits show the two women together, then together with Matsura. The main difference from the Timento photo is fashion: Matsura dons modern settler wear, while the women display a more distinctively Indian style, with their heads wrapped with scarves and, conspicuously, their blankets around their shoulders. Modern and traditional not as opposed, but complementary: this is no endorsement of assimilation; rather, it is a visual assertion of survivance through adaptability and coexistence.

In contrast, a four-shot series with Timento's niece, *Matsura and Miss Cecil Chiliwhist*, also known as Cecil Jim, circa 1910, seems more decidedly modern in

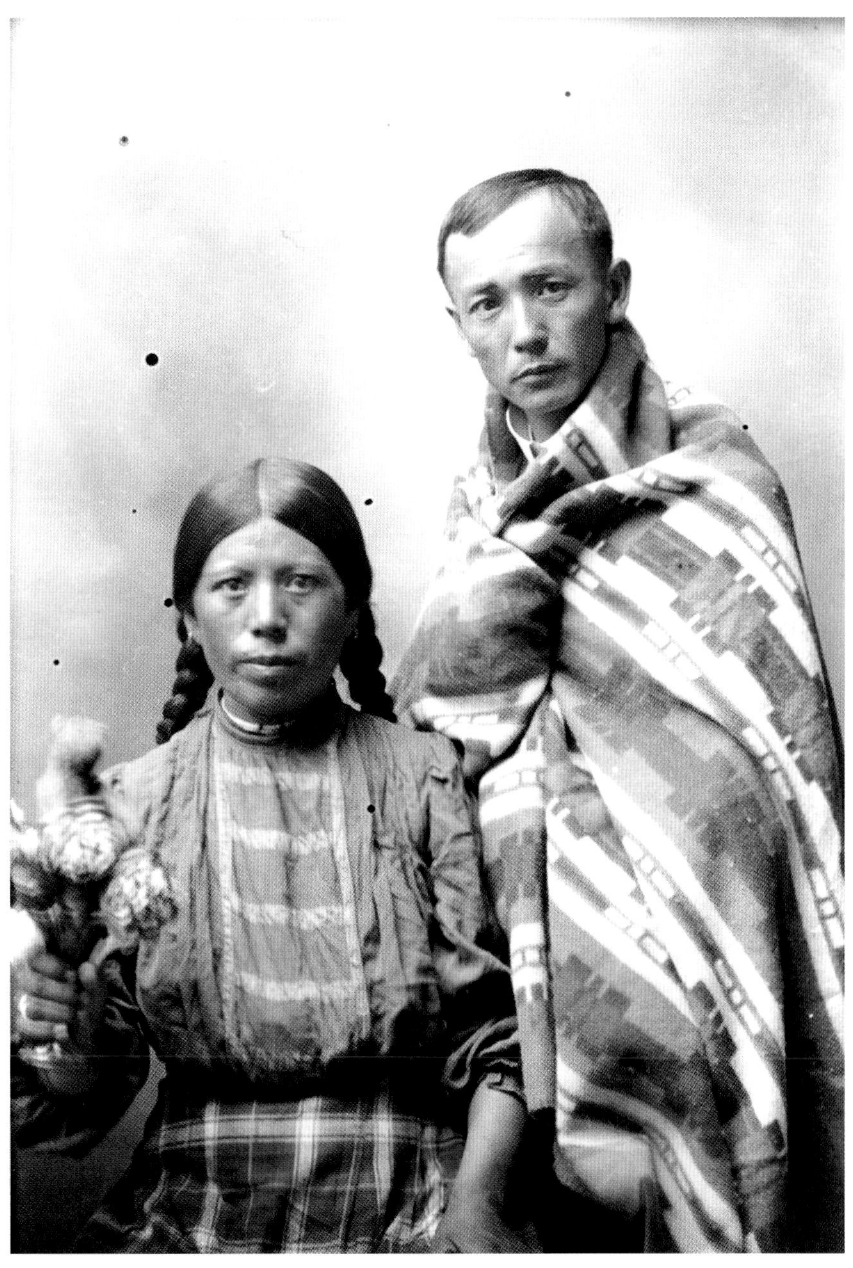

Matsura and Susan Timento Pose at Studio, ca. 1912.
Matsura and Susan Timento pose for a picture in his studio in
Okanogan. Matsura stands with a blanket wrapped around his
shoulders. Timento sits in a chair beside him, holding a teddy
bear. She is the aunt of Cecil Jim.

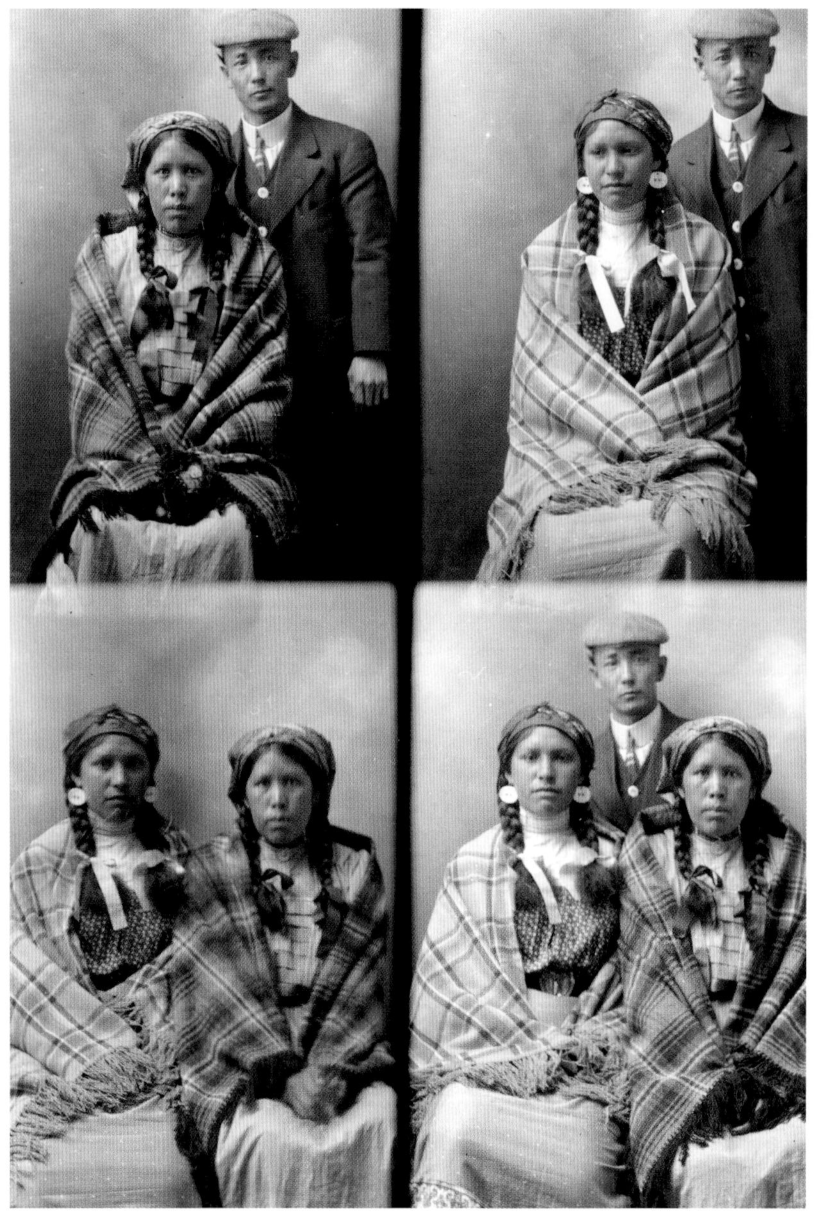

Matsura with Two Young Indian Women, ca. 1909

Matsura and Miss Cecil Chiliwhist, ca. 1910

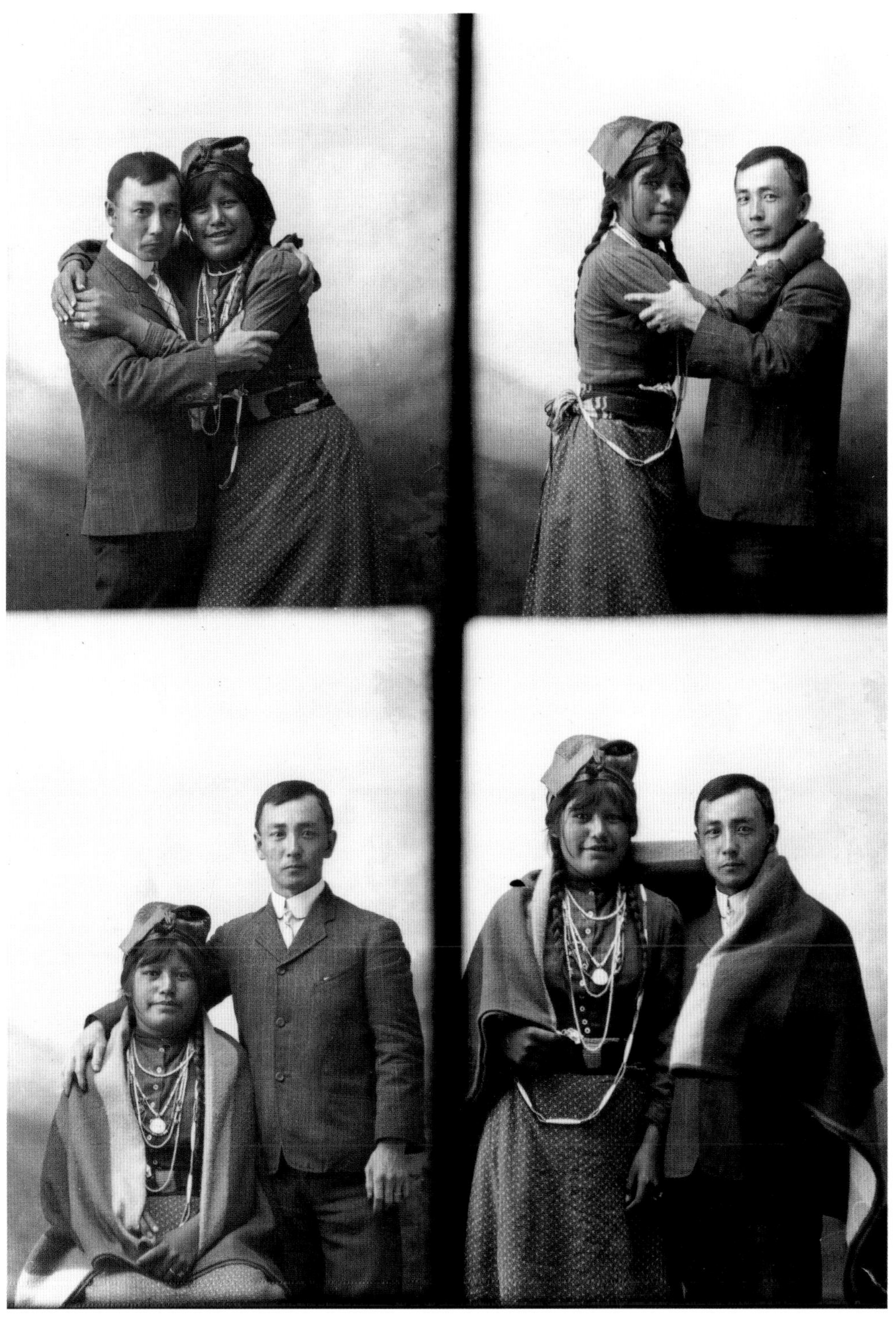

its fashion and its departure from the photographic conventions inherited from portrait painting. The lower left image hews formally to aunty Susan Timento's later circa 1912 portrait, except the subjects' fashion is inverted: Matsura is not playing Indian; rather, Jim is being and wearing modern, as she does in several other photographs (perhaps most memorably paired with another Native woman on a Victorian fainting couch). But unlike in the Timento portrait or the four-shot with the two young Indian women, here, Matsura's arm clearly wraps around Jim, hand on shoulder. In the top two frames of the series, this small, campy gesture displays their affection, with Matsura, in ShiPu Wang's terms, playing the part of spouse or lover—a role-playing that he appears to relish in numerous portraits with women. But in the fourth frame, lower right, we see a variation of a telltale gesture particular to Matsura's portraits with Indian women: in addition to Matsura wrapping himself and the two young Native women wrapping themselves, here we see his friend Jim wrapping them both, together, with her blanket. In Coyote-like fashion, things are not always as they appear to be, indeed.

Matsura's portraits of and with white women render the sexually transgressive nature of Matsura's photographic miscegenation perhaps most explicitly. In a four-shot series from circa 1912, for example, a matronly white woman wearing glasses and a white blouse with a tight, neck-high collar sits for straightforward portraits in the top two. In the bottom two, however, Matsura enters the frame, and we see the woman toying with a seated, straight-faced Matsura in the bottom left. In the bottom right, the two are seated together, heads leaning in and touching, with Matsura embracing the woman with his right arm: a couple's portrait. In another stamp-photo series, Matsura and his friend Norma Dillabough sit through a romping session composed of twenty shots in which they act out the role of lovers. Except, we are led to believe, the series is "obviously" staged since they engage in the whole hat-swapping routine and, in two silly shots, adorn themselves with strings of his real photo postcards and playing cards. And yet they lift each other's chins, Dillabough sits in Matsura's lap in a half-dozen shots, and they close in the bottom right frame "kissing" behind the brim of a hat. Dillabough's father, it merits noting, owned the Elliot Hotel in Conconully, and he was the first to hire Matsura as a cook and cleaner when he arrived in the county several years earlier.

One may wonder if such photographs were shared relatively publicly—or at least, say, with spouses and family—or were kept for private titillation. Two other photographs, while they do not resolve the question of circulation,

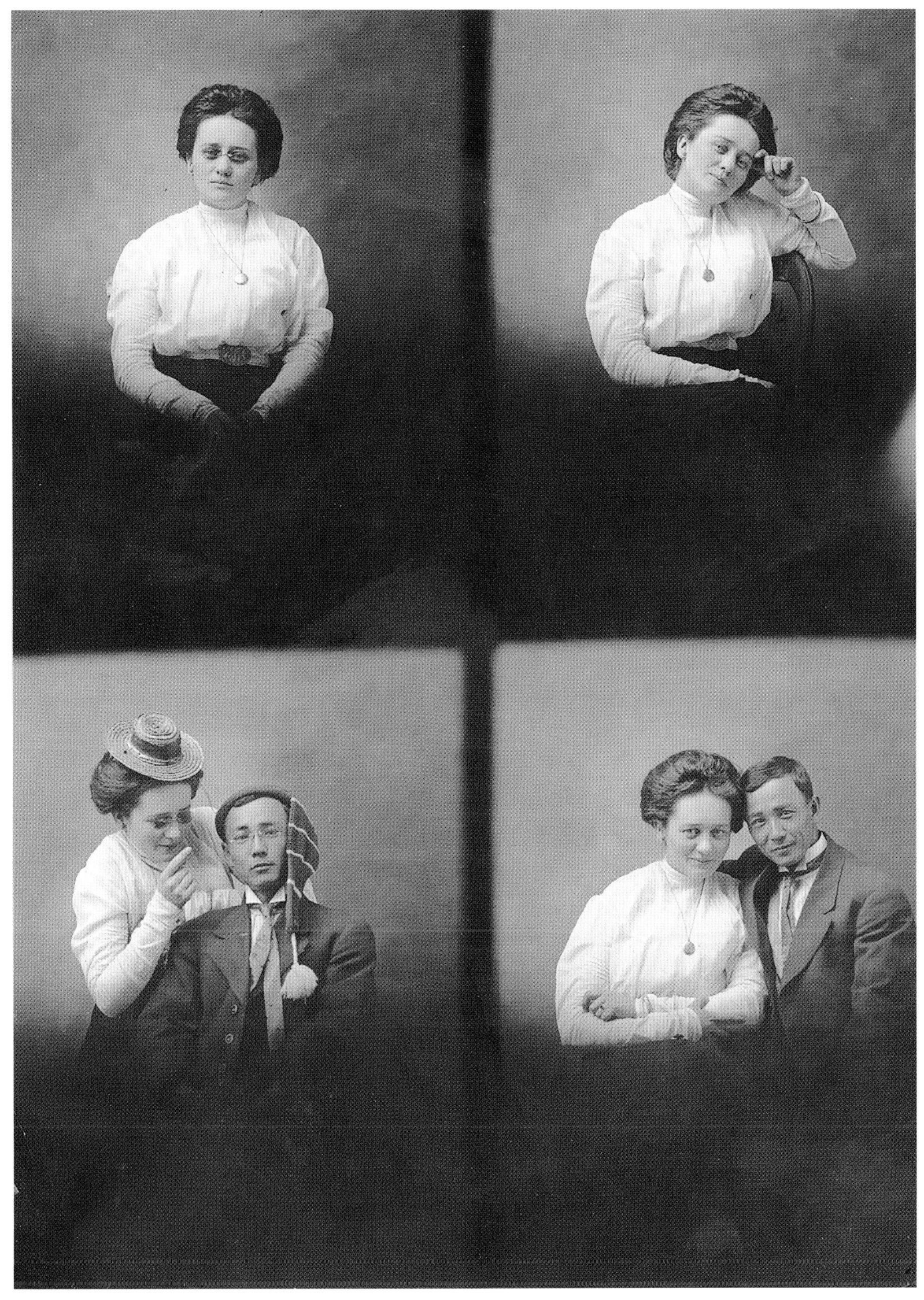

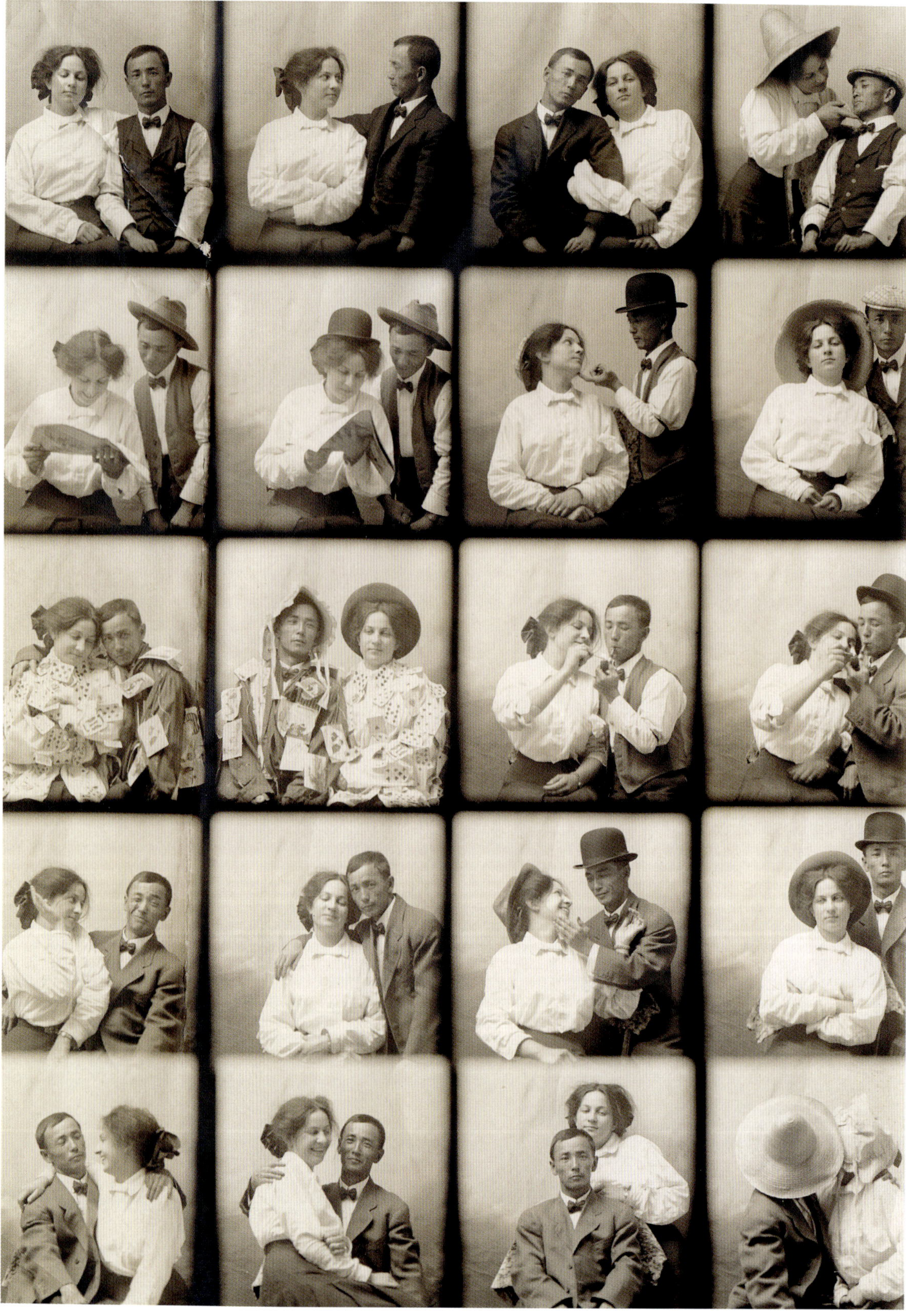

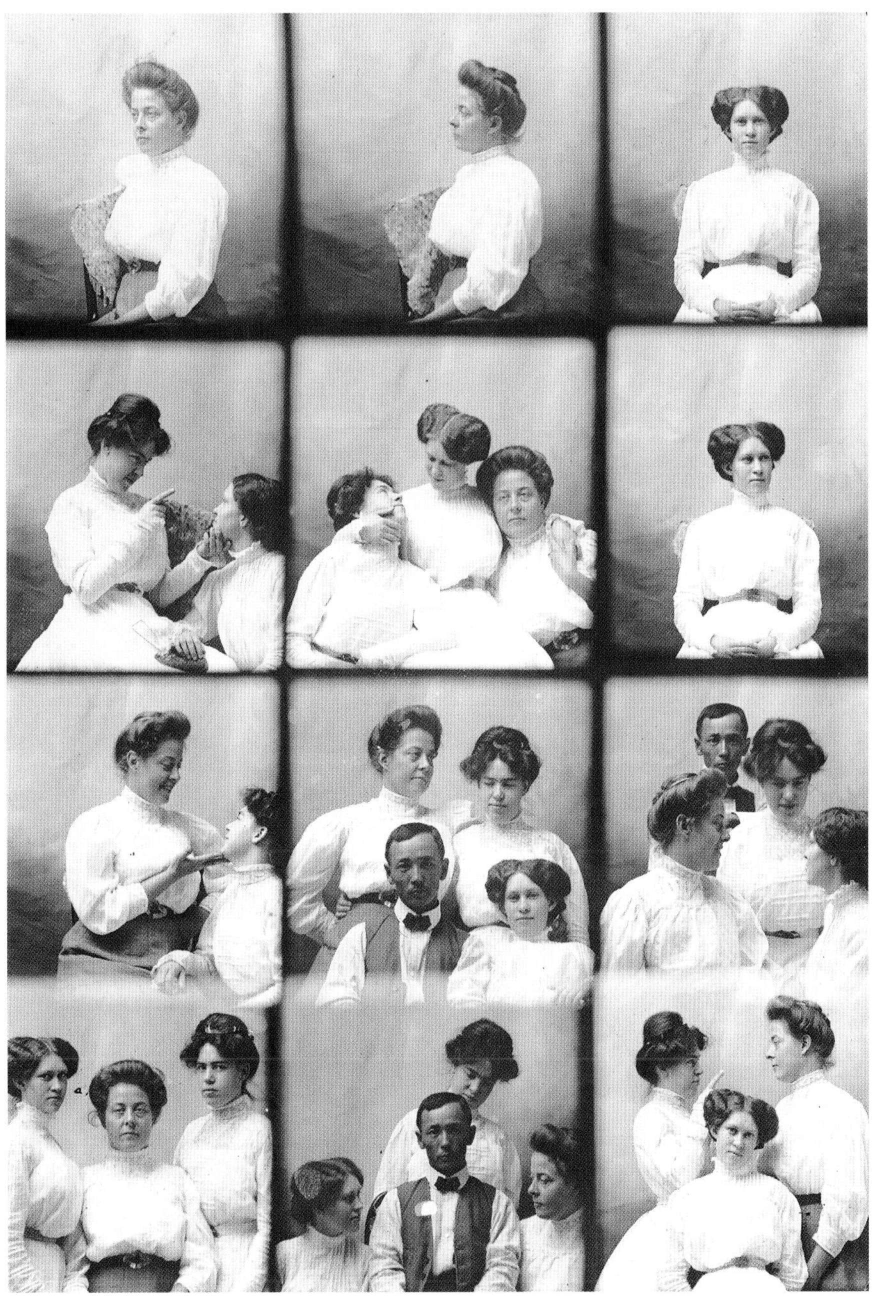

OPPOSITE
Norma Dillabough and Matsura Pose at His Studio for Portraits, ca. 1911

ABOVE
A Mother and Two Grown Daughters Pose with Matsura at His Studio, ca. 1911

complicate the issue from the performative side of the camera. In one, a twelve-shot series shows a white mother and her two white daughters sitting for a portrait session. All appears to be going well when—surprise—Matsura shows up in three of the last five shots. In the first, he appears to insert himself into the foreground of a family portrait almost surreptitiously: the women pretend not to see him. In the second shot, Matsura appears to be excluded from the three women's conversation, or perhaps he is eavesdropping? In the third, he is now front and center and scrutinized from each side and from behind by the women, as if visually vetoing any desire or attempt to pose as spouse or lover.

In the second twelve-shot series, Matsura joins a young white couple in all but three shots, in which the couple poses together and each alone. They engage in the hat wearing and swapping game and goof around throughout. In three shots near the end of the series, Matsura appears seated to the woman's left side (viewer's right), where her husband or lover typically would be. If Matsura is playfully iced out by the mother and her two daughters, he is welcomed as an equal in this photographic ménage à trois with the young white couple. These two series may not be as racy as the previously examined series, but they introduce figures—mother, romantic companion—whose authority might be expected to intervene in such suggestive theatricality. Instead, they, too, participated.

Not all of the cross-cultural traffic recorded by Matsura went against the grain of prevailing ideologies or sentiment. Among the forms of cultural consumption enjoyed by the county's settler colonial communities were older-school, racial-gendered practices that reflected tastes and investments that were both cosmopolitan (like orientalism) and national (like minstrelsy). While most studio portraits of women present their subject seated, one subset depicts them standing fully in frame: white women wearing silk kimonos.

The photos capture one way in which Okanogan County's settlers, however geographically remote, remained connected to fashion-forward trends: in this case, the interface of a burgeoning Art Nouveau and theatrical Japonisme, both of which linked their tastes not to East Asia to the west but to the "far east" of Western Europe. After Japan's forced reopening to trade with the West in 1853, Japanese art and crafts flooded European markets and immediately impacted its art world, most notably a fascination with ukiyo-e wood-block prints that transformed Impressionist painting. Japonisme, or Europe's aesthetic and cultural reanimation through its market-driven encounter with Japan, reached a fever pitch on the stage with Gilbert and Sullivan's comic opera *The Mikado* (1885), followed

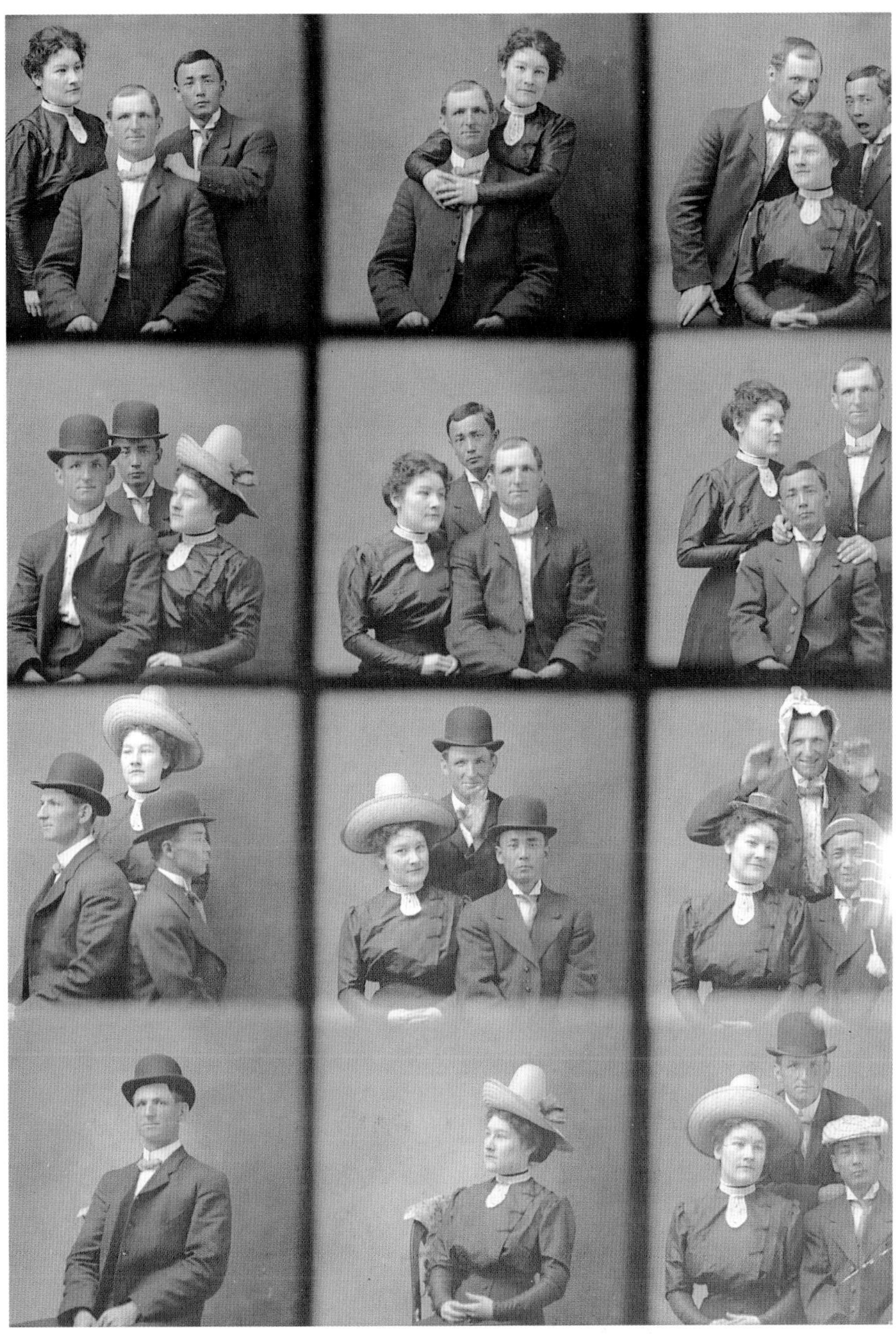

*Matsura and a Young Couple Pose for Portraits
at His Studio*, ca. 1911

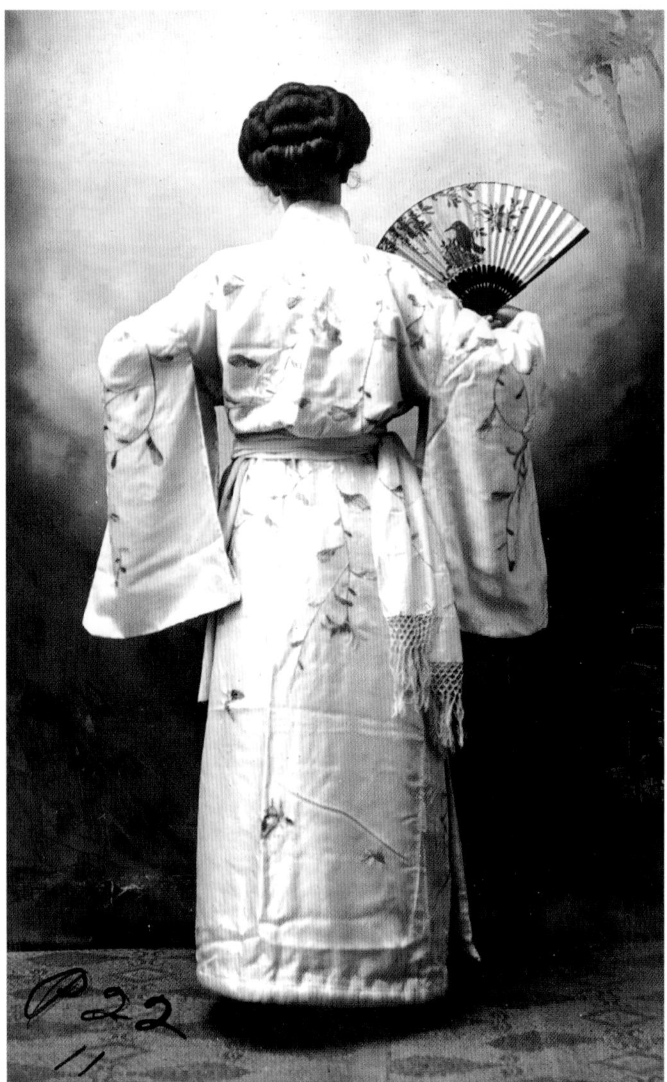

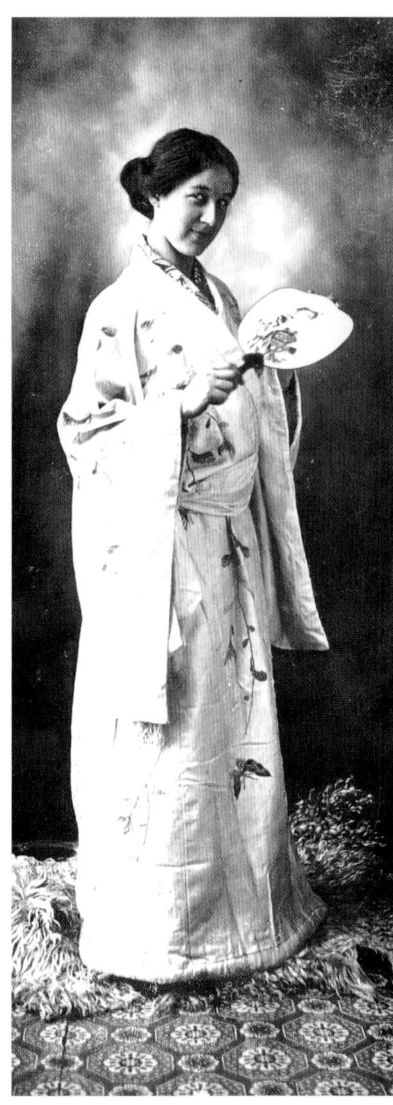

LEFT
A Woman in a Kimono, Back Turned toward Camera, ca. 1910

RIGHT
Woman in Kimono Holding Fan, ca. 1912

by Sidney Jones's Edwardian musical comedy *The Geisha* (1896), and immortalized by Puccini's *Madama Butterfly* (1904)—all popularizing the alluring figure of the geisha. These performances fueled European bourgeois consumption of oriental bric-a-brac like lacquers, fans, and, most prized of all, the silk kimono, which in turn influenced the rise of Art Nouveau in fine and decorative arts and fashion.

Hence, in these two photos, vertically long and horizontally narrow in the manner of Art Nouveau painting, these two women do not merely display their orientalist regalia, they perform it: mysteriously back-facing in one and, in the other, turning seductively to the camera, head slightly bowed in shadow, casting a sideways glance—fans poised artfully in both. One wonders about such moments

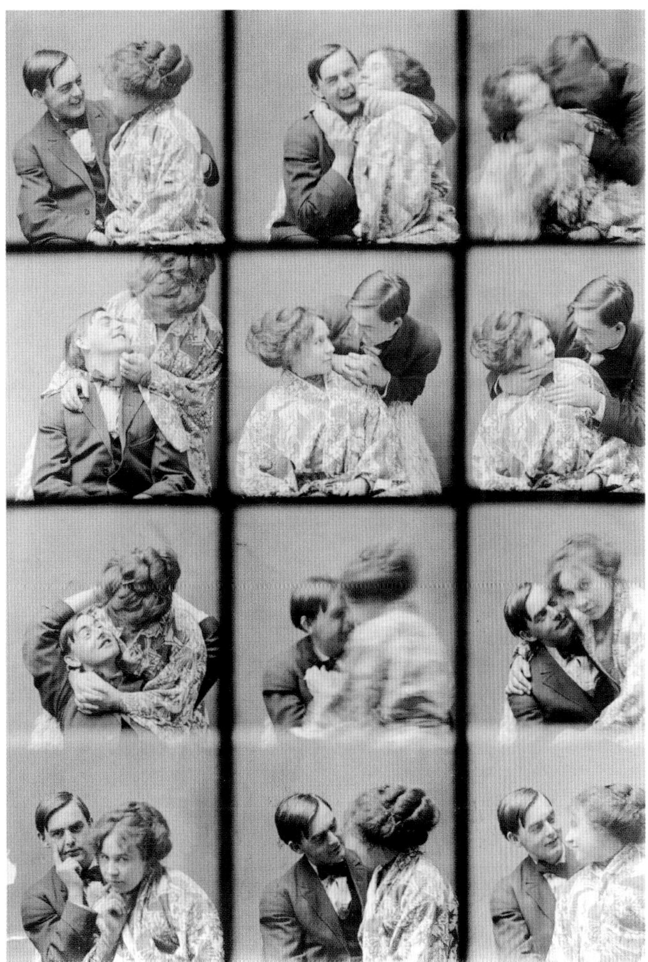

Mathilda Schaller in Kimono with Friend at Matsura's Studio, ca. 1912

of Okanogan settler femininity projecting European taste, masquerading as Japanese refinement, in a Japanese immigrant's studio just across the river from the Colville reservation: did she ask Matsura if her presentation was authentic? And what might have been the difference between what he thought and what he said? Did *he* care if she got it right? Perhaps not: witness Mathilda Schaller, who, at least in this instance, bought that spendy silk kimono, which traveled from Japan to Europe to Okanogan County through the Eastern Seaboard, only to wrinkle it by horsing around with a friend.

In this case, the playfully permissive space of Matsura's studio divests the kimono of its orientalism—settler colonial counterpoint to the Indian blanket?— and instead turns it into a classic Matsura serial photograph.

If regaling oneself in a kimono was cutting edge and its consumption and performance a decidedly "adult" form of self-gratification, blackface minstrelsy was low family entertainment: backward and, by the turn of the century, bordering on the archaic. And yet in an early image in Matsura's archive, and perhaps one of its more unsettling, we see Matsura center stage in a local talent minstrel show in circa 1906.

It isn't one of his better photos: the camera flash catches the small metal divider between performers and audience, which flattens the main scene behind, lending the image a dusty atmosphere rhetorically fitting for its antiquated subject matter. But it still reveals and fascinates. Several of the other men are in blackface and costume, and Matsura, seated in the middle, wears a burlap sugar sack with, according to its WSU caption, "clown makeup and a pointy, striped hat…playing the triangle." (And let us not overlook those…painted whiskers?) He appears ghastly: is his role in this blackface show, in Indian country, to perform as an honorific white man in whiteface? Was this photo a rite of passage for Matsura to demonstrate his obedience, devotion, trustworthiness to the local whites, many if not most of whom were also recent arrivals, anxiously or aggressively asserting their propertied citizen whiteness as they homesteaded lands taken from the long-standing local Natives?

As we know, unlike most of his white neighbors in the settler colonial community, Matsura will befriend those local Natives and, so it appears, come to recognize something of himself in them. Six years later, as he cloaks himself in the "Indian blanket" sitting for a self-portrait with Susan Timento, he forsakes not his Japaneseness nor his affinity for Native peoples, but rather whiteface and the lure of assimilation on display in this minstrelsy record. With Art Nouveau

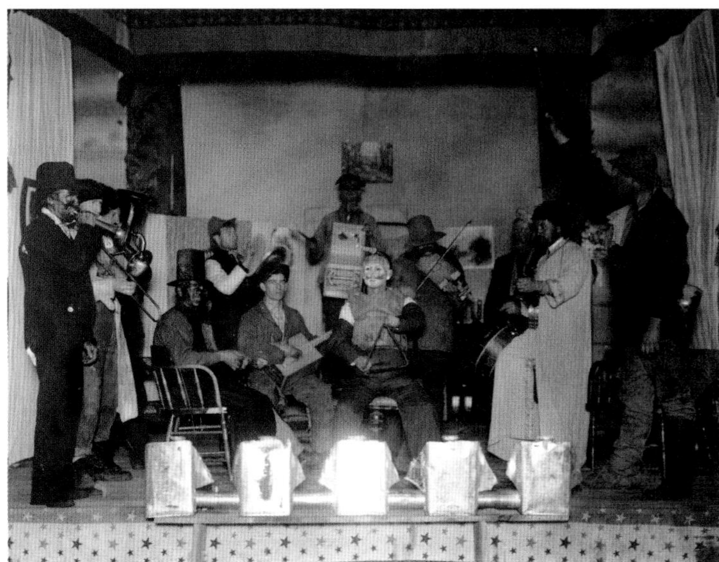

*Local Talent Minstrel Show,
Conconully, Washington,* ca. 1906.
"Squeedunk" Orchestra, Matsura in
clown costume with triangle.

self-decorating, this blackface performance suggests the spectrum of racist settler entertainment and cultural consumption in Okanogan County; and in the broader context of Matsura's archive, it appears not only out of step in time but also out of place in the larger Indigenous Plateau.

Among his portraiture work, curiously, Matsura does not appear to ham it up with Native men, at least not in front of the camera. In this respect, his portraits of Native men overall represent some of his most "typical" photographs: in contrast to the savage-paradigm rhetorical gesture of canonical Indian photography—nostalgically saving them for posterity, before they vanish into the past—perhaps Matsura reserves the painterly, dignifying, and humanizing conventions of studio portraiture most of all for Native men. This appears to be consistent whether the photographic occasion is casual or formal. A circa 1912 six-shot series presents two Native men, one older and one much younger—related, or just friends?—dressed in heavy coats for colder weather. As in other serials, we see them exchanging and playing with prop hats, as well as a long pipe: they're evidently enjoying themselves, but Matsura doesn't join in the fun with them, and they don't cut loose in the way that many of his other subjects do—Native and white women and white men.

In a more formal series from circa 1911 (following page, bottom), a Native mother and son sit together for three shots and solo for the following nine: three for mom, six for son, both sporting Euro-American fashions with modern

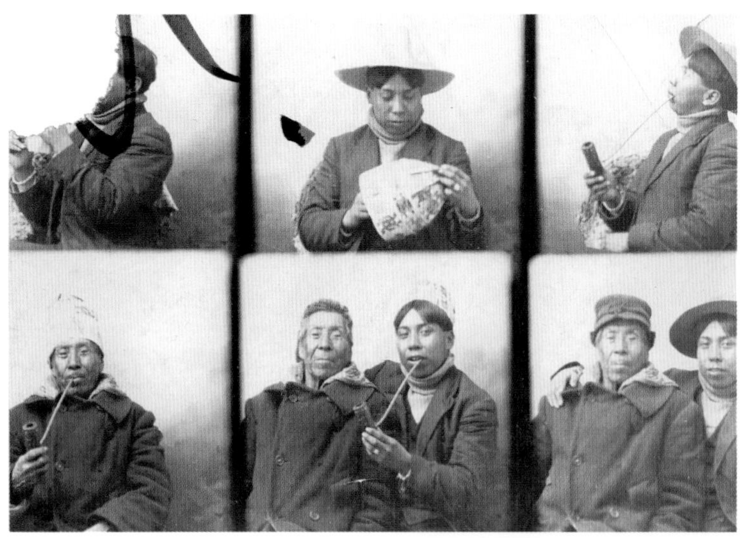

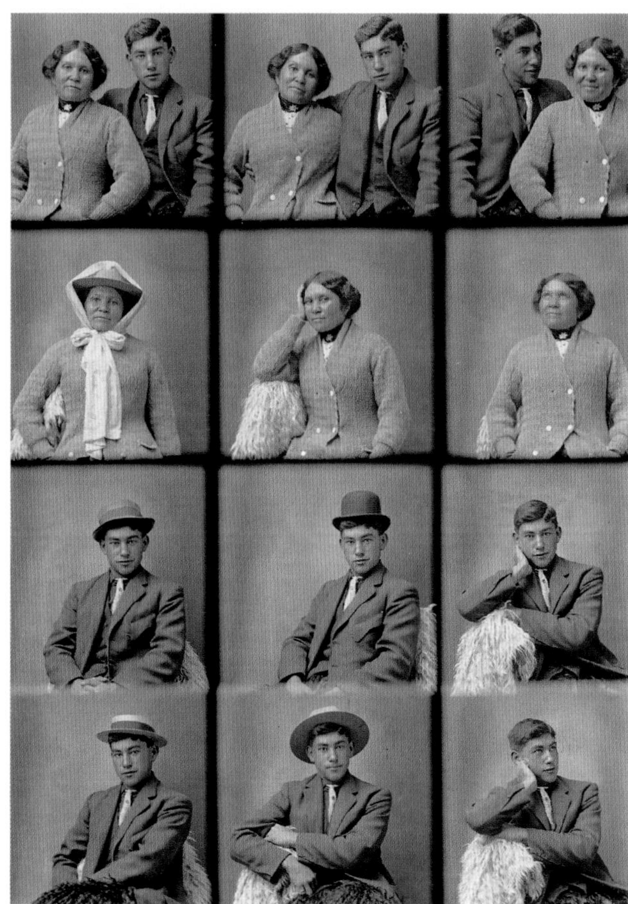

ABOVE
Two Native American Men Pose for Portraits at Matsura's Studio, ca. 1912

RIGHT
Native American Mother and Son Pose for Portraits at Matsura's Studio, ca. 1911

hairstyles. The mother wears a cardigan sweater over a high-collared blouse with an inset cameo; the son wears a three-piece suit with a necktie. The mother tries on a hat with a large bow, and the son tries on three different hats; but they use the props as they are conventionally intended: as accents for their relaxed, confident poses, not as sight gags or playthings. This twelve-shot sequence is among the most endearing, beautiful portraitures in Matsura's archive.

A final example here is among the most striking: a majestic portrait of Chiliwhist Jim in Matsura's studio (see page 68). Seated upright, legs apart, hands on his thighs, he appears at ease yet distinguished. He is also attired in the same traditional regalia that he is wearing on horseback by the broken clock in the photograph discussed earlier; perhaps his business in town was this portrait session? Capturing his friend in his entirety, rather than cropping his portrait at the knees or bust, Matsura presents the medicine man as he wishes to present himself. The long shot encompasses the bottom of the painted screen behind him, with the floor stretching forward from below. Seated not straight on along the photograph's two-dimensionalizing 180-degree angle, but instead at a slight angle, Chiliwhist Jim is figured three-dimensionally, a robust and dignified presence, further accentuated by his magnificent bird headdress in sharp relief against the white reflection of the artificial light on the backdrop, itself encircling his solemn expression, beaded necklaces, and hide-lined shoulders like a nimbus. We don't know if this session was taken for Chiliwhist Jim or at Matsura's request, but the respectful trust between them is evident in the portrait itself. Given its vivid, formal composition, beyond its private value or purpose, this image was used as a postcard—an emblem of the region for personal but mass circulation beyond its boundaries. Its reception at its various points of destination is largely unknowable, but in the context of Matsura's archive, it rightfully bestows high esteem to a Methow medicine man dispossessed of his people's land.

What's in a Landscape?

In relation to his manifestly trickster portraiture, Matsura's landscapes, agricultural studies, and scenes of town and country may appear value neutral or less ideologically unfettered. But are they? In a very different context, distilling his views of *fûkeiron*—the "landscape theory" arising from 1960s Japanese political cinema—the radical filmmaker Masao Adachi provocatively asserts, "All the landscapes which one faces in one's daily life, even those such as the beautiful sites shown on a postcard, are essentially related to the figure of a ruling power."[13]

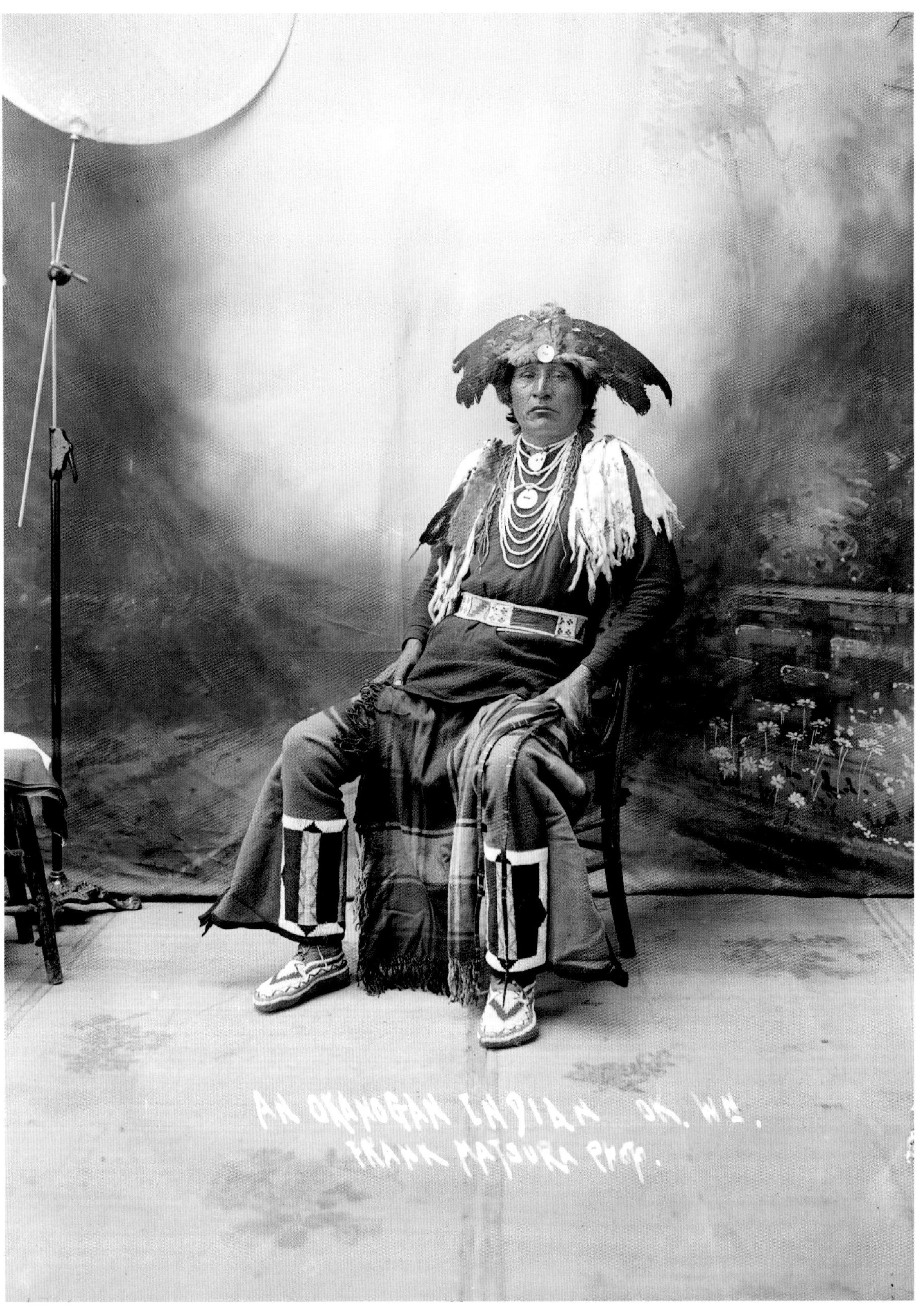

AN OKANOGAN INDIAN OK. WN.
FRANK MATSURA PHOT.

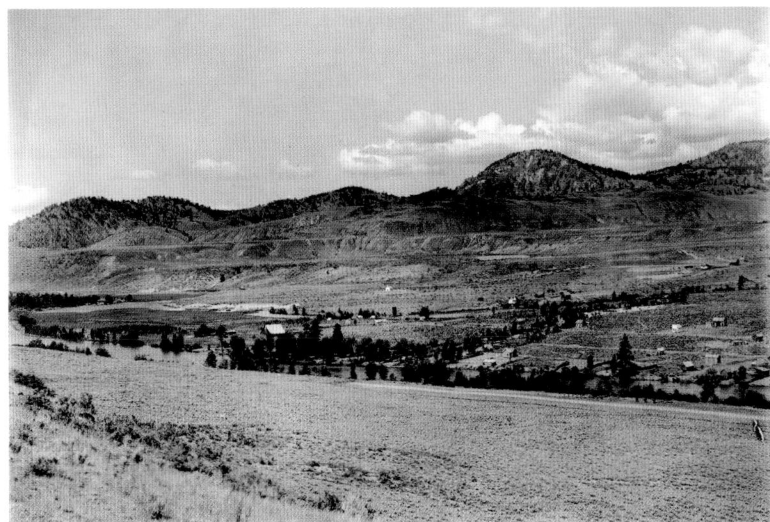

Perhaps unsurprisingly, the ur-text of *fûkeiron* is photographic: the hauntingly deserted streets and interiors of old Paris captured by Eugène Atget, whose urban landscapes on the verge of transformation were roughly contemporaneous with Matsura's work and which also distinctly departed from the prevailing photographic codes and conventions of his time and place. One of Atget's exponents, German critic Camille Recht, remarked that his photographs share a likeness with crime scene images—an observation taken up and elaborated by Walter Benjamin in his widely influential 1935 essay, "The Work of Art in the Age of Mechanical Reproduction," from which Adachi and his Red Army comrades formulated their landscape theory and practice. And the "figure of a ruling power" latent or implicit in a landscape—or its "hidden political significance" in Benjamin's terms—is the historical violence of capitalism that pervades, circumscribes, or conscripts the landscape for its own purposes. In Matsura's scenic photography, Benjamin or Adachi might say, the landscapes of the Indigenous Plateau are crime scenes of westward colonial expansion and settlement.

Adachi and his comrades eschewed the more legible, even confrontational political ideas and approaches of their internationalist filmmaking contemporaries, like the Latin American proponents of the Third Cinema movement, in favor of the slower, oblique, contemplative engagement that landscapes oblige of their viewers. Matsura's scenic imagery, with or without intent, similarly refrains from the aesthetic or social didacticism of his American photographer contemporaries.

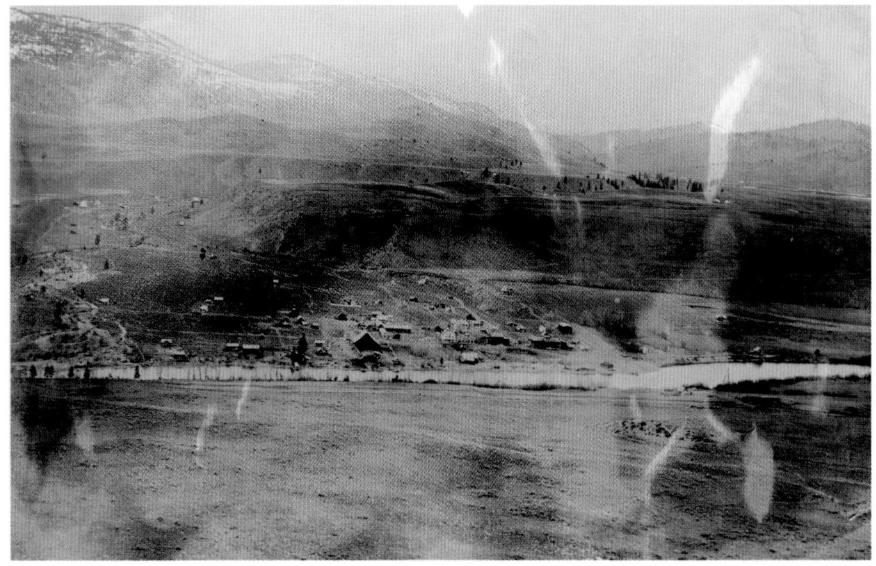

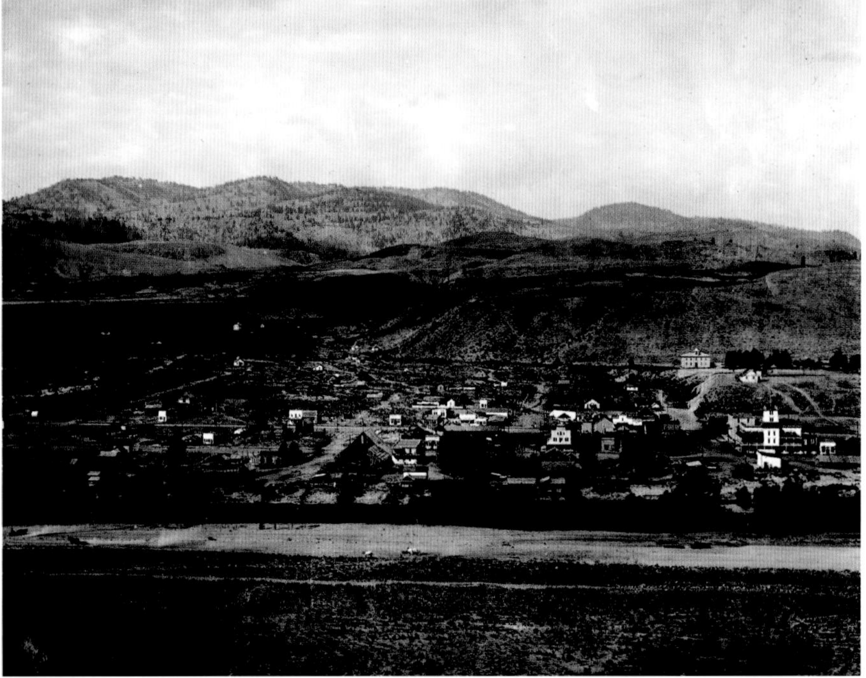

TOP

Early Overlook of Okanogan, ca. 1907. Location, south of the town of Okanogan at the mouth of Salmon Creek on the Okanogan River.

BOTTOM

Scenic Overlook of Okanogan, ca. 1910

Instead, Matsura's landscape details, their contextualizing interrelations across different photographs, and, in some cases, serialization in similar photographs over several years, invites scrutiny of the scenes' "figure of a ruling power": to see, Coyote-like, how things may not be as they appear.

Hauling his camera and other equipment up the ascending slopes on the eastern side of the river, Matsura took three panoramic views of the site where the town of Okanogan was built: two in circa 1907, with a follow-up in circa 1910. Together, these landscapes depict Okanogan before, during, and after its construction as a town. The first, tracking down the Okanogan River running northeast to southwest, is taken facing east to west. It identifies the site chosen in 1897, by the mouth of Salmon Creek, which would incorporate the smaller towns of Pogue and Alma into what would become Okanogan. The second, taken later in the year, looks directly across the river, southeast to northwest; although cloudy and marred, the image provides a visual record of the town's layout and early development. The third was taken approximately three years later, from roughly the same spot as the second photograph; somewhat underexposed, it provides a detailed picture of Okanogan as a burgeoning town.

With the portraiture of the region's newer and long-standing residents, white and Native, as a salient reference, another detail of this three-part historical sequence becomes conspicuous: the river bisecting their overlapping photographic space is the region's material and symbolic boundary. It divides this part of the Indigenous Plateau between the growing settler colonial community, benefiting from the region's agricultural development, and the western border of the Colville reservation. Across the three photographs, as the town grows above the river, below its demarcating line, nothing changes. At the time, for years, threats were repeatedly made to open the Colville lands east of the river to settlement, which did not materialize. Today, the 12 Tribes Omak Casino Hotel does brisk business just northeast of Okanogan, and a few scattered homes dot the hills on the river's eastern side. Otherwise, it appears largely the same as it did during the founding years of the settler town and eventual county seat. Hence, Matsura's three photographs symbolically express the unequal material legacies and uneven historical consequences of colonial settlement for Native and white stakeholders in the fate of the Indigenous Plateau.

By the mid-1800s, growers discovered that the Yakima, Wenatchee, and Okanogan valleys were ideal for apples, and with the development of large-scale irrigation by the 1890s, Washington's apple industry expanded rapidly, becoming

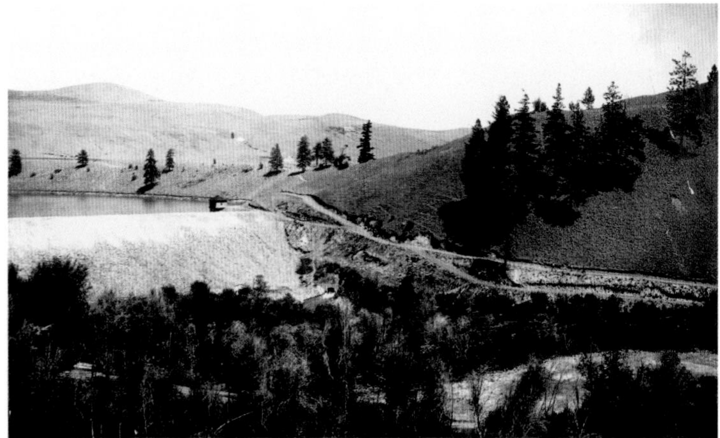

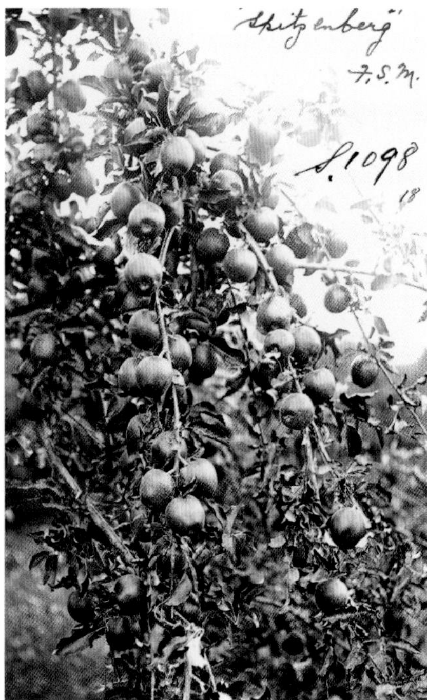

ABOVE
Conconully Dam and Diversion Tunnel, ca. 1910

RIGHT
Branches of a Spitzenberg Apple Tree, ca. 1910

the world's premier apple producer by the 1920s. Okanogan's settlement was driven by the demand for apple production, as well as other agricultural initiatives. In the mountains northwest of Okanogan, the Conconully Dam was built concurrently to help irrigate the region's massive expansion of agriculture. From an engineering standpoint, its water diversion tunnel may pique specialist interest; but otherwise, the dam itself is architecturally unremarkable. Nonetheless, dedicated to documenting seemingly every component of the region's transformation, Matsura's circa 1910 landscape of a near-complete Conconully Dam records a significant if largely invisible—out of the way, relatively inaccessible—component supporting the region's settlement.

From a commercial standpoint, Matsura's orchard scenes ranked among the most interesting and viable for advertising what cultural historian Jackson Lears might call the region's "fables of abundance." Images like one of the branches of a Spitzenberg apple tree served as the sublime object of the apple industry: so laden with ripening fruit, the branches are bent like vines downward to the ground. Vertically long and narrow in width, Matsura's photograph appears to be an Art

Nouveau rendering with its decadent bounty enticing its potential consumer; it is primed for enlistment as an advertisement. But if this image appears ready-made for commercial use, others resonate more obliquely, perhaps even ambivalently.

In a handful of his apple orchard scenes, Matsura solicits white women and girls only to pose in the frame: to give scale to sprouting trees at different stages of their growth, yes, but also, suggestively, to romanticize the orchard as a prelapsarian garden? In one image, a young woman and a younger girl, both dressed angelically in white, stand gaily amid a tree's overgrowth; the woman enticingly displays a glorious apple before her, as the girl cannot wait to bite into hers. No doubt this would be a pleasing memento for the ladies themselves, their families, perhaps even the grower. But what might it say beyond its local viewing? Unlike with the Art Nouveau apples, the messaging here is ambiguous: a fall from grace; or the serpent was right? Once again, Matsura's most affecting images tend to be about and for the local community and not, as a default, easily translatable to the interests and language of commercialization.

Another subset of Matsura's photographs that illuminate settlers' impact on the land is comprised of outdoor hunting scenes. Contrary to Native peoples' sustainable, reciprocal relationship with the land and its inhabitants, white settlers in these images appear to habitually engage in hoarding, collecting, and banal cruelty. In one such scene, a group of local sportsmen with the then newly

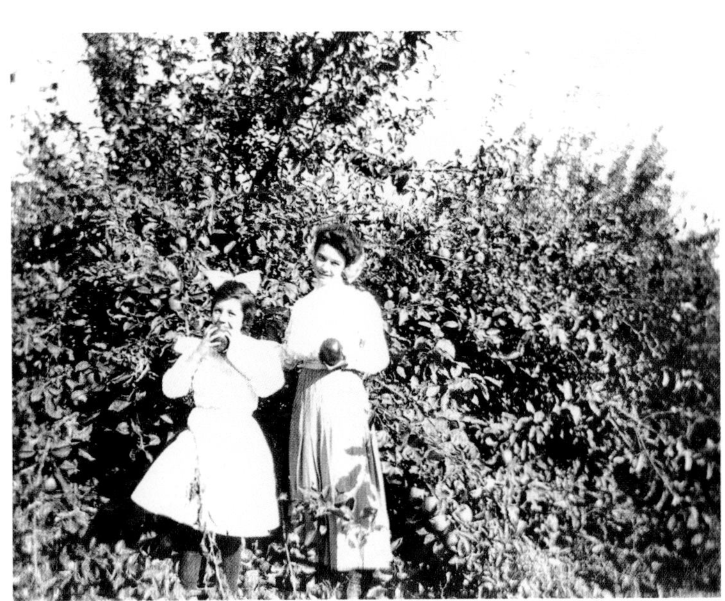

Two Young Girls Pose in Front of Tree Holding Large Apples, ca. 1910

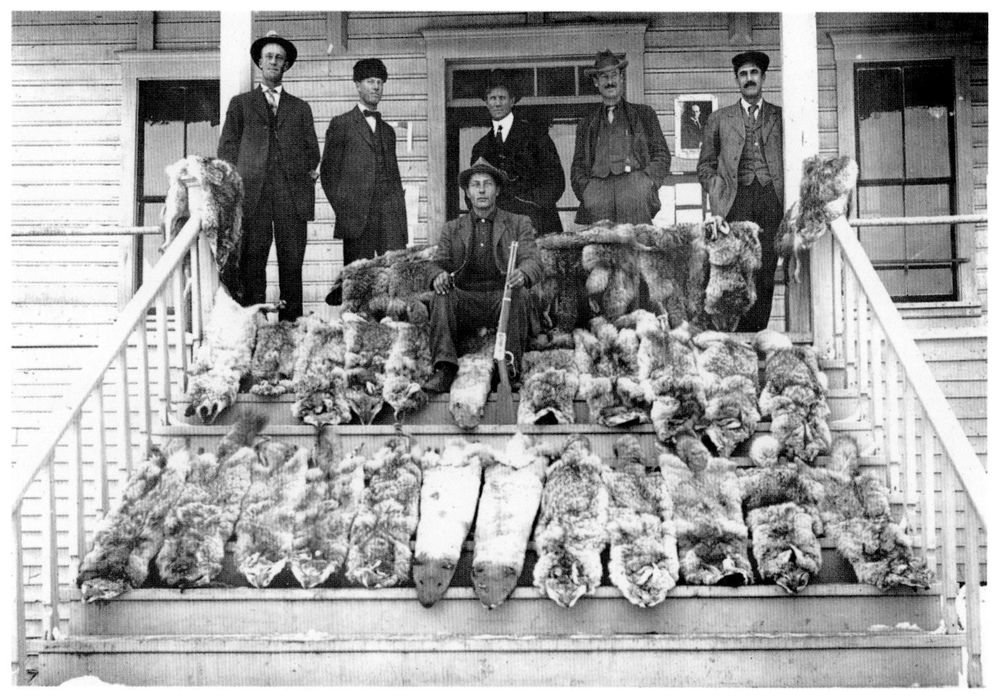

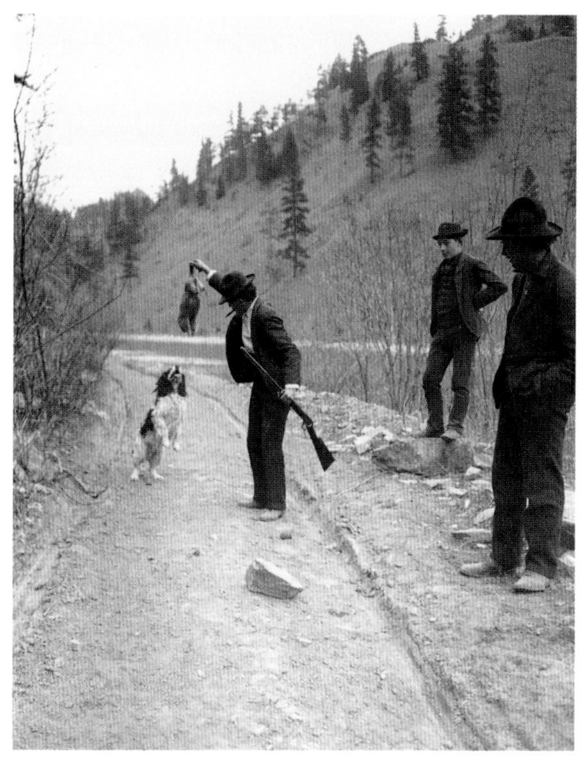

ABOVE

Members of the Game Protective League Sitting with Recent Bag of Coyote, ca. 1910. Location, Conconully Courthouse steps. The county paid bounty for coyotes.

RIGHT

Two Men and a Boy Tease Springer Spaniel with Recent Marmot Kill, ca. 1910

formed Okanogan Game Protective League display their bounty on the steps of a lodge: an array of pelts from coyotes, "considered a nuisance" for "[killing] the very game birds the men hunt," according to the WSU photo caption.

The caption begs the question that, no doubt, Native people would want to ask: who are you calling a nuisance? Or rather, who are you to regard coyotes as the nuisance? Native peoples likewise might want to consult with the game birds to see whom they regard as the greater nuisance: coyotes or white settler hunters? Apparently, the coyotes did not willfully assimilate to white settler ideas of civility, either. And Matsura's outdoor scenes reveal equally the intergenerational nature of such aggressive, normatively cruel "sportsmanship": in one of these photographs, two men teach a boy how to taunt their dog with a fresh kill of marmot. In another, we witness the casual, learned cruelty of two white children playing with a chained, captive bear, possibly orphaned following the hunting death of its parent? In each of these three outdoor scenes, the dominance-over-nature mindset of westward-moving white settlers—meticulously researched and written about elsewhere—is brought into stark photographic relief.

There are, of course, different ways to relate to the natural world and its long-standing, nonhuman inhabitants. The region's Indians—salmon people—developed methods of reciprocal and sustainable relations with their region's ecosystem, ensuring the health and balance of its food chain.

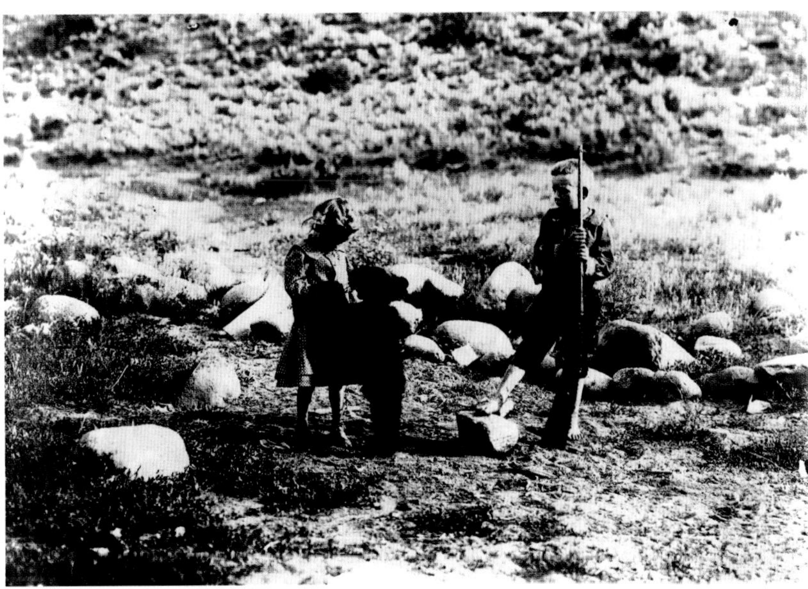

Two Young Children Playing with a Bear Cub, ca. 1908

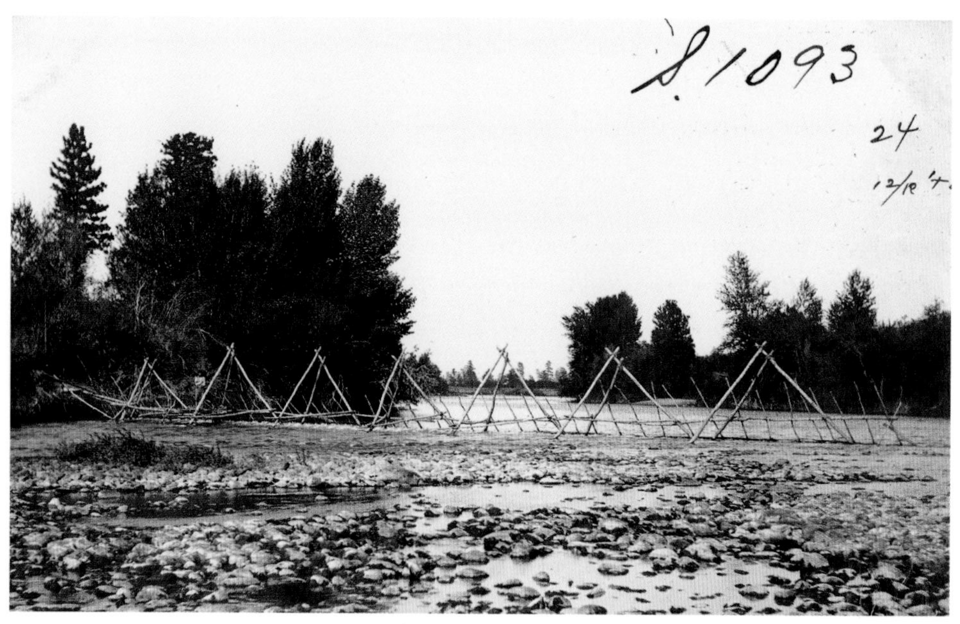

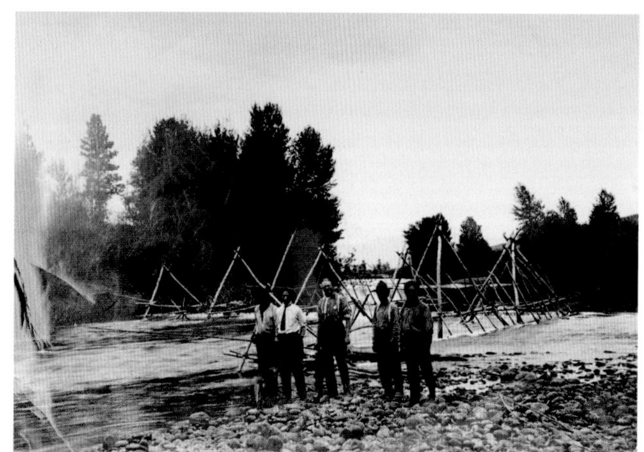

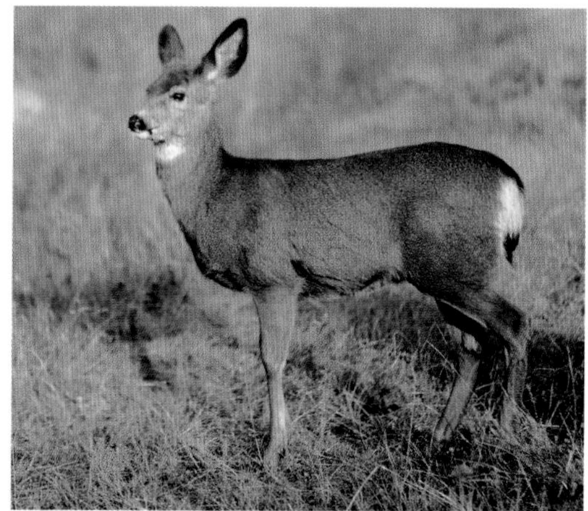

BOTTOM, LEFT
Fish Trap on the Okanogan River, ca. 1911

BOTTOM, RIGHT
Close-up of a Deer, Colville Indian Reservation, ca. 1909

Their fish traps for catching runs of salmon—netted walls made of wooden poles bound together with strips of willow bark—were developed over generations of trial and error. With his insatiable interest and curiosity, Matsura took photographs of recently installed fish traps along the same spot at the mouth of the Chiliwhist Creek, off the Okanogan River. As for Matsura himself, his sustainable method of hunting was apparently with his camera. A frequent visitor to the Colville side of the river, Matsura, by his own account, befriended a deer, or vice versa, that he named "My Pet." Ironically domesticating name aside, he photographed several encounters with his nonhuman friend (a mule deer doe: another lady, of course)—a relationship that the local Indians, no doubt, understood and appreciated. In one of these photographs, Matsura's lady friend poses patiently—they are just feet apart, with the camera set up to his left—and his shadow falls behind and across his friend as he squeezes the shutter release. Hinting at a human-nonhuman relationship characterized by reciprocity, in contrast to the largely unilateral, unequal relations of power imposed by settler colonialism, this landscape-cum-portrait makes for arguably the most interesting, if unexpected, image of self and other in Matsura's archive.

Coyote Finishes the People?

To return to *The Vanishing American* for a moment: When Zane Grey pens his conclusion promising impending marriage between Indian hero Nophaie and white companion Marian, he isn't foretelling a future of peaceful, mutually flourishing coexistence. Rather, as literary historian Walter Benn Michaels shows in *Our America: Nativism, Modernism, and Pluralism* (1995), he is alluding to a complicated but powerful white nativist discourse at the time. Grey named his novel not *The Vanishing Race* (after Edward Curtis) or even *The Vanishing Indian*, but instead *The Vanishing American* for two seemingly contrary reasons: it acknowledges that American Indians were the "first" Americans by birth, but more significantly that the melancholic disappearance of the Indian was, for white nativist modernism, the tragic but necessary precondition for whiteness to become the properly modern inheritor of "American" identity. By the end of World War I, the model American was no longer the European white ethnic immigrant who *became* an American through hard work; instead, white nativism had successfully asserted the primacy of American identity grounded in inheritance and birthright. Thus, it opposed all immigration, including from Europe, resulting in passage of the 1924 Immigration Act. Just one week later, predicated on the same logic, Congress enacted the 1924 Indian Citizenship Act, which granted citizenship to all Natives born in the territories of the United States, who were American by birthright, and that alone was prized and envied by white nativists. Hence, in the novel, the implication was not that Nophaie and Marian's children and grandchildren would identify as Indian, or even mixed race; rather, they would identify as white with birthright claims to "first" American identity through their extinct Native American lineage and recuperate their whiteness with each successive generation. Nophaie must not only die; his Indianness must die with him for his white children to become fully American. Only his attachment to the land would live on through them.

In his reading of *The Vanishing American*, Michaels reveals another historical anxiety underwriting the literary and cultural debates of the day. White nativists opposed, for the first time, all immigration because they feared American-born whites would be overwhelmed by their European immigrant counterparts—that white ethnics would come to outnumber and dilute American-born whites. This anxiety was especially keen after the war because in World War I—which white nativists regarded as a global "white civil war"—in the eugenicist eyes of white nativists, the strongest and bravest whites killed each other off, thus leaving American identity vulnerable to the less brave and intelligent, lesser stock "Mediterranean" whites. The real vanishing American of the 1920s onward, white nativists worried, was the "lost generation" of American-born WASPs themselves.

Of course, as we've seen, to the endangered white nativist fear of being replaced by newcomers, Natives from the Colville reservation and elsewhere might well reply: welcome to the neighborhood. In the ensuing one hundred years, as many Native writers have pointed out, this endangered yet empowered whiteness has endangered not just Indigenous life, but the health and well-being of the planet itself. In his 1978 novel, *The Dreams of Jesse Brown*, Abenaki writer Joseph Bruchac recounts Old Man Coyote's encounter with a terrifying, burned white creature seeking to destroy everyone with great fire, whirlwinds, and then a rain that will eat those who survive from the inside out. Old Man Coyote tells the creature that he wants to help and tricks the creature into telling him how to prepare the world for his arrival. The creature tells Coyote to get everyone out into the open because his magic does not work against the earth. Coyote points the creature to the great cities of the Whites, then runs to tell all of his People to hide deep in the caves and underground: "Thus, when the bombs fell, most of Old Man Coyote's people survived."[14]

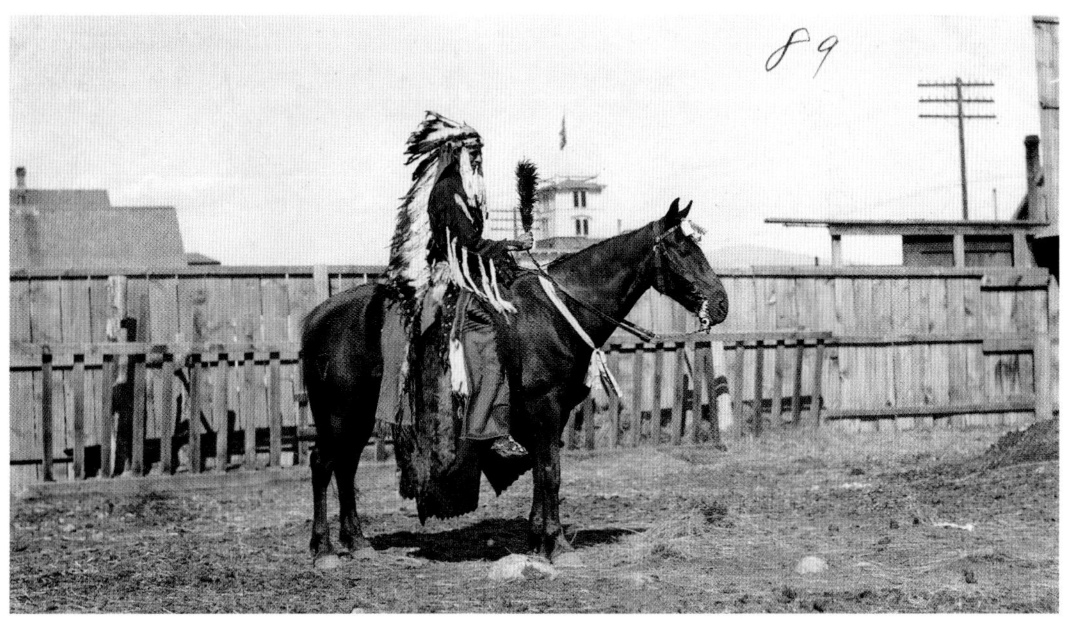

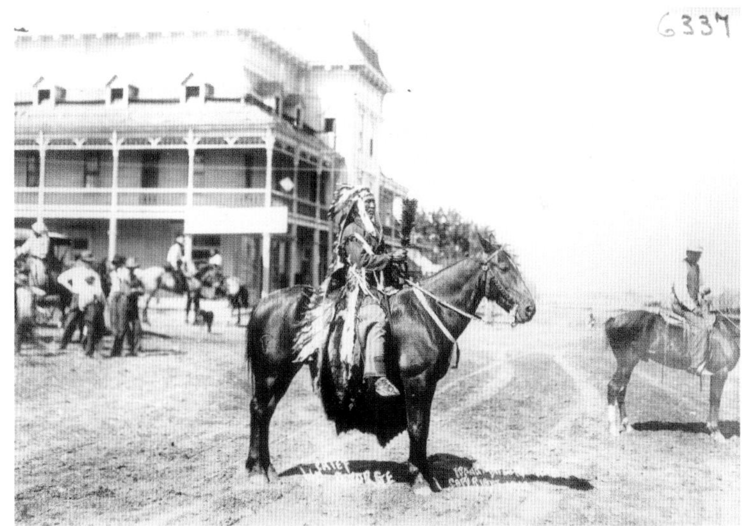

ABOVE

Man in Indian Costume on Horseback, ca. 1910. A white man in full feathered headdress poses in regalia identical to one wore by Chief Koxit George in a similar Matsura photo.

RIGHT

Chief Wm. George on Horseback, ca. 1910. Chief Koxit (William) George on a horse in front of the Bureau Hotel. This may have been taken at the 1910 Fourth of July celebrations. Eilers Music Store opened in the Bureau Hotel in 1910. Their first ad was in the *Okanogan Independent* on July 22, 1910.

Bruchac's story is a clever account of Native survivance, and an alarming rejoinder to white settler colonialism that mistakes its own death drive as civilization: vanishing Americans, indeed. But does it have to be this way? The Colville (Entiat) engineer and writer Wendell George, whose grandfather and father befriended Frank Matsura and were photographed by him, envisions Coyote saving not just Natives, but all people. George, one of the first members of the Colville tribes to attend college, joined Boeing and helped NASA land a man on the moon, before returning home to help establish the Colville Business Council and the Wenatchee Valley community college system. Thus, he has a capacious understanding of the threat that technology poses to humanity, and its potential uses for collective survival. In George's account, Coyote's role, among others, is to spread the Indian way—reciprocity between people and with nature, toward a sustainable future—to whites and others, because everyone's fate is ultimately interdependent. In this vision, Native people, not whites, bear the capacity to universalize a peaceful, collaborative, and sustainable humanity—for Coyote, in George's words, to "finish the people."[15]

Matsura appears to have learned this wisdom, likely from the local Natives and possibly from George's grandfather Chief Koxit George (Lahompt). And if he was unaware of the vanishing Indian mythos, he was certainly familiar with the white obsession with playing minstrelsy blackface and geisha yellowface and the similar fascination with playing Indian as a failing means to reanimate nativist settler whiteness. Not surprisingly, he took its picture: an unabashed white man, reportedly with Indian permission, dons the exalted feathered headdress and regalia of Chief Koxit George, then mounts a horse to have himself recorded in the likeness of Lahompt in one of Matsura's most famous photographs. The white man, playing Indian in some stable, is a failed copy of the original. In that august photo, Chief Koxit George pauses for Matsura's camera before the Bureau Hotel; he is in town for the 1910 Fourth of July celebration to show that he is not vanishing or going anywhere—a Coyote image of survivance.

In this way, Matsura's archive unveils the difficult world negotiated by Chief Koxit George and later envisioned by his grandson Wendell: one in which Indians may well need to salvage whites from the consequences of settler colonialism, self-destructive as well as destructive for others and of the planet. Or at least show a different way—something that Matsura's work shows us of life on the Indigenous Plateau of the early 1900s. Wendell George writes, "And so Coyote left his comfortable life to help the People.... He hoped they would give him a chance to prove himself. Eventually, he knew he would need special powers to be effective."[16] George isn't writing about Matsura, but again, Matsura appears to have understood the lesson, shared perhaps by his grandfather Chief Koxit George or other local Natives.

This essay closes with a self-portrait: Matsura with his camera and tripod in or around 1909, on or near the future site of the Great Northern Railroad depot for its Wenatchee-Chopaka line, built in 1913 but relocated thereafter north of the settler town of Omak. He is taking a picture of himself shooting a landscape of the nascent development of Okanogan town from the other side of the river—from the point of view of the Colville reservation.

In the end, Frank Matsura was a Japanese immigrant who became neither white nor Native, but a culturally hybrid, adaptive citizen of the Indigenous Plateau who helped to make it a better place. He certainly did not "finish the people," but his work illuminates a starting point on that long path toward a Native-centered, reciprocal, cooperative, sustainable humanity. And—impeccably dressed as always, to invite the gaze of others or of his own camera—he looked dashingly good doing it.

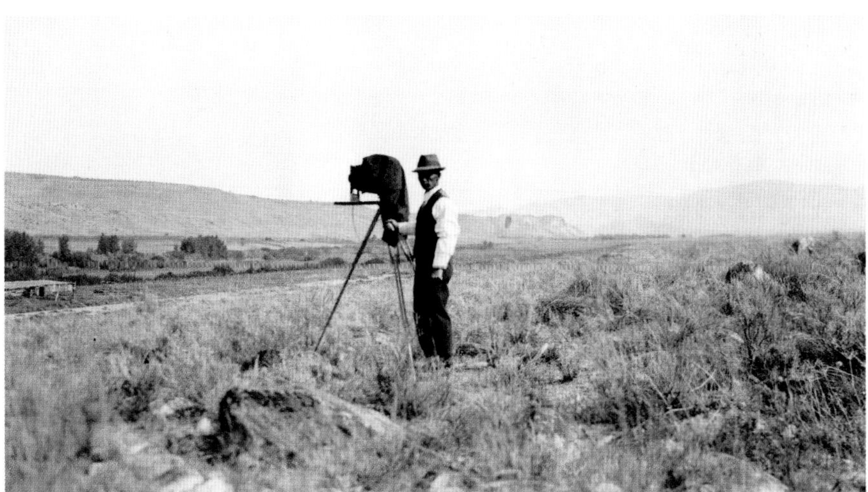

Matsura in a Field with His Camera, ca. 1909. Matsura poses for a rare self-portrait at work. The location appears to be near Suzanne Leo's place and the site of the Great Northern Railroad depot built in 1913. Okanogan is across the Okanogan River and to the left.

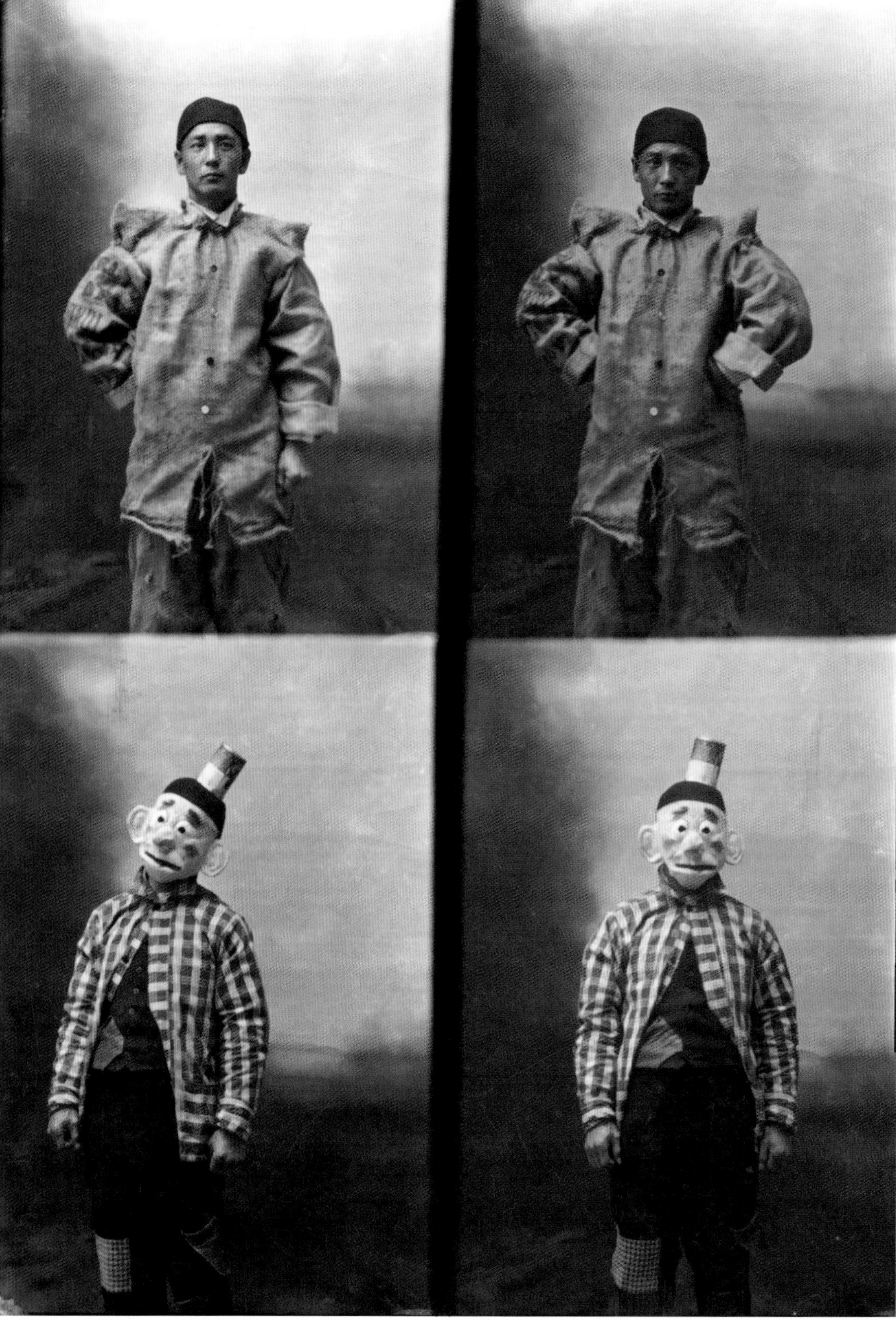

PHOTOGRAPHY, PLAY, AND DISSONANT SEEING

Maki Fukuoka, PhD

**Note on names: Japanese names in this chapter follow the Japanese order with family name followed by given name. In the case of Frank and other Japanese who have published in English using English order or given name followed by family name, I have adapted this order for clarity.*

During the short thirty-nine years Frank Sakae Matsura lived, between 1873 and 1913 in the Gregorian calendar, he appears to have been pulled toward transforming things and people, while everything around him was also constantly and rapidly changing. Tokyo, where he was born, underwent enormous changes on many levels—political, cultural, economic, and social. Okanogan County, Washington, where he died and is buried, was also going through noticeable and significant transformations, although distinctly different in their scale and characteristics from those of Tokyo. In addition, Matsura's personal life was marked with and shaped by a few significant changes from the early years. For example, he became the heir of the Matsura family at the mere age of four after his mother passed away. Around ten years later, after his father died, the Matsura family broke

OPPOSITE
Clowning Around, ca. 1903–1913. Four comical self-portraits by Matsura taken in his studio; Matsura poses wearing clown costumes. The clown mask and soup can hat were used as props by several of his clients.

up, and young Frank was sent to live with his uncle Masashi. In 1889, at sixteen, he was baptized by Kimura Kumaji, who had studied at Hope College in Michigan and returned to Japan as a Christian missionary.

As if these drastic transformations were warm-ups, Matsura left the port city of Yokohama in 1901 with a newly issued Japanese passport in his hand. He appears to have traveled to Seattle, Washington, and Juneau, Alaska. In terms of environment, both places would have been unfamiliar and even uncomfortable for someone with Matsura's background. Or at least, I imagine it must have been both exhilarating and exhausting every day to make minor adjustments to make things comfortable, understandable, and doable. He had learned English before leaving Japan, but the linguistic barrier was not the only challenge when emigrating. Slight differences in social protocols, etiquettes, and expectations add up at a surprising speed and amount. Matsura seemed skilled at adjusting to these changes and internalizing these transformations despite their scale and the demands they created for him. As someone who also migrated from Japan to the United States at a similar age, I remember these moments of confusion and reassessment vividly. The circumstances and conditions differ greatly between Matsura in the early twentieth century and me in the later twentieth century. However, as young adults, we both felt a delight and challenge in transcultural experiences that engendered and amplified the sense of elevations and slump that often comes with the age.

What kept running through his mind at and through each of these transformative moments, and why did he make yet another decision to change? As with many other aspects of his life, currently there aren't many clear and straight answers. Perhaps more fundamentally, I wonder if I want to have all the answers, for it is his enigmatic biography and photographic practices that constitute his appeal.

Some of the changes appear to have been made for him by other adult family members, while others were made by him. The name change is perhaps a good example of changes he made for himself. By the time he was living in America in 1901, he began to use Frank as his first name in addition to his given Japanese name Sakae.[1]

From this point of view, it is perhaps not too surprising that in 1903 he answers an ad for a handyman at the Elliot Hotel in Conconully, Okanogan County. This is a most decisive decision that, in hindsight, is pivotal to the emergence of our Frank Matsura, mourned by a whole community of Okanogan only a decade later. The man and his work we are coming to know rose out of this deceptively simple act of responding to a local newspaper ad. His activities in the next ten years form the basis upon which we come to respect and adore this idiosyncratic individual.

Matsura's increasing public role in documenting the events and lives of the people of Okanogan is well established. Here, both archives and historical newspapers offer useful evidence. Matsura photographed group portraits for basketball, baseball, and football teams at local high schools and the teachers institute's annual gatherings. He photographed numerous weddings, local parties, and balls. In 1906, he began to sell picturesque souvenir postcards that incorporated some of his landscape photographs. His business card notes a range of photographic services and products on offer: "souvenir post cards, season post cards, views post card albums, developing plates or films, printing from negatives, picture frames made to order, portrait works, scenic views, stamp photos taken, photos enlarged, photos on pillow tops."[2] His portrait photographs include all sorts of sitters: young white settlers, members of local Native American tribes, travelers passing by, young couples, close friends, mother and child, brothers, multigenerational family, and local businessmen. Matsura's business was as enterprising as the county in which he chose to live.

Indeed, the images in the databases at Washington State University and the Okanogan County Historical Society give an unwavering sense of the popularity of his photographic service. It is also quite clear that his practice came to be interwoven with many aspects of the social fabric of Okanogan. Looking through these images, I am most struck by how many play upon the forms and processes of transformations and include Matsura himself. The numerous selfies, as we might call them today, are a tantalizing starting point. By often posing with his sitters, dressing them in a variety of outfits, and enacting theatrical scenes, he extended and tested the limits of transformation to create a sense of what one might call *tableaux vivant*. Here, his attraction to and familiarity with visual techniques to highlight transformations appear to be key to the interpretive process.

I hope to suggest that the fact that Matsura lived with and through transformations in two locations, Tokyo and Okanogan County, and the sense of the unpredictable and nonconformed that we witness in Matsura's images are not only related but also perhaps a deliberate approach that marks his creative output. He encourages change as a creative mode. To start with, let's consider the techniques of visual transformation that Matsura would have been familiar with in Tokyo.

Asakusa, Photography, and Dissonant Seeing

The area called Asakusa became a hotbed for photographic studios in the 1870s and 1880s in Japan. It is no coincidence that photographers wanted to open their studios in this area. Historically, it has been (and continues to be) a well-known entertainment area for the ordinary citizens of the capital city. People who came to Asakusa could expect to experience the latest forms and types of amusement. Around the 1870s and 1880s, the area hosted various forms of attractions, including Kabuki theater, puppet plays, storytelling, magic lantern shows, magic, circus, and temporary traveling shows known as misemono (literally "showing things"). In 1875, Shimooka Renjō, the pioneer of photography in Japan, moved to Asakusa and began orchestrating his own shows using photographic images and more.[3]

Asakusa was a vibrant neighborhood centered around the Senso-ji Temple. One striking feature of the various types of amusements in the area is what I have termed "dissonant seeing."[4] Dissonant seeing plays upon the habitual and familiar ways of appreciating representation by adding a surprising twist. Deliberately tapping into the gap between what the viewer sees and what the viewer thinks the image is, dissonant seeing interferes with the process of seeing by subverting or twisting the expected structures between what one sees and what one thinks they see. The elements of surprise and absurdity of the final reveal were key to delivering this experience efficiently. It often deployed visible physical transformation as the platform upon which the dissonant seeing unfolded.

A typical and popular show, for example, would take a famous actor in Kabuki and make him a life-size doll using chrysanthemum flowers. The characterization becomes the recognizable ultimate pose of the theatrical production. Another common example would be using dried fish to form Buddhist statues. Attraction and entertainment based on this type of pleasure explore optical illusions that play upon a perceived gap between the subject in reality and its representation. To put it differently, it lays bare the relationship between what is shown and what it is, or between visible and knowable.

One of the most readily available approaches to establishing dissonant seeing is transgressing the divisions separating different media forms and worldviews. So, an infamous gruesome murder is re-created with lifelike paper-mache dolls, for example, while a cultural icon, such as a Chinese dragon, is represented by assembling everyday kitchen utensils. The embedded assumption in the various plays of dissonant seeing is that crisscrossing between different media,

OPPOSITE
Three Men in Masks at Matsura's Studio, ca. 1912

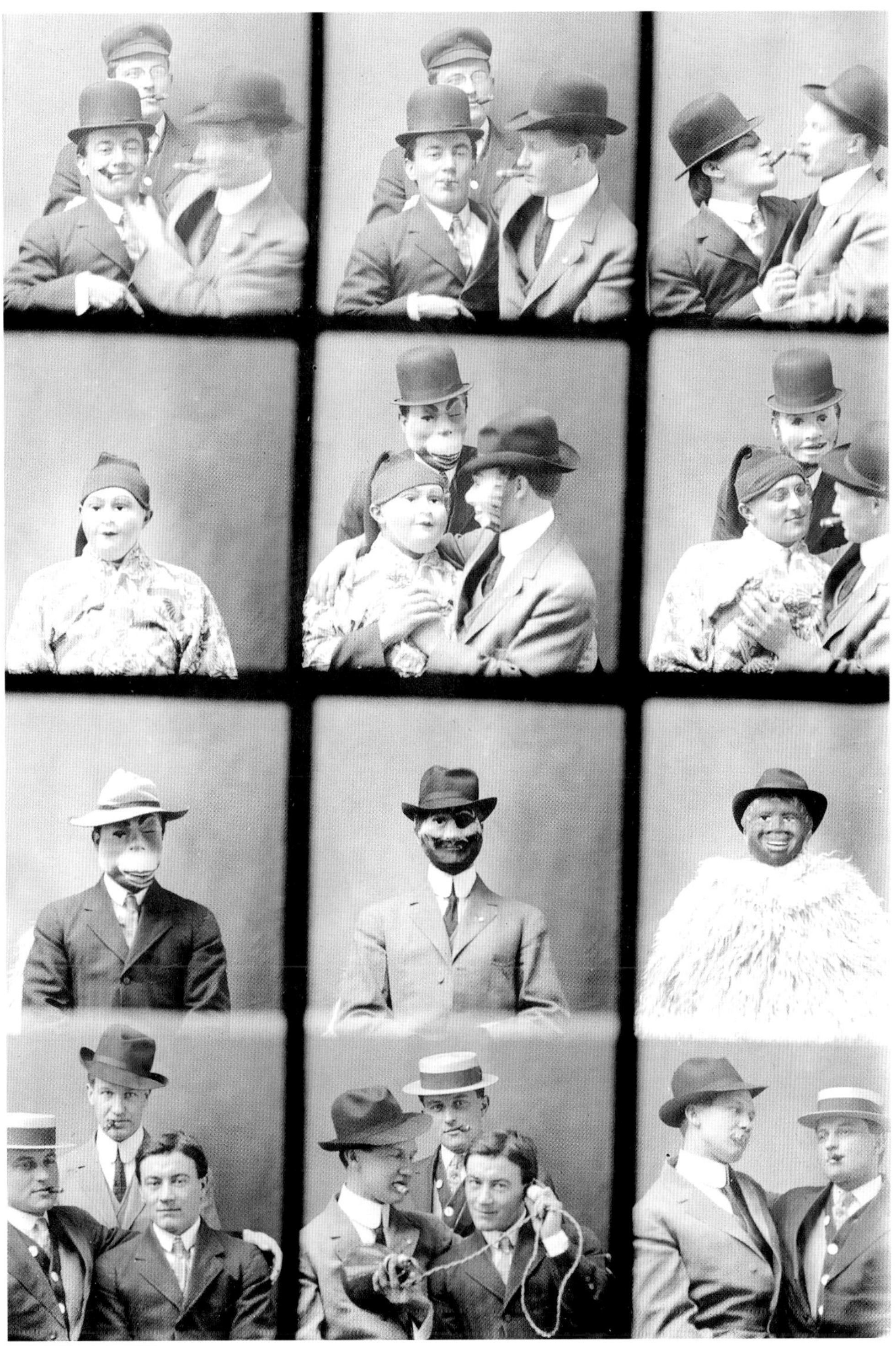

established meanings, dimensions of the visible and known world, and forms could and would lead to surprising pleasure, and this sensation of the unexpected would satisfy the crowds who came to Asakusa looking for such extraordinary entertainment.

It is quite telling that the photographic studios thrived in this context. In fact, many photographers incorporated these playful experiences into their own work. In 1881, Kitaniwa Tsukuba, a famous and successful photographer of that time, produced sixteen life-size photographic images of old men. For a banquet for his studio, he placed the figures in the poses of famous Buddhist arhats, highly evolved practitioners who had reached the status of enlightenment. He also placed several clothing items on the figures as if to suggest that these figures were alive.

Although we do not have direct evidence to know where and how Matsura picked up the knowledge of photography, it is tempting to consider the possibility that he had been familiar with these local and popular ways of playing with photographic materials and more broadly the prevailing applications of dissonant seeing in Asakusa. In fact, Matsura wrote about his visits to Asakusa at least five times in 1893 and 1894, including seeing the reenactment of the murderous scene called Kawachi juningiri (murder of ten in Kawachi region) in lifelike paper-mache dolls in March 1894.[5] I'm going to postulate that he was thoroughly entertained by the possibilities of transformation and the jolly and skillful ways of adapting the theatrical elements available in Asakusa, particularly the experience and sensation of dissonant seeing.

Transforming Subjects

Matsura's images exude energy, especially in portraits. He brings out the sense of a person with a gentleness and humor that defies the norm of commercial studio photography of that time. In this group studio session, the viewers see the jovial gathering, suggestively exuberated by drinking alcohol. The two bottles on the flimsy table encourage our interpretation. The two photographs are, though, also noticeably different from each other. For example, there are four members in the image on the left, and five in the one on the right. The man with a straw hat in the center of the right-hand image is the addition, not included in at left. He appears to have taken the white fur collar scarf that sat near the floor at left. Even the men who are in both photographs wear different hats in these two images. The quick decision to change their hats and poses (the man with his feet on the table becomes almost invisible in the right-hand image) adds to the

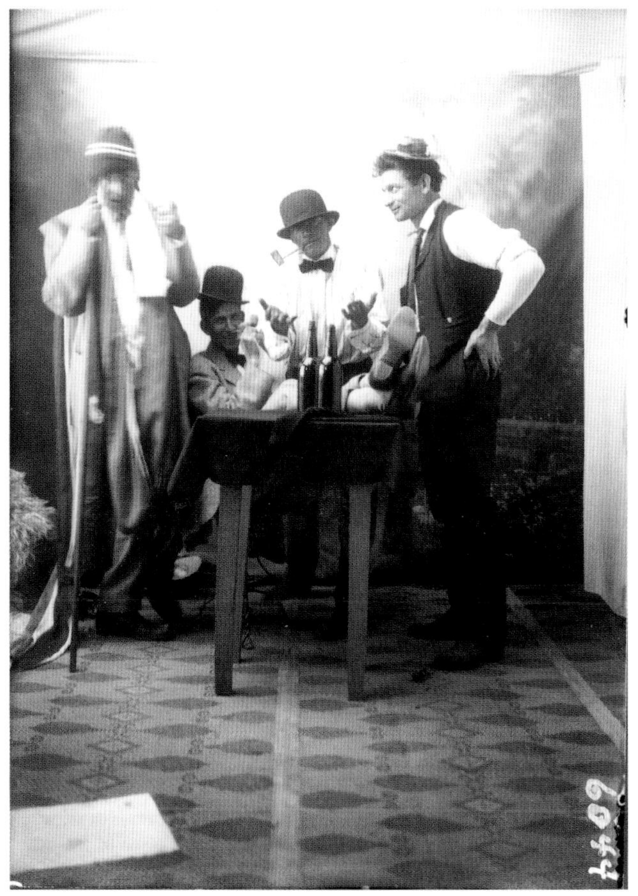

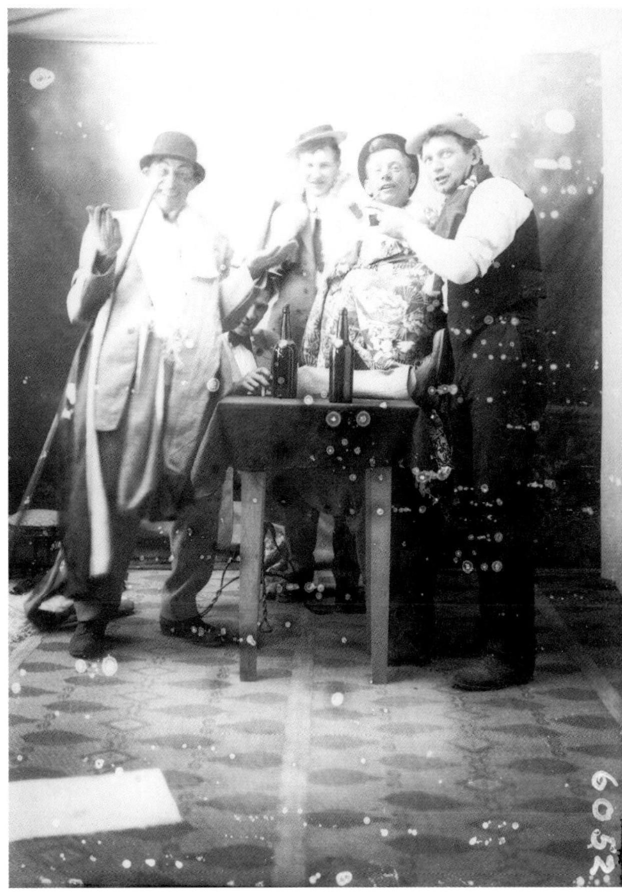

LEFT
Comedians' Portrait, ca. 1903–1913

RIGHT
Comedians' Portrait, ca. 1903–1913

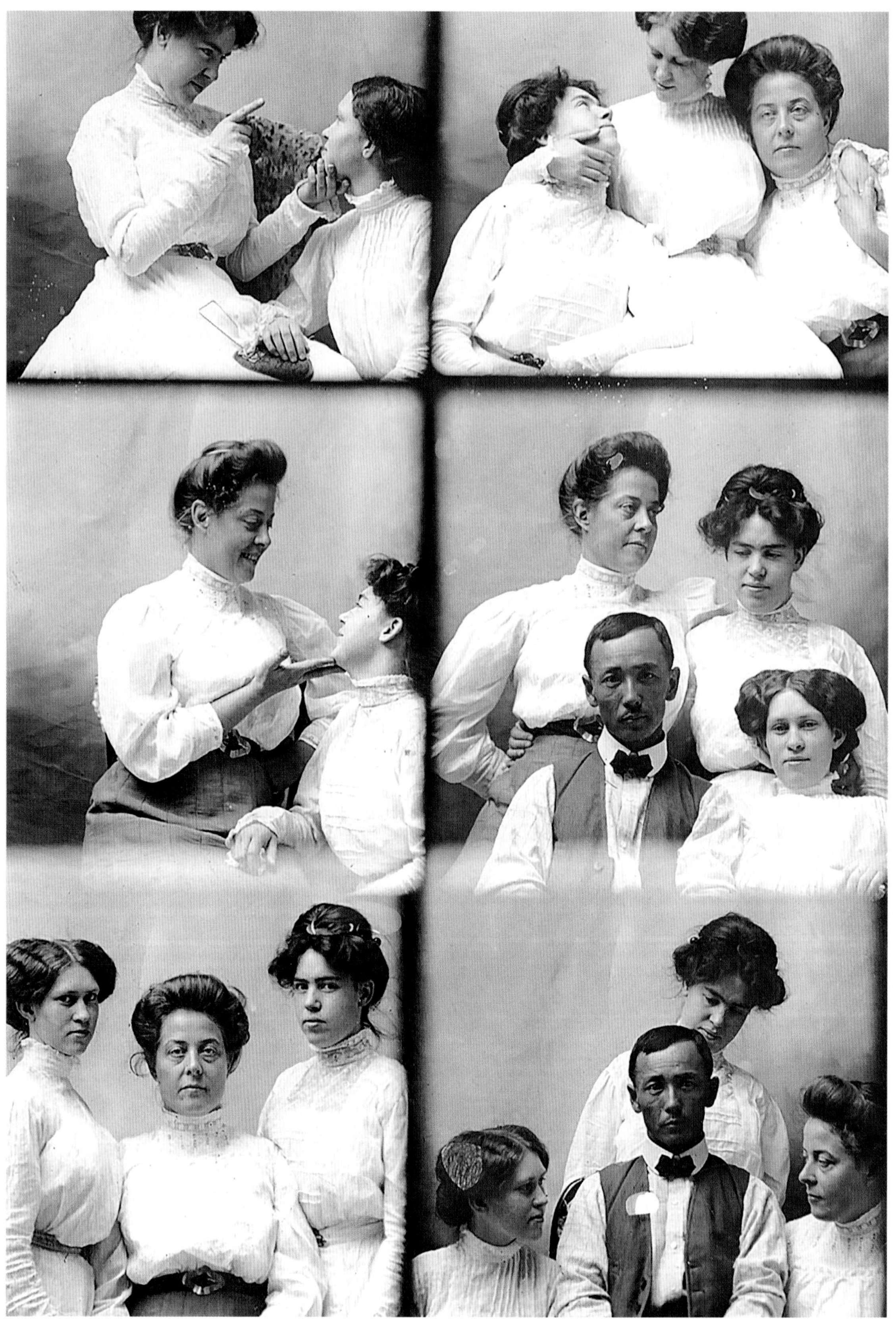

ad-lib atmosphere that surrounds the occasion. From one scene to the next, as Matsura would have been, the viewers, too, are drawn into the changes within the photographs.

In this sequence of studio shoots, the viewers are led to see them almost as if a broader narrative structure supports these images. It might be in part because several images (the top row plus the right image on the second row; see full image on page 59) appear to suggest some regularity, with two shutter presses for each woman sitting on the same chair. The similarities in their puffed-sleeve white cloth shirts, long A-line skirts, and visibly tight belts, as well as their hairstyles, give a sense of coordination to the images. The narrative evolves around the dynamics among the three women, a type of insular negotiation that only these women are familiar with. The hand gestures are particularly expressive in showing the viewers the quibble and the praise passing among them. When Matsura enters the frame in the bottom two rows, it surprises the viewers. The stealthy entrance to the narrative framework without any explanation or prelude alone is surprising and comical. He also holds the same still expression in all three frames. The darker tone of his suit and skin adds another visual element of contrast. In the center image on the bottom row, all three women take notice of him momentarily, after which Matsura disappears from the viewfinder. The visual trickery, combined with the elements of coordination, surprise, and contrast, draws the viewers in, some hundred years later, to join in their creative process at his studio. These tropes of changing stories, narratives, and appearances constitute distinct aspects of Matsura's work. Indeed, he seems to be particularly fascinated by the changing appearances and roles of women in many of his photographs.

These series of "trick photographs" are examples that further show how Matsura focused on aspects of transformation and change in his production process. Here, by combining a few negatives, Matsura generates a composite of multiple views of the same model. It is not merely the angle of the camera that is altered. Their actions, too, are changed in each negative so that, seen together, the model appears in an unfamiliar and uncanny visualization of "keeping one's own company."

Indeed, "trick" photography like this was established quite early in the twentieth century in the United States. In contexts such as spiritualism, multiple exposure was a popular and accepted use of the technology. The way Matsura deploys it, though, strikes me as worth noting precisely because it is in line with

OPPOSITE (DETAIL)
A Mother and Two Grown Daughters Pose with Matsura at His Studio, ca. 1911

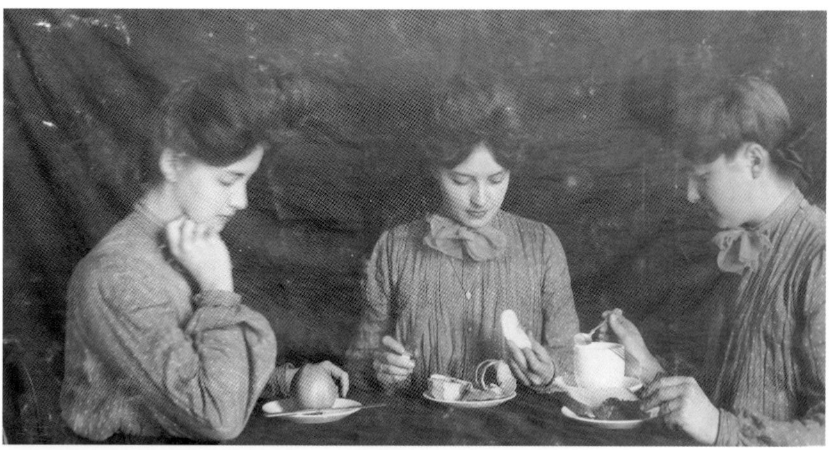

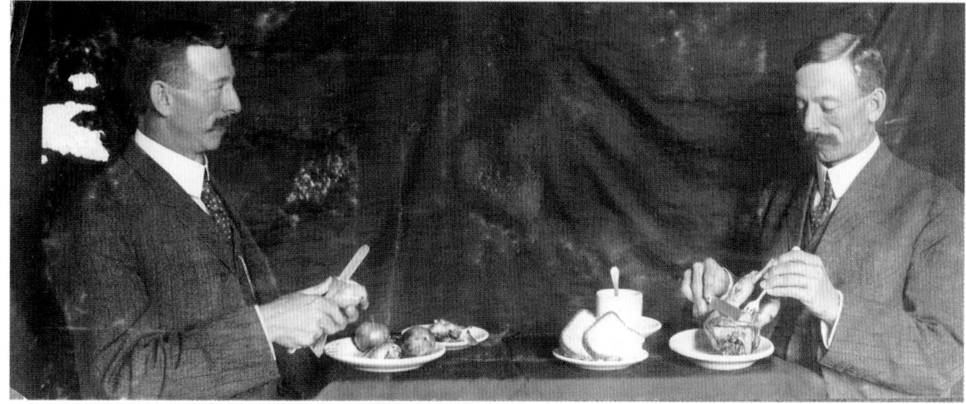

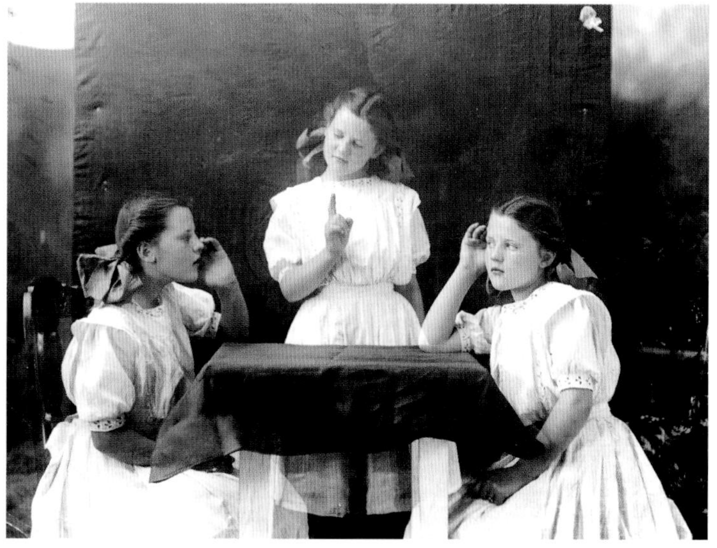

TOP
Untitled, Frank Matsura photograph,
ca. 1903–1913. Multiple negative, three
views of the same woman.

MIDDLE
Untitled, Frank Matsura photograph,
ca. 1903–1913. Multiple negative, two
views of the same man.

RIGHT
*A Girl Doing Three Things—Pointing,
Speaking, and Hearing*, ca. 1903–1913

his focused attention on the transformations of a person. In one composition (opposite, top), the same young white woman is shown three times, wearing the same dress shirt and a ring on her ring finger, sitting before small plates of food. On the left, the model appears to contemplate a whole apple. With her right elbow on the table and her hand under her chin, she looks as though she is deeply lost in her own thoughts, unaware that she is being photographed. The middle image reveals the (same?) apple peeled and sliced, showing the transformation of the fruit in two distinct states. Here, too, the woman looks down, focusing on the piece of peeled apple held in her left hand. In the right image, a set of new items are on the table: a fork, spoon, cup, and saucer, and a small plate with what appears to be a slice of white bread and possibly a piece of pie. Perhaps it was a piece of apple pie? As with the other two figures, the woman is looking downward at her food, focusing on the small teaspoon with which she is stirring her drink.

In another photo using multiple exposures (opposite, bottom), Matsura generates a composition using suggestive gestures. Although its iconography is difficult to identify, to my eyes it appears to be a staged conversation between the two girls sitting, one whispering and the other intently listening. The central figure, standing above the two in discussion, appears to intervene in the conversation.

In the case of Tokyo, as you might guess, Asakusa played the central role as a site of manufacturing, distributing, and offering performances of magic lanterns. The topics of magic lantern shows varied widely—from biology, folklore, and religious teaching to the temperance movement. As a form of audiovisual entertainment, its popularity peaked between the 1880s and 1890s. In fact, from the center of Asakusa, we have a case of a *rakugo* (storytelling) performer who incorporated a magic lantern into his performance from 1878 until the end of the century. In other words, just as in the case of photography, the magic lantern, too, came to play a part in a culture that thrived on dissonant seeing.

It is also noteworthy that alongside these developments and synergetic mergings in popular entertainment, the magic lantern came to play a central role in education, especially after 1880 in Tokyo. For example, in 1883, the Ministry of Education placed orders for a mass production of educational magic lanterns to be used in primary schools with two photographers, both of whom had their business headquarters in Asakusa.[6] By 1890, in both education and popular entertainment, magic lantern shows had become a common and familiar form, especially for someone like Matsura, who taught at Sunday schools at Daimachi church and the Shoei Girls' Elementary School in the 1890s. We know from his diary that Matsura attended various magic lantern shows between 1892 and 1894, including a lecture on the Red Cross and a few sermons at church.[7] The temporal sequencing and visual demand for narrative structure, along with the seriality of images, are characteristics of Matsura's images that leads one to imagine that Matsura might have not only enjoyed magic lantern shows but drawn inspiration from their serial narrative format and embedded visual trickery.

"Education of the Japanese Women"

At this point, I want to consider the newspaper article published under Matsura's name in the *Okanogan Record* on March 31, 1905. His surname is still spelled with two *u*'s, Matsuura, and he had not opened his photo studio yet in Okanogan. The article is titled "Education of the Japanese Women," and it was supposed to have been followed up by another piece by him, which did not happen. Even though it is incomplete as a thought piece, it gives us a contour of Matsura's view, especially that of women in his community. It is helpful to remember that before he left for the United States, Matsura taught at Shoei Girls' Elementary School, a Christian school founded by his uncle Okami Kiyomune. The interest in this subject, then, is not new for Matsura. Rather, it is a subject he had an extended experience with and time to form his opinions about before moving to Okanogan. It is also notable that Kimura Kumaji, the pastor who baptized Matsura, focused his missionary work on the education of women when he returned to Japan. Kimura opened Meiji Jogakkō in 1885 in Tokyo as a unique institution that offered its own curriculum and pedagogy for educating women, rather than relying on Christian pedagogy devised outside Japan.

Matsura opens the article by summarizing English philosopher John Stuart Mill's view on the relationship between society and individuals. He agrees with Mill's assertion that strengthening individuality will lead to a stronger nation. And a national framework is the context in which Matsura considers the role of women and the necessity of their education.

It is not surprising that Matsura would be familiar with Mill's work, in part because Mill's "On Liberty" was a bestseller in Meiji Japan. It is also helpful to consider that Matsura published the piece during the Russo-Japanese War, and he indeed makes multiple explicit references to the current geopolitical armed conflict between the two nations. In this light, the article functions as a platform to explain to his readers in Okanogan that his homeland Japan had, historically, treated women as equals at a time when masculine and imperial "progress" was being made by force in a far distant context.[8]

Matsura notes how, many centuries ago, women had been treated with the same consideration as men in Japan. "In the olden times, spiritual education seems to have been the backbone of training. To women, as also to men, respect for deities, purity, resoluteness, faithfulness, and loyalty were necessary qualities that made up womanhood," he asserts.[9] In fact, he notes how there had been princesses and empresses who hunted alongside men, as well as women who were equipped with artistic talents in poetry and the arts.

The curious move he makes—and this appears to be the point he wants to underscore in this piece—is that introductions of Buddhism and Confucianism have had a detrimental effect on the social position of women. While he does not offer specific examples or aspects of how gender inequality was introduced by these ways of thinking, he claims that they repositioned women as "sinful by nature" and "inferior by birth." The equality that existed between men and women was recalibrated through these hierarchical views. In other words, Buddhism and Confucianism were structural mechanisms that constituted the sociocultural privilege of men.

One could imagine that Matsura's time teaching at Shoei Girls' Elementary School provided him opportunities to help young women to flourish as individuals unfettered by the older approaches to gender articulated by these two modes of thinking. One might also imagine that in the context of Okanogan, Matsura came to know many women who had not experienced the gender adversity he identified in his article. Whether belonging to Native American tribes or white settler communities, women he met in Okanogan were most likely not familiar with either Confucianism or Buddhism. This article from 1905, coupled with many transformative images of women he generated in photography, begs us to consider his approaches to women and their role in his photographic works.

Equal Share with Women

For example, we find several cases where Matsura places himself as an equal to the female sitter, both in the sense of importance and the physical space they occupy. In a portrait with Susan Timento, Matsura stands beside her while she sits with a bundle of something in her right hand (see full image on page 53).

The portrait sitters share the space equally, and their poses are contained in their own way. One person does not suggest the dominance of one over the

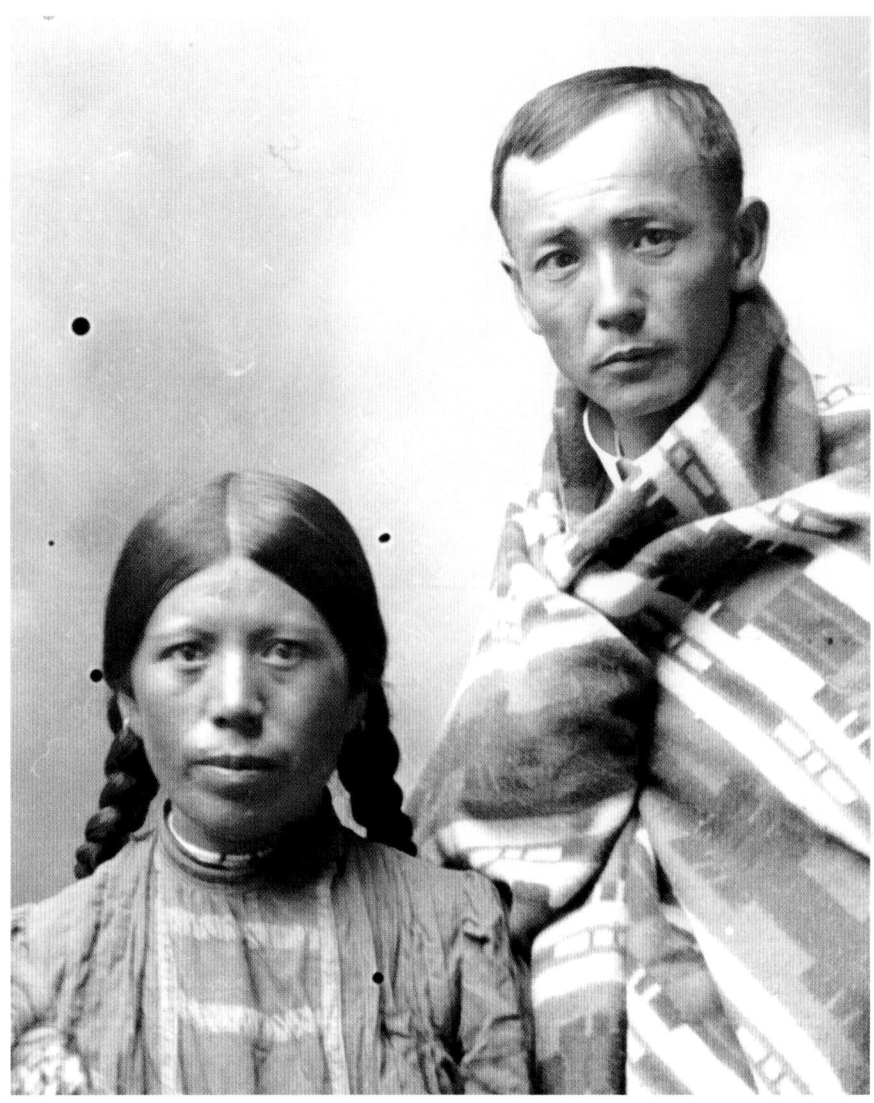

ABOVE (DETAIL)
Matsura and Susan Timento Pose at Studio, ca. 1912

OPPOSITE
Matsura with W. R. Kahlow, ca. 1911. Matsura and
friend W. R. Kahlow, originally from Minnesota. Kahlow was
a teamster and fought at the Battle of Birch Coulee during
the US-Dakota War of 1862. In 1904 he erected the Alma
Hotel in Alma, a small town incorporated into what later
became Okanogan in 1907.

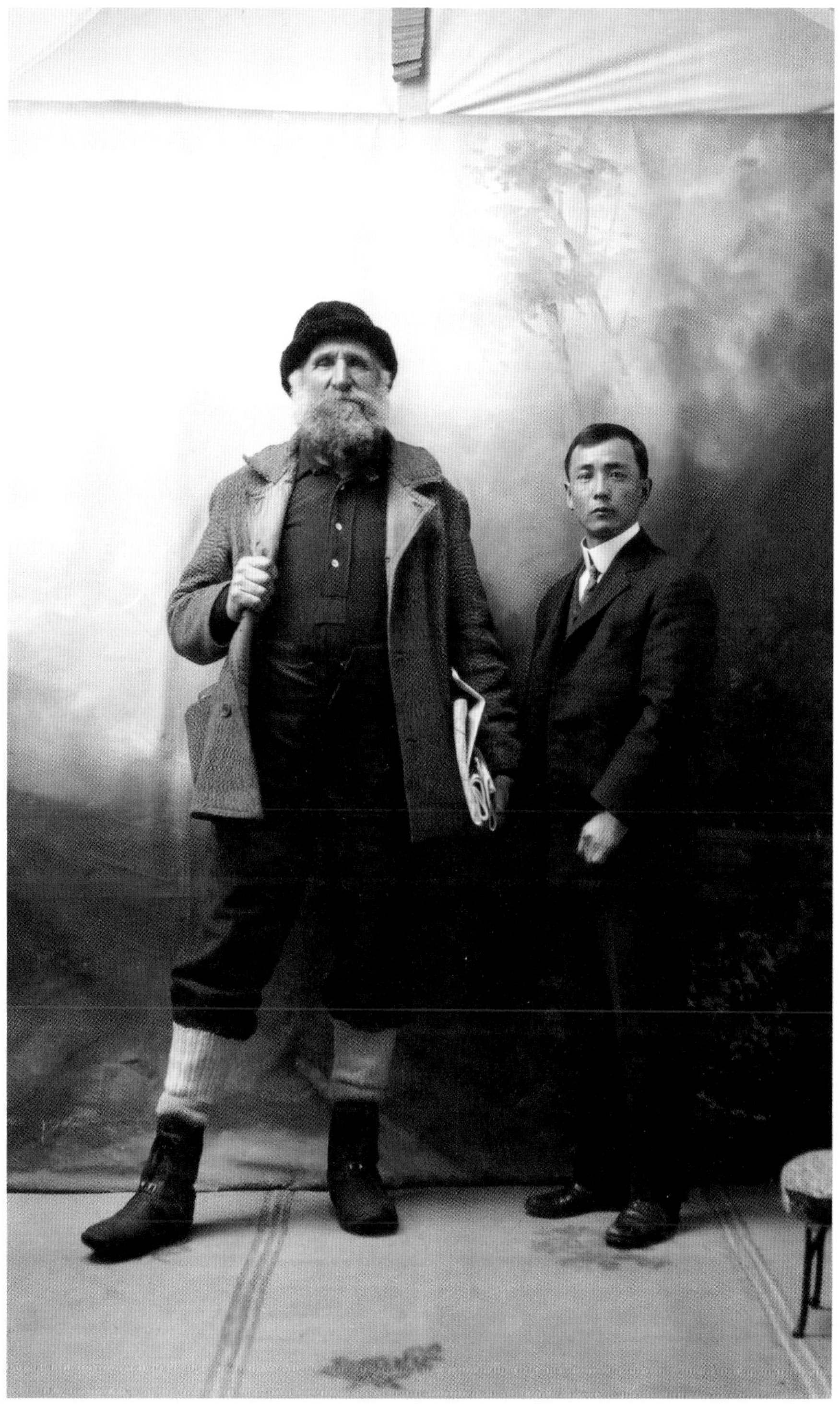

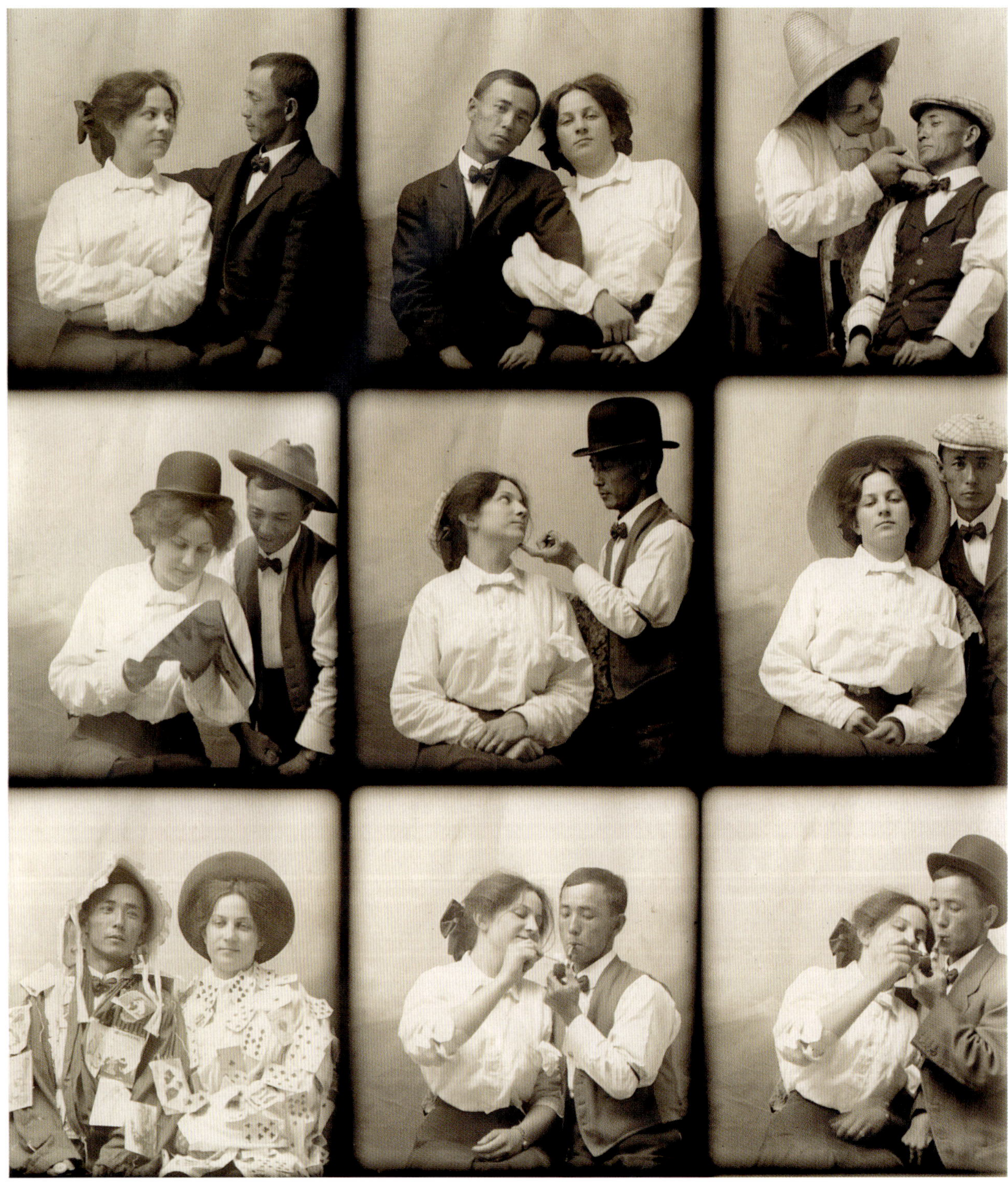

other. Covering himself with a blanket completely, Matsura appears to ignore the differences in sex and putative social roles that some photographers might exaggerate and instead co-occupies the studio space. Together, Susan and Matsura stare directly into the camera.[10]

Compared to this portrait with Timento, another portrait, with W. R. Kahlow, takes a different approach (see page 97). Here, Matsura poses with the large and tall Kahlow, a local businessman and an owner of the Alma Hotel in Okanogan. Rather than placing the camera closer to the subjects and focusing on the midlength portrait, as was the case with Timento, Matsura framed Kahlow in such a way as to demonstrate his height and presence. Kahlow's pose, gripping the lapel of his blazer and pointing his right foot, adds to the weight and formality of his representation. Matsura appears standing next to him to serve as a measure, a reference point to assert the statuary bearing of Kahlow.

With his friend Norma Dillabough, whose father hired Matsura initially as a handyman for the Elliot Hotel in 1903, Matsura shows many directions and textures of transformations: they change clothes, hats (Matsura wears six different hats), positions, and props repeatedly and consistently throughout this session (see full image on page 58). In the right frame of the first row, Dillabough chucks Matsura under his chin, and in a later image, second from the right in the second row, they reverse the roles. They are goofing around with an affection and playfulness that reveal the physical and visible changes and the level of acceptance and comfort they have in each other's company. In two images on the left, in the third row down, both are dressed in smock-like coats, one covered by playing cards and the other with what appears to be repro-duced postcard images. Frank wears a woman's bonnet, while Dillabough wears a wide-brim western hat. In the image above, they act as if they are reading the newspaper together with equal interest. In the left frame of the fourth row, Norma appears to have lightly smacked Frank with her right hand. These playful changes end with the anticipated frame of a kiss between the two, an embrace that is alluded to but shielded behind large hats. In the images of Timento and Dillabough, women do not carry the normalized signs of diminished status in patriarchy, often articulated by standing a step behind a man or appearing placid with exaggerated ornaments around them. Timento appears dignified, and Dillabough appears to have an equal role in their partnership, performed or not. To evoke Matsura's own phrase, the women in these images defy the putative inferiority of women or sinfulness of women. The transformations of Dillabough, in this particular case, are as much led by Dillabough as by Matsura.

Staging Scenes and Drag

As we interpret his photographs along with his article and exposure to dissonant seeing, it is particularly revealing that Matsura staged and produced several photographs where women perform the roles of men.

While it is hard to trace exactly where and how these ideas emerged in the context of Okanogan in the early twentieth century, it is worth noting that staging photographs appear often in Matsura's body of work. Here, too, I want to consider his images in relation to dissonant seeing. In the context of Kabuki theater, which Matsura would have known, what in English might be deemed as drag has been a standard practice since the seventeenth century, known as *onnagata* (literally "female role").[11] Indeed, there have been many famous Kabuki actors who specialized in *onnagata* and rose to the fame precisely because of their appearances and acting skills as female characters in drag.

What stands out is the fact that Matsura reverses the familiar to produce *otokogata* ("male role"), as it were. In these images, it is the women who dress up as men and perform the role of heterosexual men (opposite). While these images are not presented in sequence in the photo album from the Okanogan County Historical Society, it is easy to see how they might work as a sequence of scenes that form one story. In one scene, Matsura uses a photographic portrait of a young woman as the key prop. It is hard to tell who is in the portrait—is it a famous theatrical actress or a portrait of the person holding the photograph? The *otokogata* is sitting back in a rocking chair, holding a cigar in "his" left hand. Dressed in a formal suit, tie, and hat, he is showing the portrait to the viewers, who can clearly see it is not the same woman as the one standing next to the rocking chair. He is looking up to her, almost with a grin on his face. She does not engage with his eyes and instead looks away to avoid meeting the eye of the woman in the portrait in his hand. Wearing a highly embroidered elegant dress, she has a frown on her face. The gesture of tilting the portrait enough to capture the difference between the two women gives a nod to the audience and an awareness of their presence. On the wall of this fictional scene, among many photographic prints, one of a woman posing in a wedding gown stands out for its color and size. These props, almost a metacommentary of the photographic commodity itself, help conjure

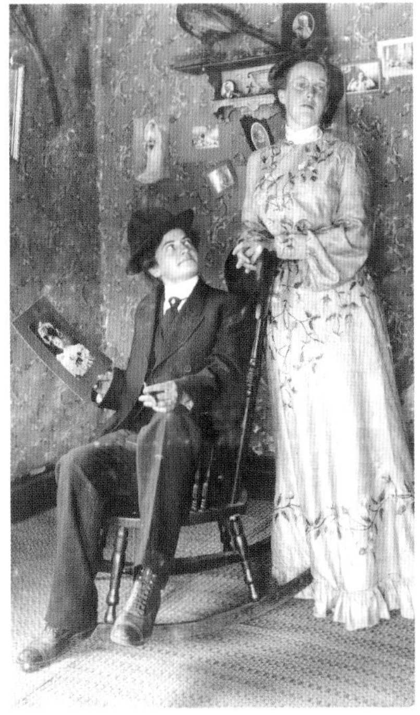

LEFT
LEFT
Untitled, Frank Matsura photograph, ca. 1903–1913.
Two women, one dressed as a man, enacting a romantic
scene in a parlor.

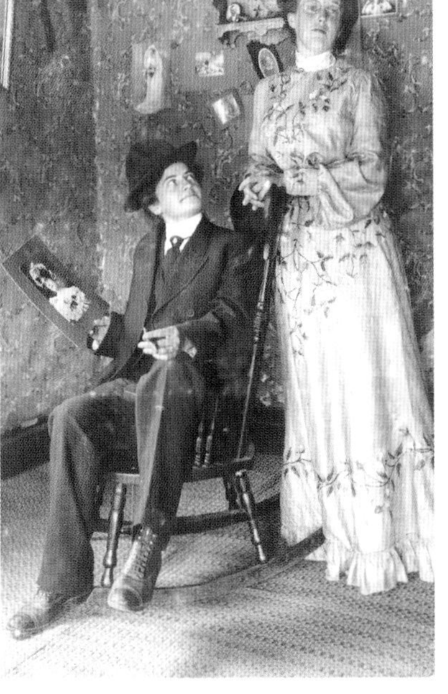

RIGHT
Untitled, Frank Matsura photograph, ca. 1903–1913.
The narrative continues with the cross-dresser in a pose
of supplication.

the romantic narrative with these two protagonists—a possibility of marriage and
the presence of another woman.

In the second image, the *otokogata* is now on one knee, holding the hand of
the woman, who sits in the rocking chair. The tension between them is less conflict
and more negotiation. He is kneeling down on her long, embroidered skirt while
she looks straight at the camera with a slight grin on her face. It is the case that
the narrative would easily change by reversing the order of sequence between
these two photographs. One could imagine the first image as a tense confronta-
tion and revelation of a secret, followed by the second image of reconciliation.
The question of sequence aside, these explorations of gender roles in romantic
scenarios create a curious parallel in consideration of Matsura's expressed concern
for the equality of women in a larger societal context. What does it mean that
women can and will perform men's roles, however brief and fictional, in these
settings? How do these role-playings sit in relation to the normative sociality of
young couples at that time in Okanogan?

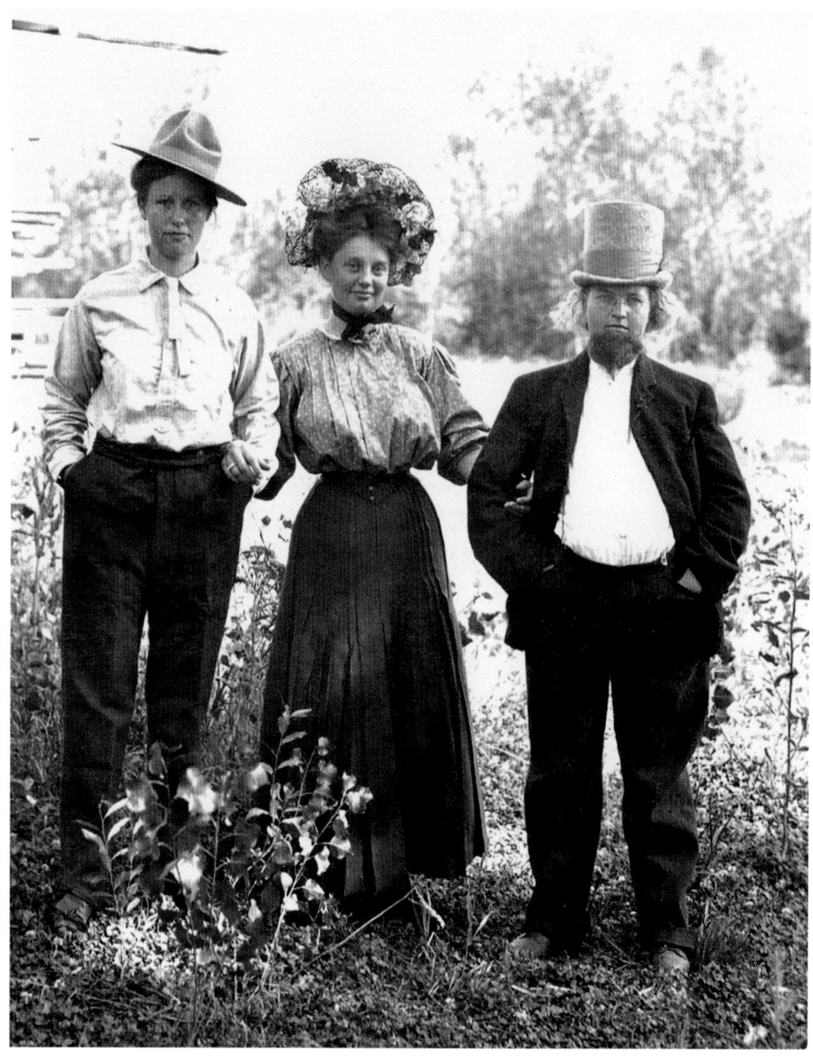

Cross-Dressing Acting Scenes, ca. 1903–1913.
Elsie Bidwell stands between two unidentified friends.

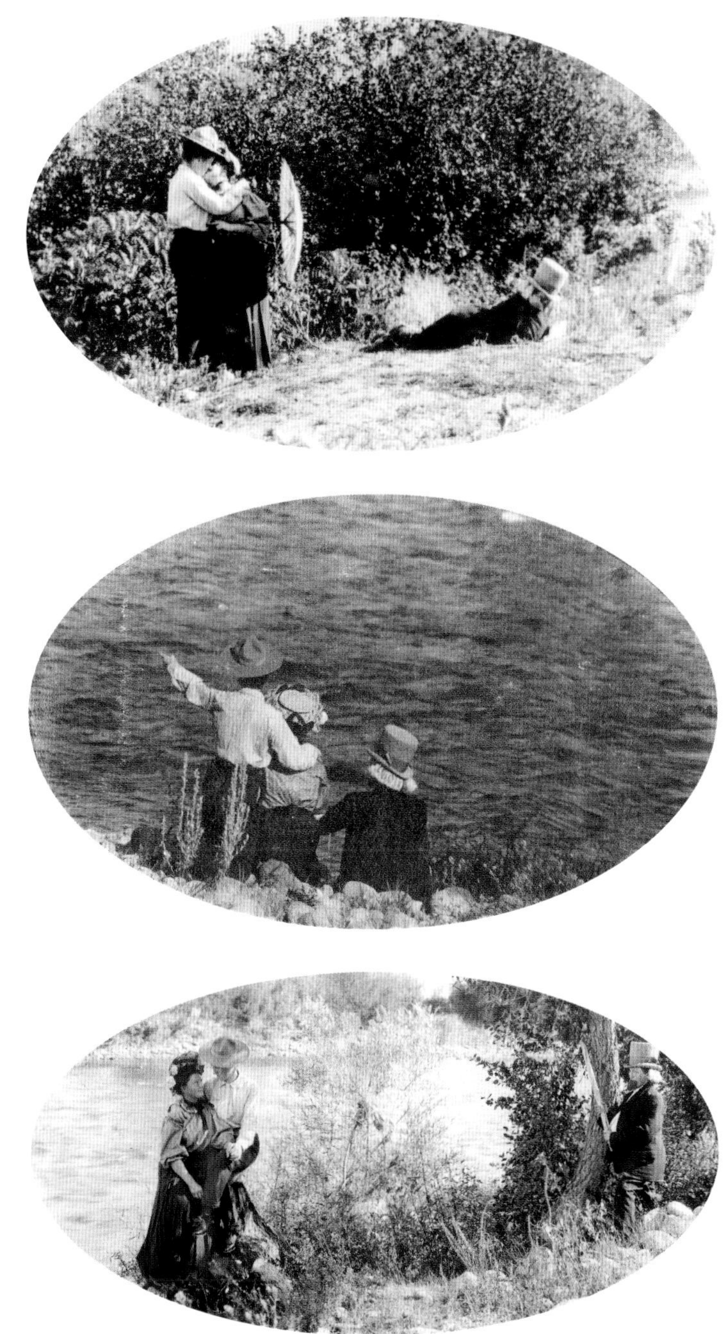

Cross-Dressing Acting Scenes, ca. 1903–1913

There is another set by Matsura worth considering in order to expand our interpretations of his work in relation to his advocacy of gender equality: a series of four images depicting three women, two dressed as men, in a pastoral landscape. Three of the images are included in a photo album in the collection of the Okanogan County Historical Society, ovals cut and pasted onto black pages. The figure playing the role of the woman has been identified as Elsie Bidwell.[12] In the image on page 102, the actors appear to be out of character with their relaxed facial expressions and linked arms. In the images on page 103, though, Matsura generates a compelling melodramatic tone in the narrative through the use of gestures, composition, and juxtaposition. Although here, too, the intended sequence remains unclear, the images do carry enough detail to know that it is about a young heterosexual couple and a third wheel, who eyes the pair from a distance. Again, it is enticing to imagine the conversation between them and Matsura as they set out to shoot on the banks of the Okanogan River. What did they envision they were playing? Did the women volunteer to perform these men's roles? In what way did drag performance feed into the friendship among them? And with Matsura?

These photographs attest to the close friendship Matsura nurtured with several women in town, especially single young women. Seeing these women in his photographs transformed and performing different roles conveys a sense that Matsura appreciated watching them become independent before his own eyes. As much as these women enjoyed visiting Matsura's studios, I imagine Matsura also welcomed them as sitters and models.

Optical Trickery and Doubles

The overwhelming resemblance to *tableaux vivant* aside, these staged images beg us to consider the availability of information, knowledge, and experiences of popular culture in a small rural community like Okanogan. The visual and narrative elements of these images reveal a striking resemblance to those elements in early cinema.[13] In fact, it is reaffirming to learn that Hub's Theater, the first permanent location for projecting film in Okanogan, opened its doors in 1910, around the time Matsura's photo business was thriving on the First Avenue. The *Okanogan Record* also shows that by 1908, a ventriloquist and a traveling performer with a film projector, King Kennedy, came through Okanogan County regularly.[14]

This image is where Matsura himself is acting out, although not in drag. In the top image, Matsura sits at the center of a large tree trunk wearing a dark

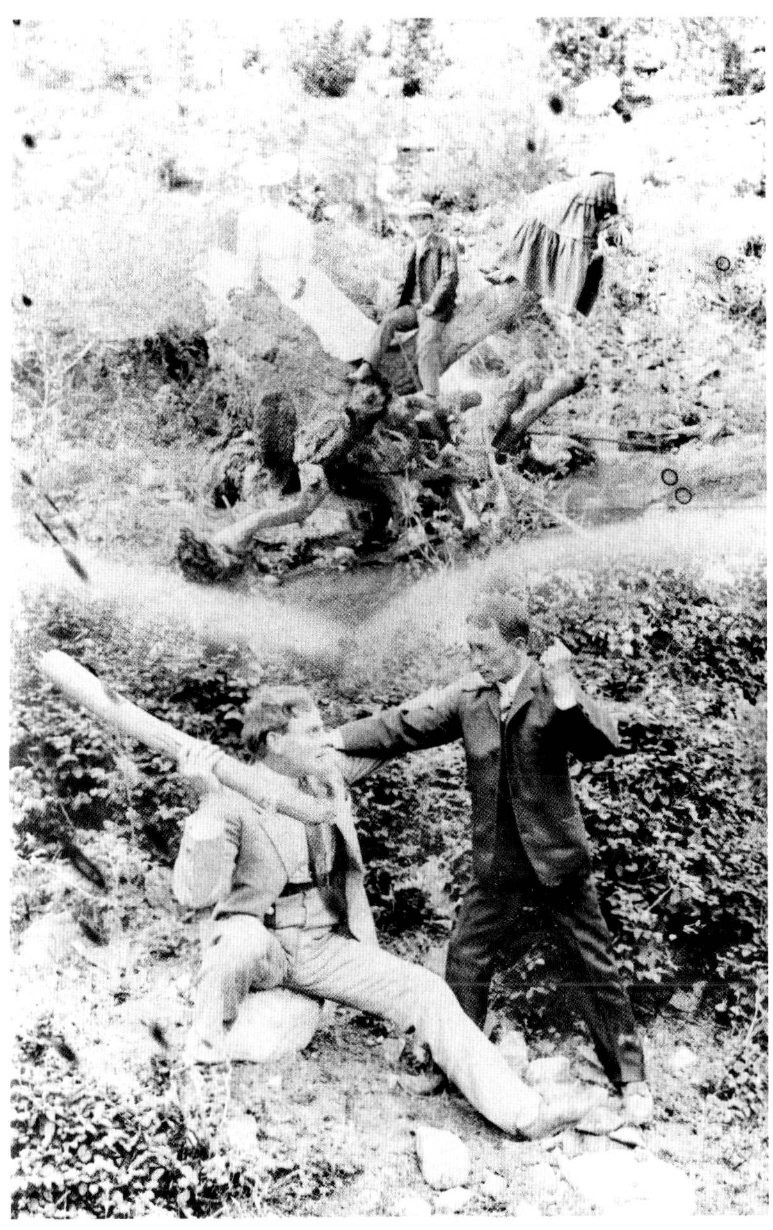

Untitled, Frank Matsura photograph, ca. 1903–1913.
Matsura acting in the scene himself, multiple exposure.

suit, with female sitters in white dresses sitting at the end of the bifurcating branch. In the bottom image, Matsura raises his left knuckle to a young guy who is holding a log and about to hit Matsura. The camera is set much closer in the second scene, to give more details of the action. The relation between these two scenes is obscure or at least not readily apparent. In the slapstick aspect of the second image, one could almost anticipate the thud sound of being hit by one of them, and the muted tone of the top image generates a further contrast. On this level, the viewers come to see two sides of Matsura, one sitting quietly and the other acting out to inflict pain on the other.

In a similar pursuit of doubling, Matsura takes advantage of the reflective water surface in the composition of an image shot at the Conconully Dam. The lone tree with its leaves leaning to the right on the hill in the background suggests how windy the area is in general. This information creates compositional tension with the central two Matsuras standing erect and still. The surface water of the dam adds further tension between the blowing gust and the seeming stillness. The

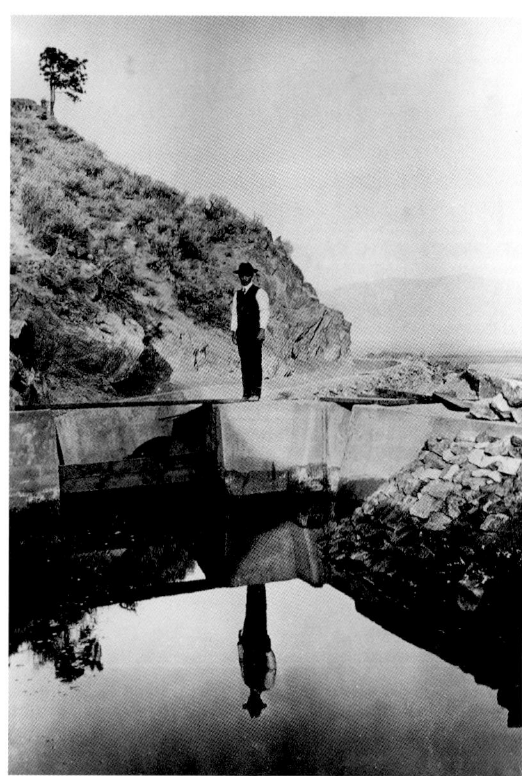

Matsura Self-Portrait over Water Tank, ca. 1903–1913. Matsura stands next to a diversion gate in an irrigation ditch lateral as part of the Conconully Dam construction by the Bureau of Reclamation for the Okanogan Irrigation District.

darkness of Matsura's waistcoat, trousers, and hat (which casts further shadow on his face) adds another contrast in this image. The edge of the dam is captured in a whitish tone, while its reflection on the water surface flips the color to pitch black. The darkish smudge around the reflected head of Matsura does not make optical sense when one looks up at the actual sky in the background. The viewers cannot find a corresponding group of stormy clouds.

Transforming Photographic Prints

The last aspect of transformation I want to explore in Matsura's work is literally the physical transformation of the prints themselves. One notices, for example, that in making the baubles out of his own prints for Christmas decorations in 1905, Matsura approached his work not only as a two-dimensional print that could be framed and placed on a wall.

On this occasion, Matsura took portrait photographs and transformed them into decorative ornaments for a festive and seasonal Christmas celebration. The bauble also includes buildings and other outdoor photographs of the vicinity of Okanogan. Along with star-shaped paper ornaments, Matsura's images have transformed, literally and metaphorically, into a different object altogether.

A page from the photo album, allegedly put together by Matsura himself, also gives us a sense of how he might have approached photographic prints as transformable objects. Here, various portrait images, mostly of infants, a few toddlers, and one adult, are cut into petal shapes to form the Imperial Seal of Japan. As far as I can tell, there is no discernible sign that these subjects form a family. I also cannot discern whether the subjects are all female or male. The choice of the Japanese Imperial Seal is paradoxical, or at least unclear. But the use of prints as material for something else, as was the case with the baubles, is evident here, too.

Matsura used photographic prints to generate and propagate further images. He also expressed double-sidedness of himself as a subject. Working with female sitters, their transformation into male roles offered another opportunity to explore Matsura's interest and attraction to transformative possibilities. Considering his newspaper article "Education of the Japanese Women," a glimpse of his investment in "restoring" gender equality through education came to the fore. His use of multiple negatives to show the multiple sides of the same subject in one view works to generate further images of the subject. I postulated how the mechanism and logic of dissonant seeing might have offered a way to imagine

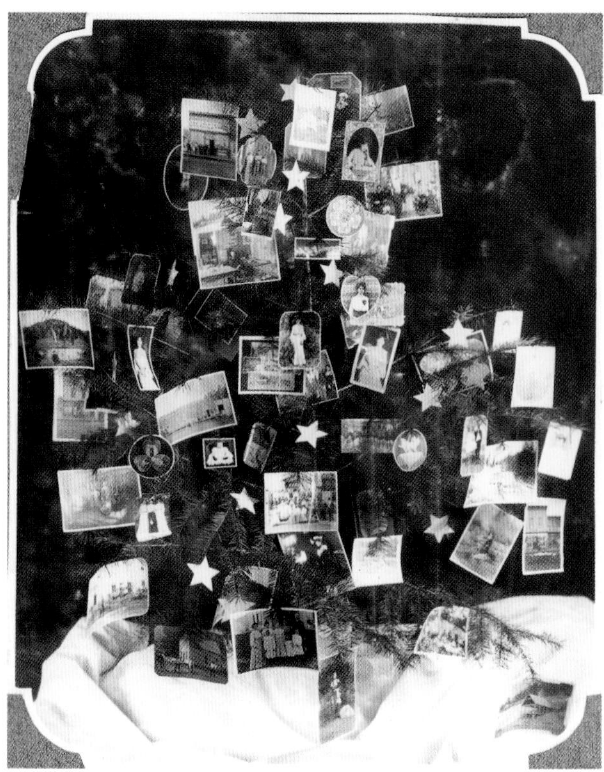

Christmas Tree with Photos as Baubles,
ca. 1903–1913. Presented to the *Okanogan Record* in Conconully in 1904.

where Matsura experienced entertaining and comical amusement before becoming a photographer in Okanogan County.

Reading accounts about Matsura, one wonders if he had his own magnetic field. Many personal and historical stories compose a picture of a man whose personality and charm pulled people from all walks of life. Traveling with his 5 × 7 view camera like a trusted companion, the pair captured images of many lives and faces. In these sessions, Matsura and his photographic subjects, often his friends, goofed around and experimented together. The photographs from such sessions served and continue to serve as storytelling boards that bring people together around Matsura's images. One hundred twelve years after his passing, his work has brought another group of people together in an orbit around his photographs. The book you are holding now is a result of this gathering. The gravitational pull of his work still elicits an atypical coming together of people. The curiosity and energy that draw us close strike me as a remarkably Matsura way of working with and through us.

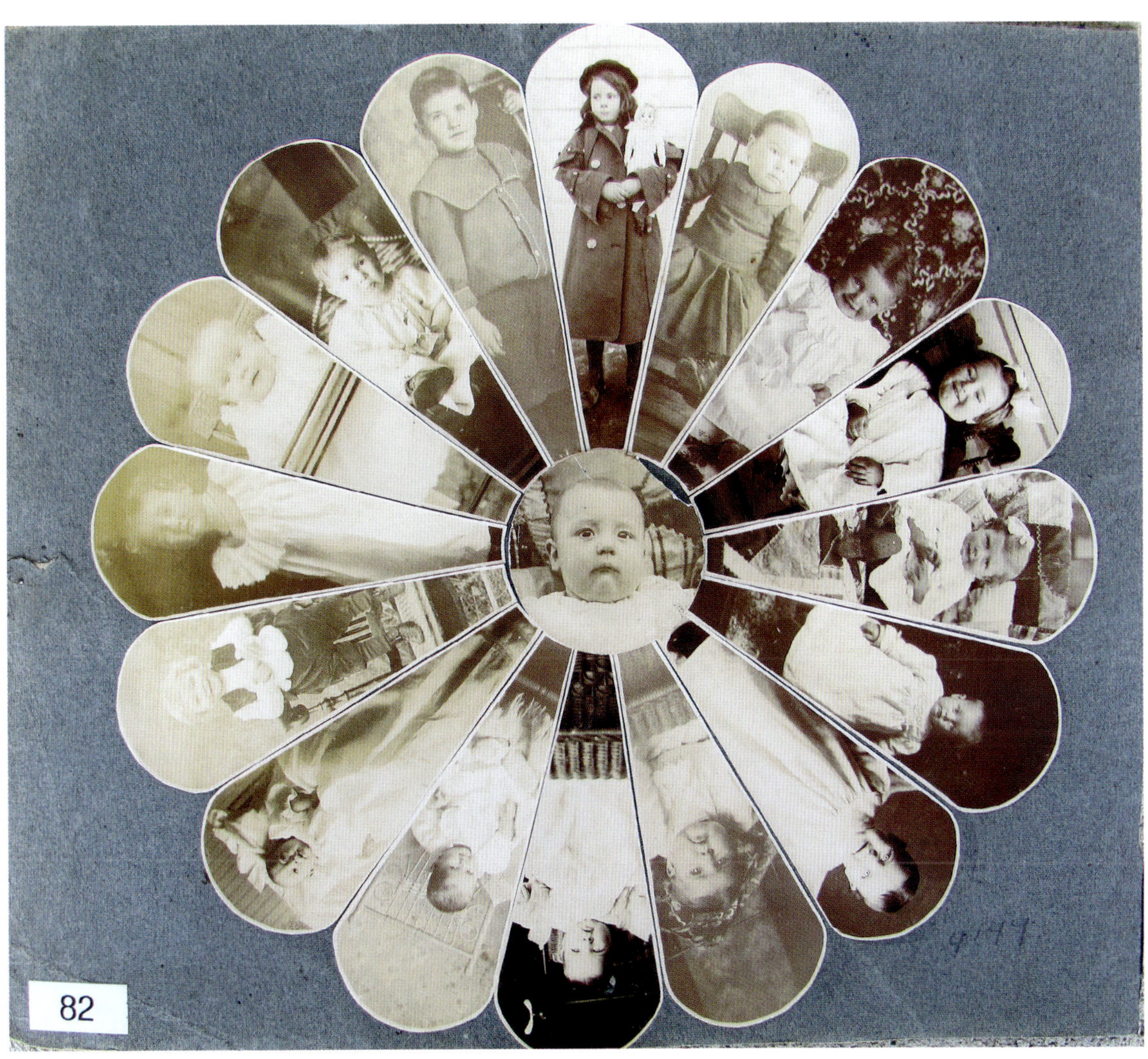

Composite in Chrysanthemum Shape, ca. 1903–1913

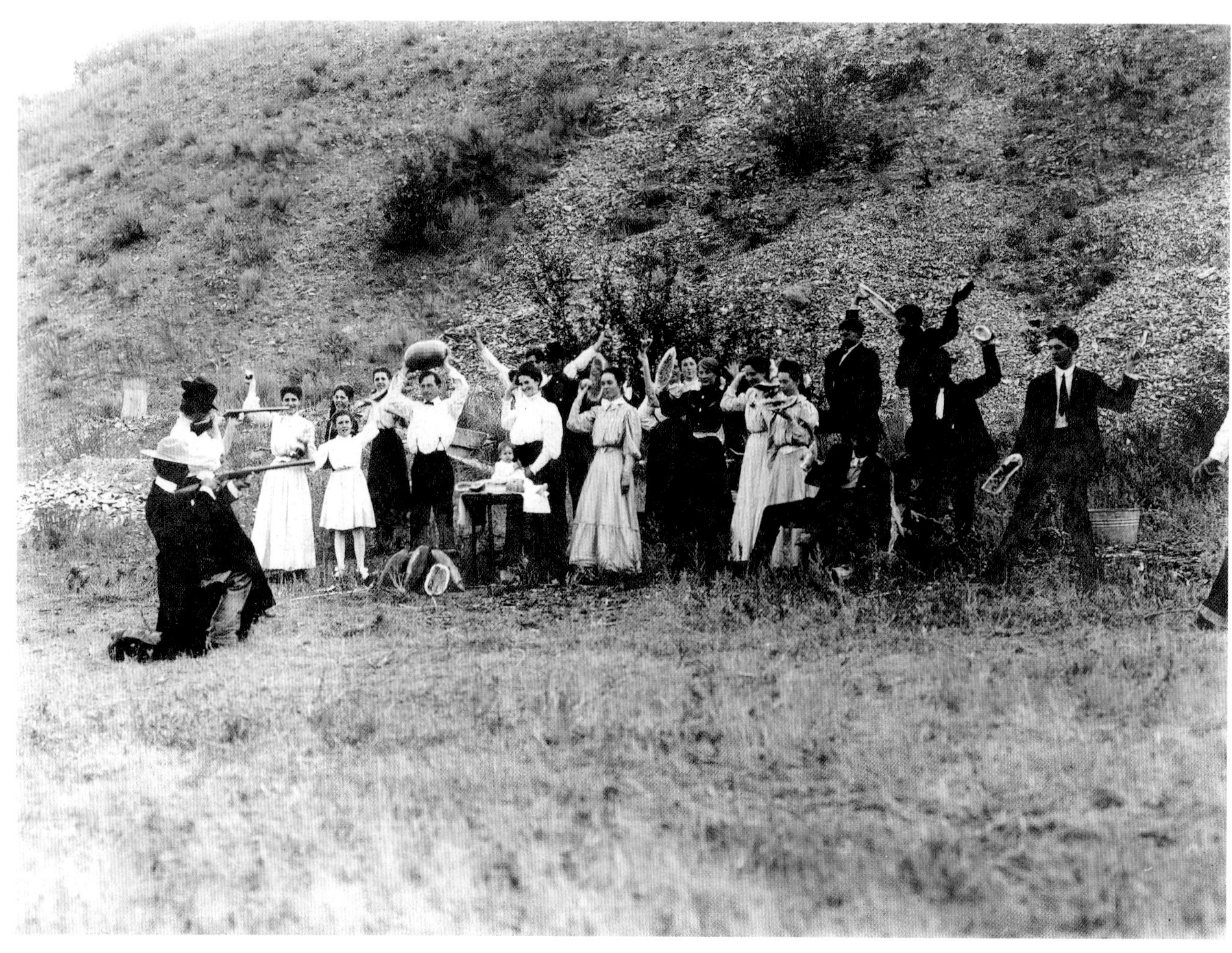

Pouge Frey George Family, 1907.
Watermelon picnic, July 1907, at Willard H. George
homestead, Omak, Washington.

CHAPTER FOUR

"MATSURA DID THEM RIGHT"

Beth Harrington

In 2002, a pit stop in Tacoma, Washington, put me face to face with the long-gone friends, neighbors, and acquaintances of an immigrant photographer from Japan. The photographer was Frank S. Matsura, and my chance encounter with his photos made over a century ago sparked an intense curiosity about this unsung Japanese artist who made north-central Washington State his home.

En route to a meeting in Seattle, I had decided to stretch my legs at the Washington State History Museum. In what I now consider a fateful decision, I visited the museum's featured exhibition, *Shadowy Evidence: The Photography of Edward S. Curtis and His Contemporaries*, curated by Rod Slemmons, who previously had been the curator of prints and photography at the Seattle Art Museum.

The work of celebrated photographer Edward S. Curtis was not unfamiliar to me. As a documentary filmmaker, I knew of Curtis's landmark body of work, *The North American Indian,* a twenty-volume set of images he had taken between 1900 and 1930.[1] The work was impressive in scope and quality, but I was well aware of the criticism it had drawn since its publication.

Rod Slemmons noted in the exhibition's catalog, "[Curtis] states categorically that he is interested in the past, not the present. He had determined to make the present look like the past, and at the same time to hide evidence of

111

cultural evolution among his subjects or of complex and imaginative syntheses of Indians by white and Indian culture."[2]

Curtis was true to his stated intent. Many of the images highlighted the photographer's commitment to a romanticization of Indigenous people, an erasure of signs of modernity, and a promotion of a narrative trope—the notion that Native Americans and their way of life were "vanishing," and that Curtis was witness to this end.

Rod Slemmons had done more than just present Curtis's works anew. He had juxtaposed other images of the same era by different creators. Some exuding a unique quality drew me in. These photos suggested a relationship and connection between the sitter and the photographer. In many, there was a sense of casual familiarity, a palpable closeness. Many of these images seemed to contradict Curtis's thesis. In these "non-Curtis" photos, one sensed personal agency. These were people being depicted as they wished, arriving at the photographer's studio dressed as they chose, and posing in ways that projected their autonomy, resilience, and modernity.

These images also seemed to cross proscribed social boundaries, and at that moment in 2002, they transcended time, with a freshness that defied photographic conventions of the day.

They all displayed the same photographer's name: Frank S. Matsura.

These images stayed with me long after I'd left the exhibition. I now know that this lingering feeling is shared by many people who have seen Matsura's photos. We comprise an informal league of devotees who have tried to find out who he was, how he wound up in the remote reaches of the Northwest, and why he stayed. I realized that Matsura had taken thousands of photos, not just of his Native neighbors, but also of non-Native settlers, other immigrants, of landscapes and regional projects, including the new dam, agricultural output, the railroad, and mining. Most notably, he took photos of himself in curious, humorous, serious, and poignant poses.

From that moment on, I did what I always do when confronted with a tantalizing story—I began to imagine what a documentary film would look like. But in 2002, there were only a couple of publications that focused on his work and biography, and I was uncertain if there would be enough of a story to tell.

Over time, I found a small but ever-growing body of writing and research by authors JoAnn Roe and Tatsuo Kurihara, tribal advocate Richard Hart, and members of the Okanogan County Historical Society, as well as the scholarship of

Dr. Glen Mimura and Dr. ShiPu Wang. By late 2021, fortified with this research and funding from the National Endowment for the Humanities, our team was able to begin work on the film *Our Mr. Matsura*. It had been nearly two decades since that first encounter in Tacoma. Matsura's work has an unshakeable grip on the imagination of those who see it.

Given the persistent mystery attached to Matsura's story, a strict historical approach to the film proved frustrating and unsatisfying. The holes in the narrative, the most commonly asked questions—Why did he leave Japan? Why did he come to remote Washington State?—could not then and, in fact, may *never* be answered.

Despite those unanswered questions, there was still powerful and ample evidence of his life in newspaper accounts of his day, in the photos he left us, and in the memories of generations of people whose ancestors are depicted in those photos.

To open the film, I concocted a "device" that I thought might engage the viewer: we would interview about a half dozen people who could point to a Matsura image and say, "This is my family at a watermelon picnic in a photo by Frank Matsura," or "This is my great-aunt in a local ice-skating party, taken by Frank Matsura." Because it had been more than a century since his death, I assumed I would find only a few people who would fit that bill, who could identify an ancestor in one of Matsura's photos and talk about the connection between the subject and the photographer. That might be enough.

Not long after embarking on this idea, I had an unexpected and welcome revelation—far more than *a few* people could make that connection. Matsura had so thoroughly engaged with people in the region, and his memory was so honored and nurtured, that I soon found I had dozens of people who could not only identify the subject of a photo but also talk about this beloved photographer. Often there were stories, both factual and imagined, that accompanied the photos.

I realized that although Matsura was "under the radar" in terms of national recognition, for the people of Okanogan County and the Colville Confederated Tribes, he remained an important figure in their collective memory. Well over a century after his untimely death from tuberculosis, scores of people from all walks of life knew who he was and what he'd contributed to the community.

Without this succession of individuals deeply caring about Matsura's legacy and passing the torch to others, knowledge of him and his work might have been lost forever.

Early in the research process, I met Georgene Davis Fitzgerald, the owner of a small produce farm in Brewster, Washington.[3] Fitzgerald's grandparents

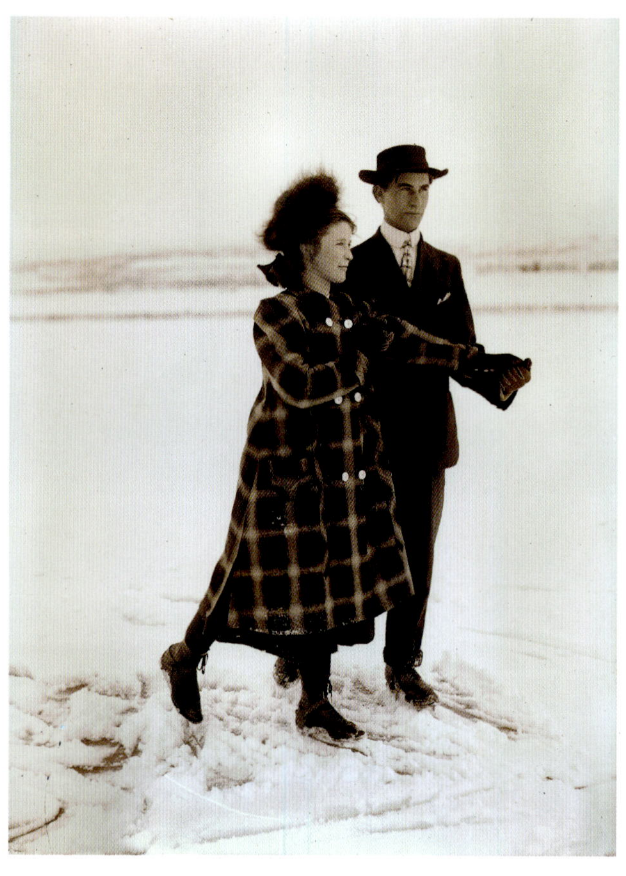

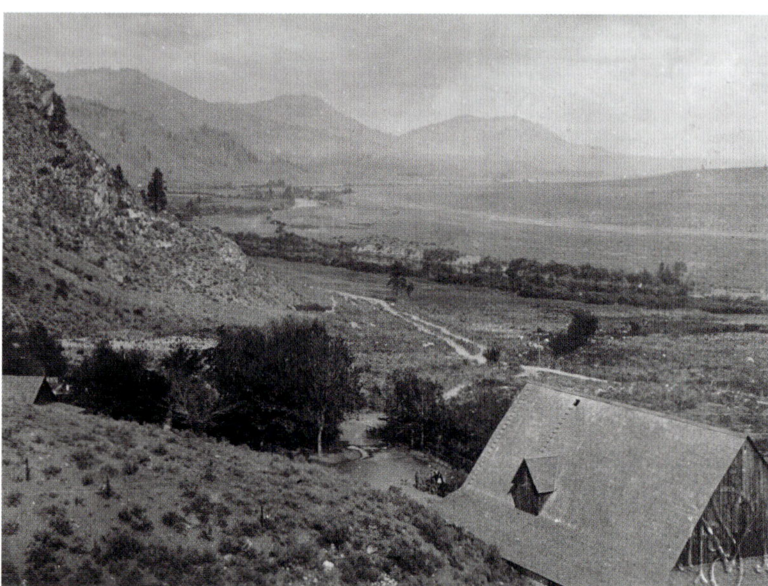

Orril Gard and Charles Herrmann,
ca. 1903–1913

Davis Farm, ca. 1903

came by horse-drawn wagon to the region in 1888, from a town near Sacramento, California. The Davises set about building the home (which still stands) and began planting fruit and nut trees. They freighted the produce to various mining camps in the area, which provided a good source of income for these homesteaders. Grandfather W. L. Davis also operated the stage route from Brewster to the town of Conconully, which carried the mail and passengers like Matsura.

Fitzgerald cited an account by local newspaper publisher O. H. Woody[4] that chronicled Matsura's long trip from Seattle to Okanogan County in the fall of 1903 to take a job as a handyman at the Elliot Hotel in Conconully. It was here he was befriended by the hotel's owner, S. J. Dillabough, and his family. Dillabough took a liking to Matsura and offered him space in the hotel to set up a darkroom for his photography.

Fitzgerald is a member of the Okanogan County Historical Society and editor of a publication for the OCHS, *Frank S. Matsura, A Scrapbook*.[5] She has spent over forty years researching Matsura's life in the county and had even kept up some correspondence with Fuku Okami, a Matsura family member, for a dozen years. Fitzgerald was quick to distinguish fact from fiction. But she acknowledged that, newspaper accounts aside, so much of what we know about Matsura can only be discerned from the evidence he left us—his photos.

Fitzgerald spiritedly contributed a narrative based on her own family photo taken by Matsura. But she qualified it as "my made-up story about the day Frank came up the valley in 1903" to make his life in Okanogan County.[6]

The photo shows the Davis family homestead, including the house, the barn, and the orchards. Careful examination reveals a stagecoach in the lower right of the frame. Fitzgerald noted that a traveler from Seattle in those days would have come by train to the town of Wenatchee. Most of the year the trip could be completed by steamboat up the Okanogan River, but this was autumn, and the water was too low for a traveler to take a steamboat. A traveler like Matsura would have taken a stagecoach for the last leg of the trip from Brewster to Conconully.

Fitzgerald then envisioned what might have come next. "In my story, of course, it was W. L. Davis's stagecoach that he got on that morning. And twelve miles north of Brewster was the Davis Ranch," a stopover where horses and humans rested and were fed.

"My grandmother Lucinda was well-known for the bounteous table that she set, and so they would've had a meal here. After lunch," she continued, "Frank, just ever on the alert for a photo op, took his camera and climbed the hill behind

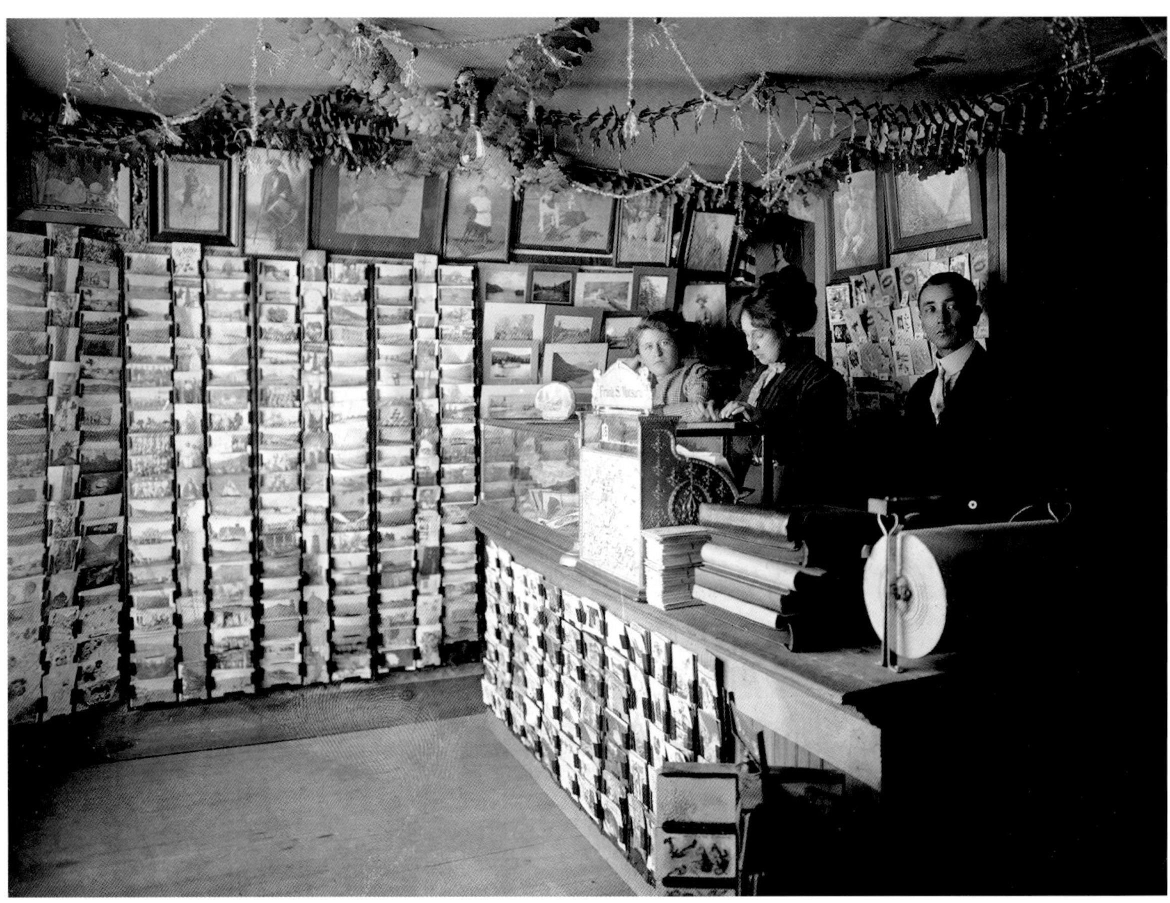

Matsura Photo Shop Interior, ca. 1903–1913. Matsura enlisted the aid of his two good friends Orril Gard (left) and Mathilda Schaller for the Christmas holiday. Matsura advertised in the local paper that a portrait was the perfect Christmas gift for a friend or family.

the then new barn and took some pictures." Fitzgerald gestured to the photo as she noted the details, "And one of them is this one looking north, showing the yard and it looks like the stage is all hitched up and ready to go and waiting patiently, we hope, for Frank to come back down off the hill and continue on" to Conconully and the Elliot Hotel.

Fitzgerald wanted to believe that this was the first image Matsura took in Okanogan County. She wistfully imagined a beautiful, blue-skied fall foliage day when Matsura "fell in love with this place and loved it as long as he lived." She shrugged and said, "Some of it *could* be true." But she emphasized, some of it "we know is true."

For the Native people of the region, Matsura's photographs help tell other stories. For many, the images bear witness to life lived in the throes of enormous trauma and upheaval. After deceptive and often ruthless machinations by American political and military entities, distinct groups of Indigenous peoples from throughout the inland Northwest ended up on a US government–established reservation, today referred to as the home of the Colville Confederated Tribes. Colville elder Randy Lewis illustrated the turmoil of this time by using his own ancestors' story, that of the Wenatchi, or P'Squosa, who were moved from a forested, stream-abundant area to the radically different terrain of the reservation.[7]

"Why would they be taking river people who were so tied to the sounds, the smell, and the life of salmon fishermen on the river and move them up here to the mountains and up here into the escarpment where there was no fish, there was no sound? Well, that's what they did, and it was intentional. It was to destroy that cultural backbone of the people." This type of disruption and more played out throughout the twelve tribes.[8]

Matsura might not have arrived in the region with knowledge of this situation, but it is hard to imagine that it took him long to grasp the forced relocation, since the hundreds of photos he took of people from the tribes suggest frequent interaction and ongoing relationships.

The images that Matsura took of people from the tribes are cherished by present-day descendants, and they often have specific stories about their family members, and Matsura himself, passed down over the years. Randy Lewis is one of these people.

Lewis has been an activist for Native American justice his entire life. His service to his people is deep and wide, starting with his involvement with the

Indian Youth Council at the age of sixteen; his organization of the national "Right to Be Indian" conference for student activists; occupying Fort Lawton in Seattle, which led to the building of the Daybreak Star Indian Cultural Center; successfully fighting the termination of the Colville reservation; working with Indigenous peoples on AIDS awareness for the World Health Organization; serving on the United Indians of All Tribes Foundation's board; and co-teaching Indian studies at Gonzaga University.

Lewis spoke of the past with a deep understanding passed down from his grandfather Jerome Miller, whose stories he recalled. Quoting his grandfather, "'I come with empty hands. All I give you are these stories.'"[9]

According to Lewis, his grandfather, also known as Kash-laxen, would stretch out after dinner for a storytelling session, encouraging his grandson to grab writing tools. "'Okay, bring your Big Chief tablet and pencil,' and he would start talking and I would just start writing....This was a great legacy."[10]

At the time of the photographer's arrival in the area, "We still had our chiefs and council, our headmen that were respected, and Matsura realized that he must talk to these people and show them, give them the respect." Lewis said that Matsura interacted with many of the hereditary chiefs or spokesmen, Indian doctors, both men and women, and shared his photography, building relationships that included getting to know members of Lewis's own family. "I know he went to my great-granddad."[11]

Lewis also spoke of his great-uncle Sam George, whose father was the salmon chief of the Wenatchi at an area known as Rock Island. George, too, was well-versed in the tribal history, which he shared with Lewis as a child. "I felt like the luckiest kid in the world having him in my life."[12]

Lewis looked at a Matsura image of a buckboard wagon overflowing with people, and he smiled and said, "I am holding in my hand one of the nicest photos." It shows Sam George; his wife, Christine George; and eight children of varying ages. He laughed and said, "It was kind of like the F-250 of wagons back then. And I don't think they could have squeezed another child in."[13]

Lewis noted that the family in the photo was headed to the St. Mary's Mission for mass. "And I love the picture because it shows that they took great pride in dressing up for this." He also pointed out how unusual the moment was. "They only came into town every two or three months with that many kids. And when I was growing up, he still had the wagon. So, it brings back wonderful memories for me. And *tupa* [revered elder] spoke about Matsura taking his picture." Lewis

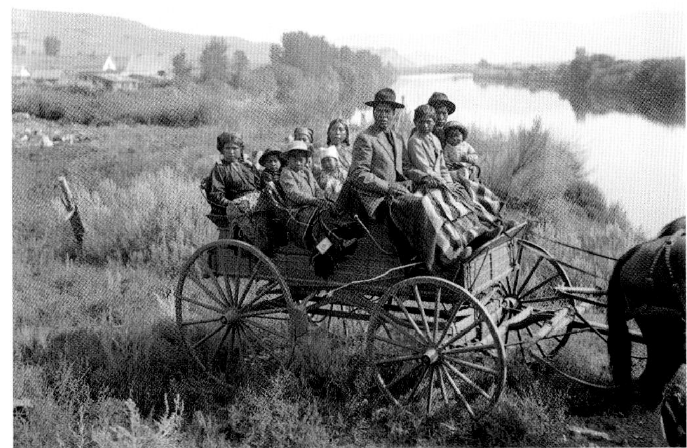

Sam George and Family, ca. 1903–1913.
George family leaving Okanogan in a
wagon. They are at the edge of the
Okanogan River. The town of Okanogan
and Shellrock Point are in the background.
The George family lived in the Omak Lake/
Kartar Valley area.

was moved that over a century later, "We're looking at that picture taken only a couple miles from here."[14]

The critical element in Matsura's photographs is obvious to Lewis. "The reason that you see them here in this photograph is that they allowed themselves to be photographed. They trusted Matsura, they loved Matsura. They did whatever they could to keep him with them. For some reason, they saw him as an asset, as an ally, somebody who's seen a lot of what they felt. So Matsura did them right.…And these families gladly and proudly hung those photos on their walls."[15]

Lewis also recalled a visit to George Burrell Ladd's photo studio decades after Matsura's death. Ladd, a contemporary of Matsura, was another local photographer well-known in the region. "Old man Ladd came out and he had Matsura's pictures, originals, and he showed them to *tupa*, great-uncle, and he reminisced with Ladd about when those were taken." Lewis spoke of the strong bond among Sam George, Matsura, and other members of the community, including the surveyor Chelsea Woodward and the Prussian immigrant, ferry operator, and hotel owner W. R. Kahlow. "[Ladd's] mind was so clear about it… they got along so well…they were good friends. All of them with my *tupa*."[16] These remembered friendships among men of different backgrounds provide a glimpse into a less understood dynamic of the community. Matsura photographs memorialize many of them.

Lynn Palmanteer-Holder, also a member of the Confederated Tribes of the Colville Reservation, has had a forty-year career as a professional educator

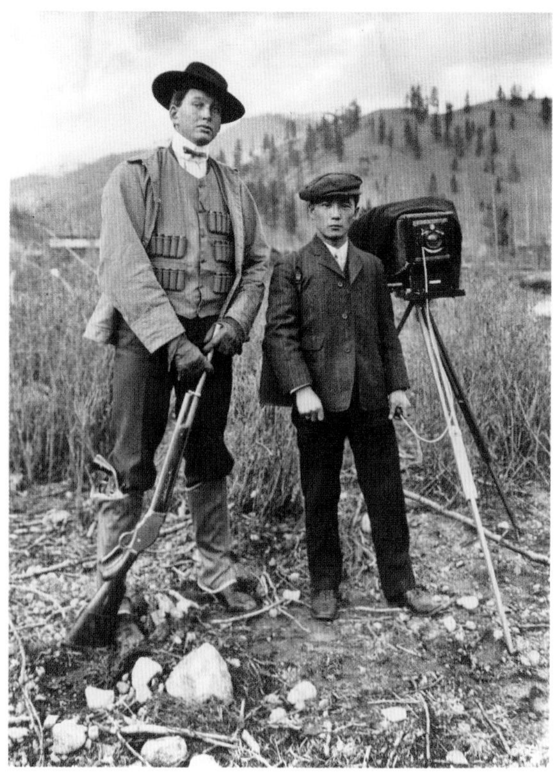

Chelsea Woodward and Frank Matsura,
ca. 1903–1913

from K–12 to post-secondary education and has been honored many times for her advocacy on behalf of Native students at the state and national levels. Before retiring, she was the first Director of Tribal Government Affairs for the Washington State Board of Community and Technical Colleges. She has also served as an elected tribal leader and has held various tribal governance executive positions.

Many of her ancestors are depicted in Matsura's work. She recalls at first being surprised by the images, since she understood that tribal elders of the time were generally wary of photography.[17] "It was feared because many believe that when that photo was taken, it was taking a piece of their soul." As a result, Palmanteer-Holder, like Lewis, concluded that for tribal families to agree to be photographed, "there had to be a lot of trust" in Matsura.[18] This is an exceptionally striking point when one considers there are hundreds of Matsura photos of people from the tribes in the collections at Okanogan County Historical Society and Washington State University at Pullman.

A man who appears in several of Matsura's images is Palmanteer-Holder's great-great-grandfather Chiliwhist Jim, one of the last leaders of the Methow tribe. Whether poised in a chair in Matsura's studio, wearing an eagle-feathered headdress and gazing confidently into the lens, or on horseback on the streets of Okanogan, posed in front of a jeweler's shop as homesteaders look on, Chiliwhist, also known as Lakekin, is a memorable presence. Family stories paint him as a charismatic figure, an accomplished horseman, someone known for his openness, affability, and, above all, diplomacy. Palmanteer-Holder also believed that he was a "man of curiosity" and that this was a trait he shared with Matsura.

Palmanteer-Holder imagined how the relationship between these men grew. "This Japanese man came into the Plateau area and wanted to learn about the history and the people and build relationships with them and eat with them." She surmises that this required spending lots of time together, and that Chiliwhist took Matsura to special places. "I just feel like there was some natural relationship

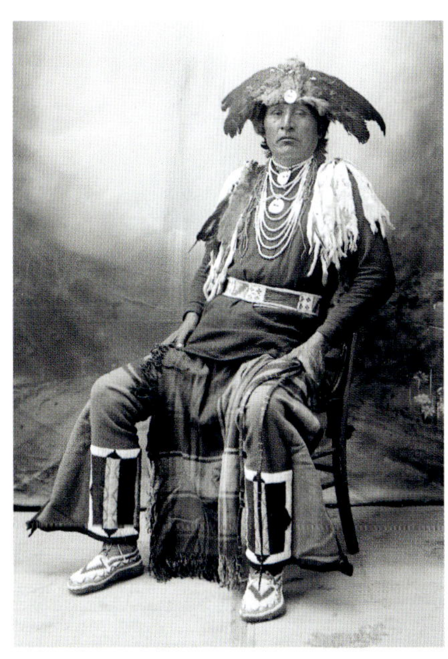

ABOVE (DETAIL)
Chiliwhist Jim (Lakekin) in the Studio,
ca. 1903–1913

RIGHT (DETAIL)
Chiliwhist Jim (Lakekin) on Horseback,
ca. 1903–1913

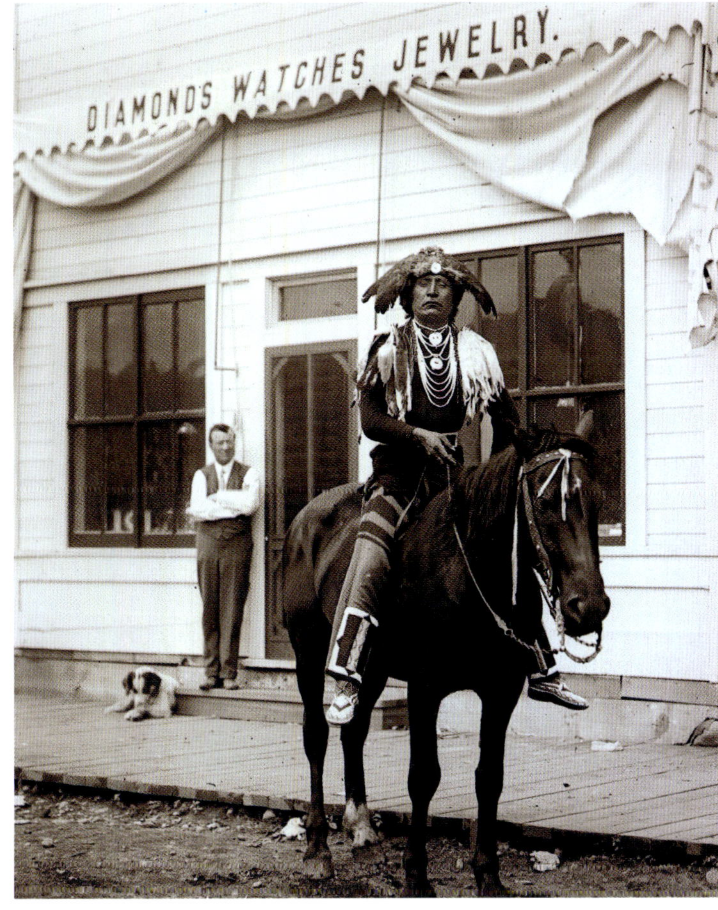

there that many of us probably won't ever know, but we can speculate that it was a good relationship between the two of them."[19]

That relationship with Chiliwhist seems to have extended to his daughter Cecil and other family members. Some of Matsura's most memorable photographs, all taken in his portrait studio, feature Cecil. These include an image of Cecil and Josephine Carden looking directly at the camera, each holding a Japanese fan; another of Cecil and Lucy Nason Walsh lounging on a sofa, appearing relaxed and perhaps a bit bemused; and a series of shots taken with a camera Matsura used frequently, a so-called multiplying camera. This apparatus had multiple lenses that made, through a series of separate exposures on one plate, various postage stamp–sized images on a single sheet of photo paper. Likened to a contemporary photo booth, the camera was used by Matsura to great effect, having the sitters change not only expression but also clothing, accessories, and props. The playful results are among some of his most interesting works. As he often did with the friends who came to play in his studio, Matsura jumped in front of the camera with Cecil. As in many of his multiplying camera photos, Cecil and Matsura are hugging, mugging, and giggling. Good humor and connection radiate from the photo series.

"They're goofing around, having a lot of fun together," she laughs. "And it almost looks, because he was shorter than her, [that] she was trying to scoot down a little bit as well because of her height."[20]

Palmanteer-Holder, speculating about the images, said, "Looking through all those photos and seeing my grandma Cecil in so many, and in such close proximity with him, many times I would be like, 'Why? Was there something going on between these two?'" But she adds that Cecil's sisters outlived her by many years and there were "never any stories about any romantic relationship." But she concluded that Matsura and Cecil "definitely got along."[21]

Palmanteer-Holder also noted that often a leader like Chiliwhist Jim would encourage family members, usually sons, to interact as emissaries to create strong community bonds. She recalled Cecil's keen intelligence and wondered if Chiliwhist Jim cast her in this role, strengthening the connection between Matsura and the entire family.[22]

Clearly, Matsura's network of friends among the people of the Colville reservation was extensive. Another leader he befriended was Lahompt, also referred to as Koxit George, the last chief of the Entiat tribe and the first of his line forced to live on the Colville reservation.

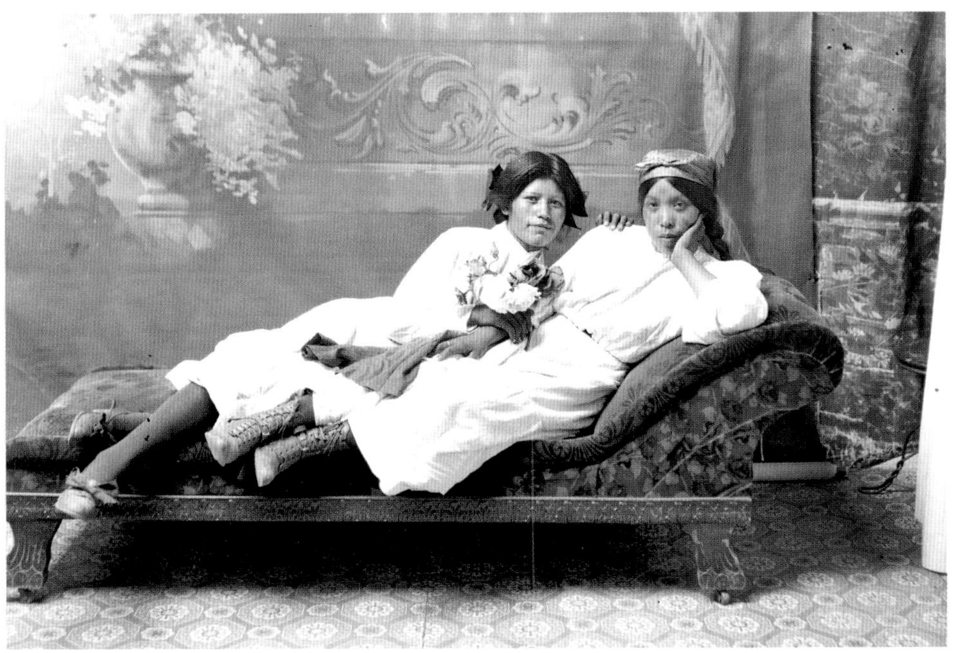

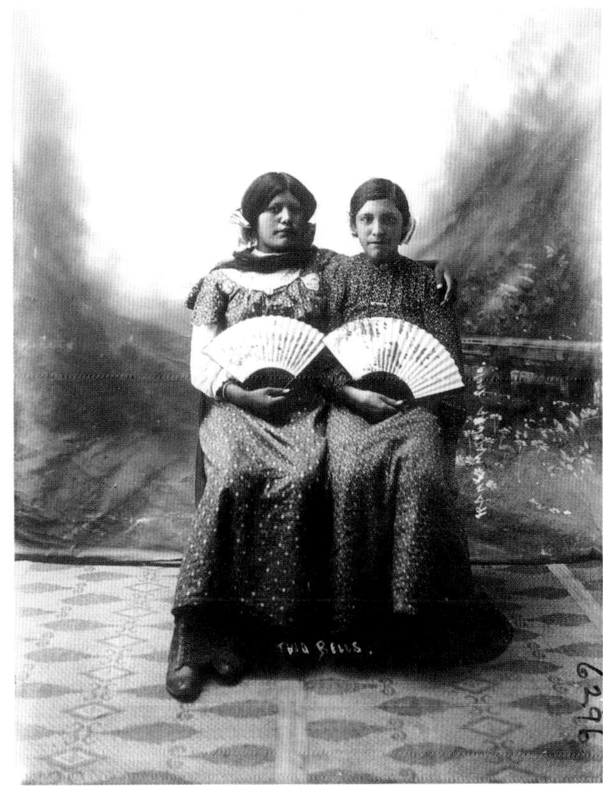

ABOVE
Cecil Jim Palmanteer and Lucy Nason Walsh, ca. 1903–1913

RIGHT
Cecil Jim Palmanteer and Josephine Carden, ca. 1903–1913

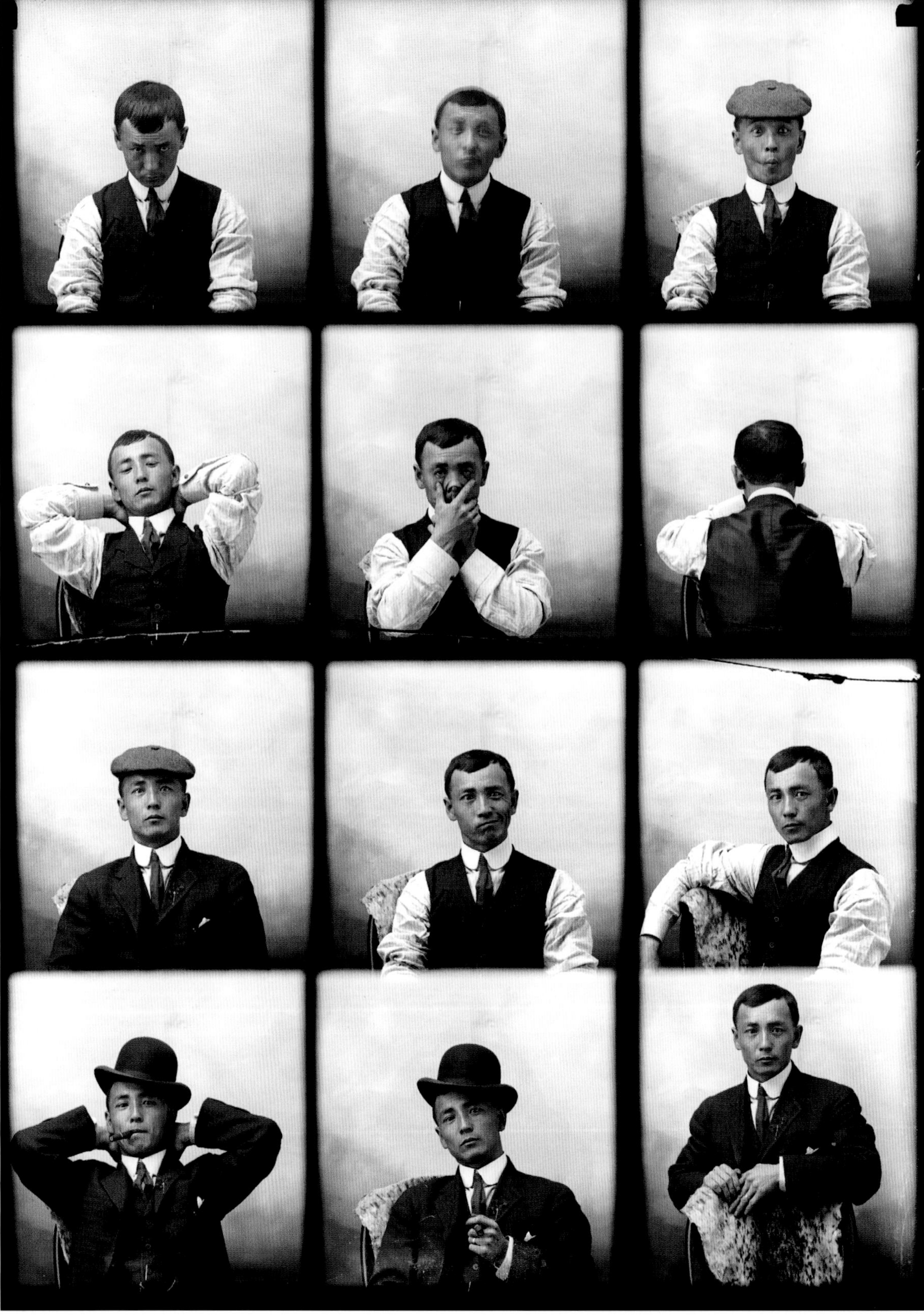

Lahompt's grandson, Wendell George, is a leader in his own right, and over his lifetime he has been active in Native issues on both the local and national levels. Attaining a degree in electrical engineering from Washington State University, George began his career working for the Boeing Company and eventually became part of the NASA effort to land the first man on the moon. Not long after, he decided to return to the reservation to help develop both human and natural resources for his people. George served on the Colville Tribal Council and the Colville Business Council and eventually became the CEO of all their enterprises. Nationally, he testified on behalf of Native people in Washington, DC, at the highest levels of the federal government. George has written extensively about tribal history and his own life's journey.[23]

His family's journey from the home of the Entiat tribe to the Colville reservation is an epic of struggle and adaptation in the face of adversity. Lahompt witnessed the double-dealing of US officials, intertribal tensions, the encroachment of miners and homesteaders on land supposedly allotted to Native people, and the tragic loss of his first wife to smallpox, leaving him alone to raise his two children. In spite of it all, Lahompt persevered, and, as George wrote, "My

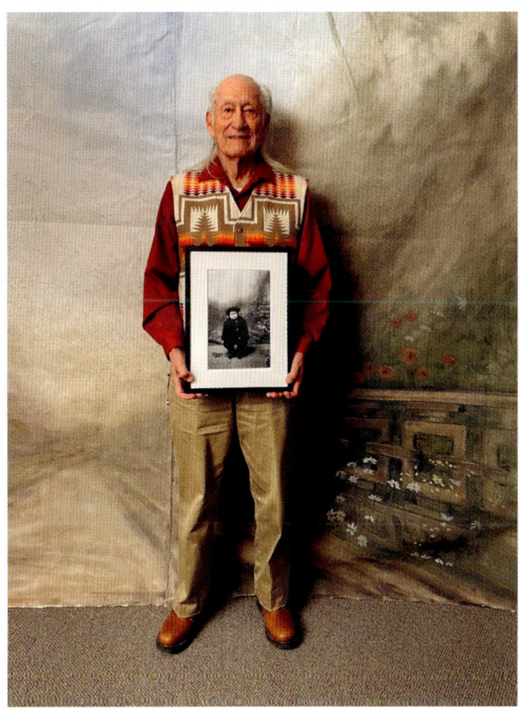

OPPOSITE
Frank Matsura's Multiplying Camera Self-Portraits, ca. 1903–1913

RIGHT
Wendell George holding portrait of Moses George, ca. 2023

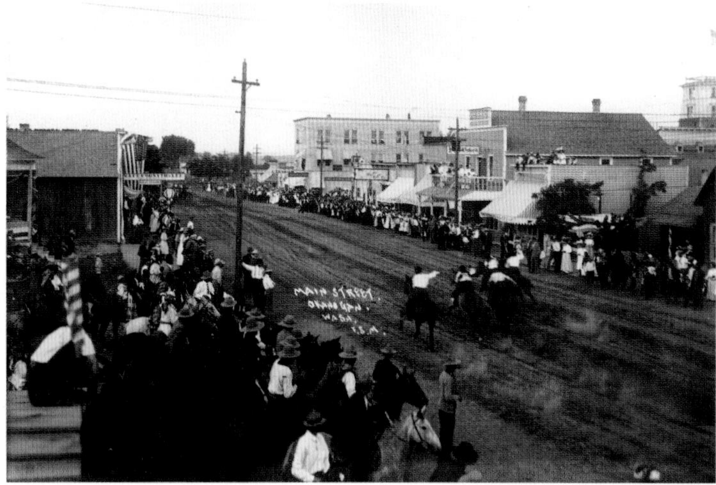

LEFT
Horse Race through Okanogan,
ca. 1903–1913

OPPOSITE
Kwa-ni, ca. 1910. Kwa-ni (Christine),
the wife of Koxit George, is wearing
a Plateau deer tail dress and a woven
basket hat.

grandfather was the first in our family to successfully make the transition from a nomadic lifestyle to a land-based commercial enterprise."[24]

Which is why the image of Lahompt in regalia on horseback in front of the Bureau Hotel in Okanogan is particularly fitting and, as George saw it, a careful collaboration between Matsura and his grandfather.

"You have to realize that my grandfather made friends with Frank Matsura. That's why [Frank] took a lot of pictures of him....They would plan all this and put together the way [Lahompt] dressed and that took a lot of work." When George, a horseman himself, examined the photo of his grandfather at the Bureau Hotel, he discerned that his mount was "well broken" by just the way he was standing in the Matsura photo. Lahompt was a successful competitive racer, and horse racing was a popular pastime in the Okanogan, a reality depicted in Matsura's work.[25]

Lahompt was a rancher, at one point owning two thousand head of cattle. Back in the early 1900s, bringing cattle to market from Kartar Valley on the Colville reservation was a difficult undertaking because there was no bridge across the Okanogan River at that time. George marveled at it. "With a few hundred head that he was bringing over there, he would have to cross on a ferry, and it took him several days to get all the herd across."[26]

George shared other Matsura images of his family, that of his grandmother Kwa-ni, Lahompt's second wife, wearing a finely detailed buckskin dress and a delightful photo of Wendell's father, Moses George, a wide-eyed toddler, taken in Matsura's studio.

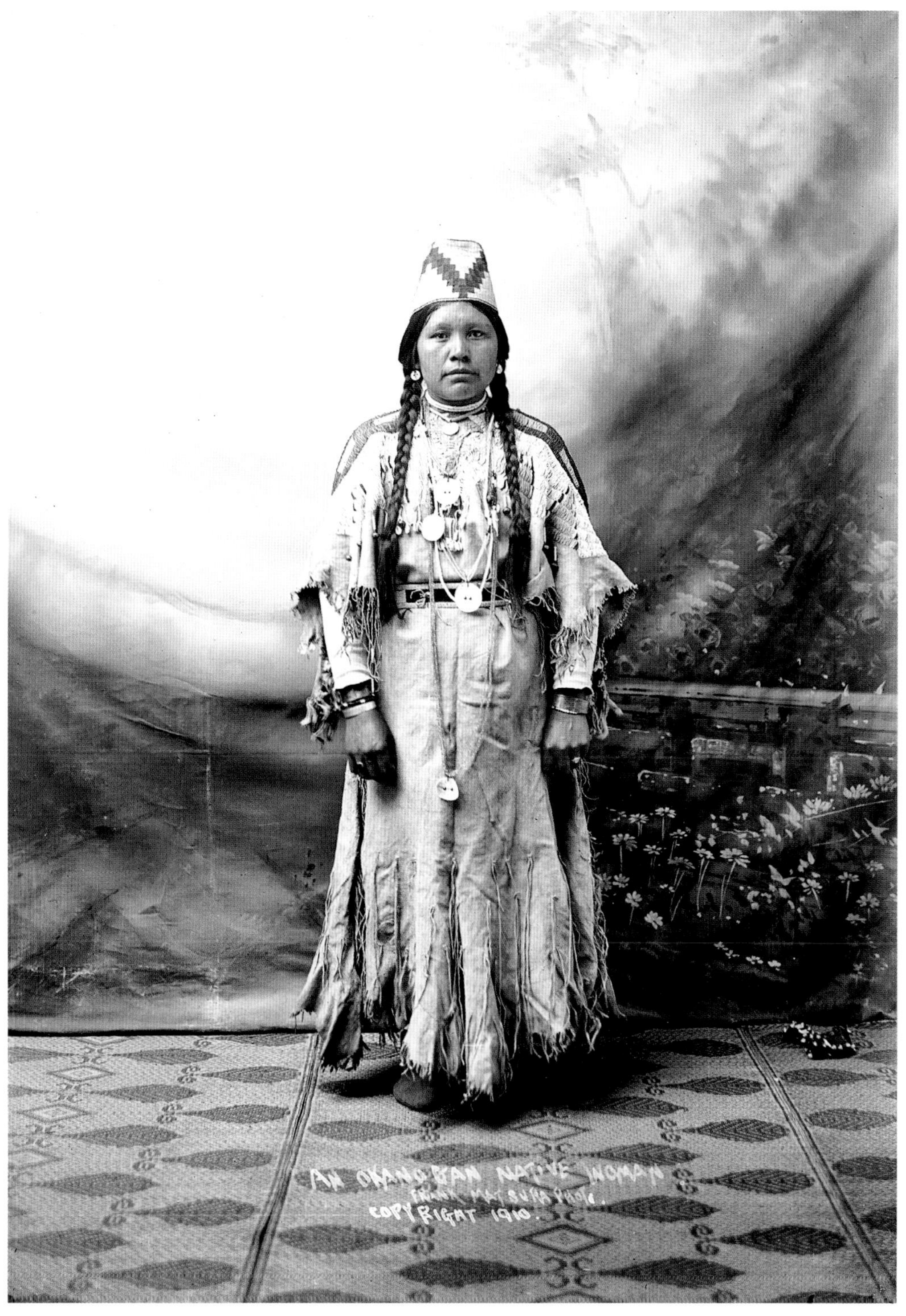

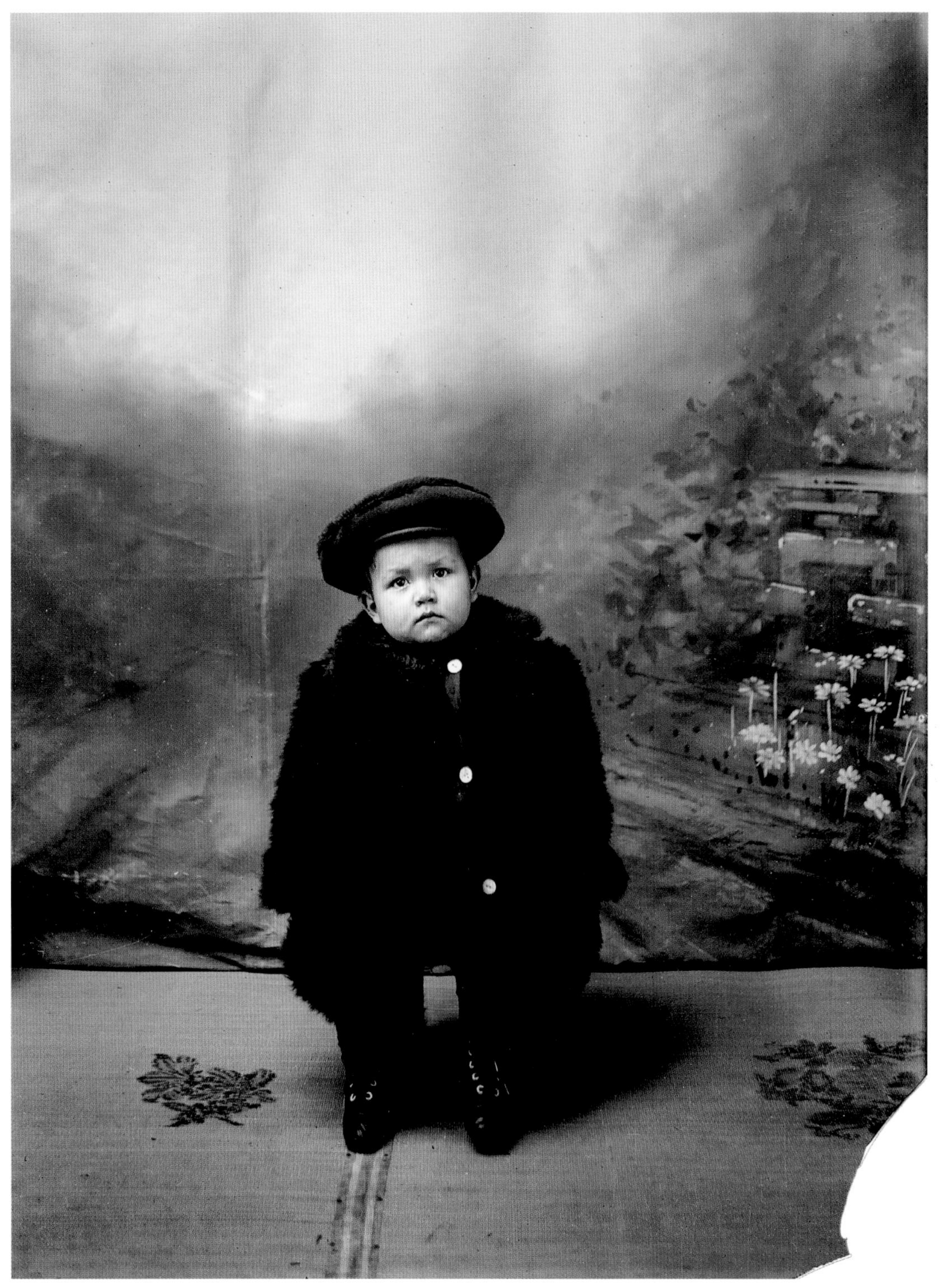

Moses George had a unique distinction, said George. "He was born in a teepee right beside the log house that they'd built. He was the last of the family born in a teepee. That was the tradition in those days." Moses would go on to become a well-regarded leader in the community and someone who encouraged his son to excel and grow in order to help their people.

But in the photo George held, there is just a tiny boy, dressed in an enveloping bearskin coat and jaunty hat, staring uncertainly into the camera. George explained Moses's bewildered expression, chuckling, "He was four years old in that picture....This was pretty new to him. He spent most of the time over in Kartar Valley and being brought into the studio and set up with cameras and that sort of thing was very new. So, he was trying to get it all, catch it all, figure out what it was all about. I think the surprised look on his face was very evident."[27]

When George considered Matsura's relationship with his family and others, he said, "Tribal people are, let's say, for the most part, friendly as a group. They will…let you prove your worth....Matsura was able to work with both people. He related to tribal people real well and also with other people." George applauded Matsura's ability to work "in between the whole thing."[28]

Matsura certainly produced a significant body of studio work, and it is understandably assumed that the heart of any small-town photographer's business was portraiture. But in the early twentieth century, an interesting turn of events in US postal rules created a burgeoning new revenue stream for people like Matsura.

Julia Dolan, the Minor White Senior Curator of Photography for the Portland Art Museum in Oregon, said of these times, "The exact years that Matsura was running a studio were the exact years that Americans and people throughout the world were obsessed with picture postcards, absolutely obsessed. And in 1907, the US government for the first time allowed people to place messages on the back of the postcard." This seemingly tiny development made an ordinary postcard that much more desirable to send.

"So Matsura is making, creating, and selling postcards at a time when technology and law allow for people to send portraits of themselves, send portraits or images of their homestead, pictures of their dog, of their baby. These wonderful personal moments can be sent through the mail and be further personalized with a message....Even if you didn't have your own photograph made at Matsura's studio, he had a wide range of postcards that you could purchase."[29]

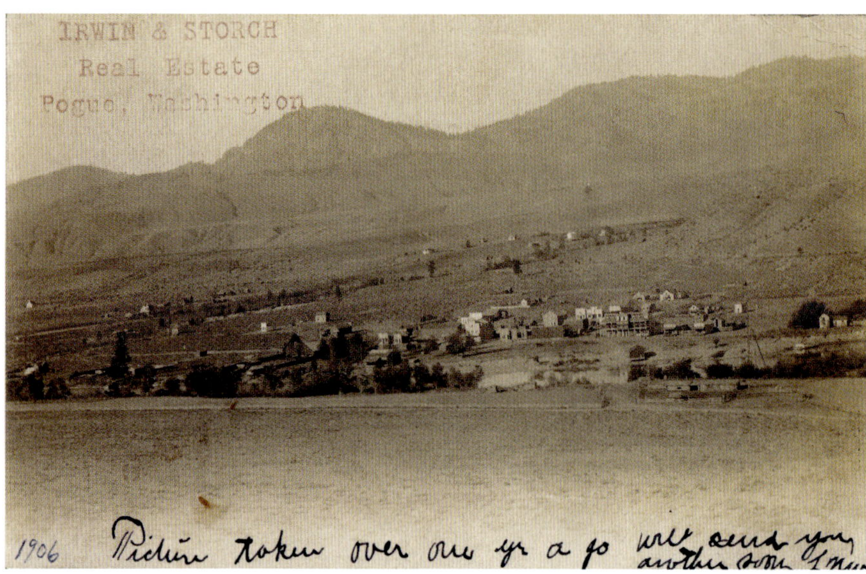

Okanogan Town Photo,
postcard, ca. 1903–1913

The medium was inexpensive, adding to its popularity. In the first decade of the twentieth century, "the United States was approaching almost one billion postcards" sent annually, Dolan said. "And I think that's such a wonderful, exciting form of communication that Matsura was able to capitalize on."[30]

Vintage postcard, photo, and ephemera dealer Michael Maslan of Seattle said these were often called "real photo postcards" and that companies like Kodak provided preprinted paper for this purpose, "It said 'Postcard' on the back" and the image could be developed directly on the paper.

With postcards being mailed at such a staggering rate, the postcard medium and by extension the photographer who produced the postcard would become essential to frontier growth. "How do you promote your town?" asked Maslan. "Well, your small-town photographer was the key to promoting your town. Frank Matsura had more imagination than almost any photographer in the way that he presented the people and presented what was happening in the town." Maslan added, "And so the photo postcard photographer, and especially Frank Matsura, were documentarians of the town....I've got to say that Frank Matsura is one of my absolute favorites."[31]

The magnetic pull of a Matsura postcard image brought many families to Okanogan. But it is unusual to find someone today who both knows the story of their family's migration to the area *and* actually possesses the postcard that spurred the move. Tacoma-based family law attorney and Okanogan-born Jason

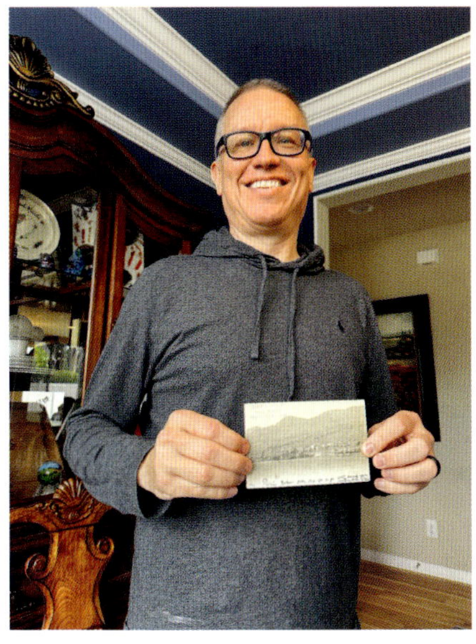

Jason Benjamin and family postcard, ca. 2023. The ca. 1903–1913 postcard by Matsura that Benjamin holds sparked the move by his ancestors to Okanogan.

Benjamin has both. "This postcard's meaningful because it's kind of the genesis of my family going to Okanogan County. I had a couple of great-uncles who went by Wag and Pete, and they were bachelors. I've never really heard the story as to why they ended up in Okanogan County, but they did. And they mailed this postcard…to my great-grandfather who was living in Sumner, Illinois.… And my great-grandfather had an adventurous spirit and took his wife and three children at the time across the country on a train, and ultimately up the Columbia River to Brewster and then stagecoach to Okanogan and bought some land and started an orchard there."[32]

Matsura's work played an outsized role in Benjamin's understanding of his family lore that goes far beyond this one postcard-assisted story of their becoming established in the area. The family and Matsura grew close, evident in the dozens of postcards in which they appear, many depicting episodes in their saga, starting with the first tent pitched while the original homestead was being built, to the success of great-grandpa's mercantile store (featuring grandpa behind the counter), to the pride of great-uncle Virgil posing with his bicycle, to a depiction of the family dog.[33]

Today, all those family images reside with Benjamin, a bequest of his great-uncle assembled in an album. "It was just filled with probably more than a hundred real photo postcards by Frank Matsura. And it had my great-grandparents, it had their kids, which would be my great-uncles and a great-aunt. And it showed

131

how they lived; it showed pictures of them at school. It showed them engaging in recreation, hunting, fishing, camping. It had photos of interesting people that had passed through the town for one reason or another. And I just became fascinated by it."[34]

The treasure trove of photos is further enhanced by an article written by Benjamin's great-aunt Mabel Wagner Schurle, late in her life, for the Okanogan County Historical Society publication, *Okanogan County Heritage.*[35]

A single young Japanese photographer, Frank Matsura, had somehow found his way up into the valley and had a little shop full of pictures he had taken of the developing country and the many people who were coming there to live....He loved flowers and had bought a lot across the street from Wag's shack. And just below our new house, he planted the whole lot to flowers, except at one end he put up a small tent to house his tools. And he also put up two swings and an exercise bar. He told us neighborhood children we could play on the swings and bar all we wanted to if we would leave his flowers alone. We spent many happy hours there and never touched his flowers, just admired them and visited with him if he happened to be working with the flowers. It was a happy arrangement for all of us.[36]

It is poignant to read her last thoughts on Matsura, "Not many years later, he died from tuberculosis....We all missed him."[37] Understanding this, it is touching to see that one of the real photo postcards in Benjamin's collection is of a young Mabel in Matsura's garden.

Benjamin found Mabel's account remarkable, wondering why she would devote so much space in an account ostensibly of her family history to this man who was not a relation. But Benjamin seems to understand the bond his family had with Matsura as something that transcended taking photographs and that Matsura's so-called "subjects" were so much more to him than people in a business transaction. "He was photographing his friends, his neighbors. For all intents and purposes, they were his family, and he considered Okanogan his home, and it's clear...through his art that he had a deep connection to the people and the land around him, and he cared about that. And it seems pretty clear that the people could tell that he cared about it. And that's why I think people remember him. I think that's why my aunt, who was ten years old when he died, I think that's why my aunt wrote in the family history about [him]."[38]

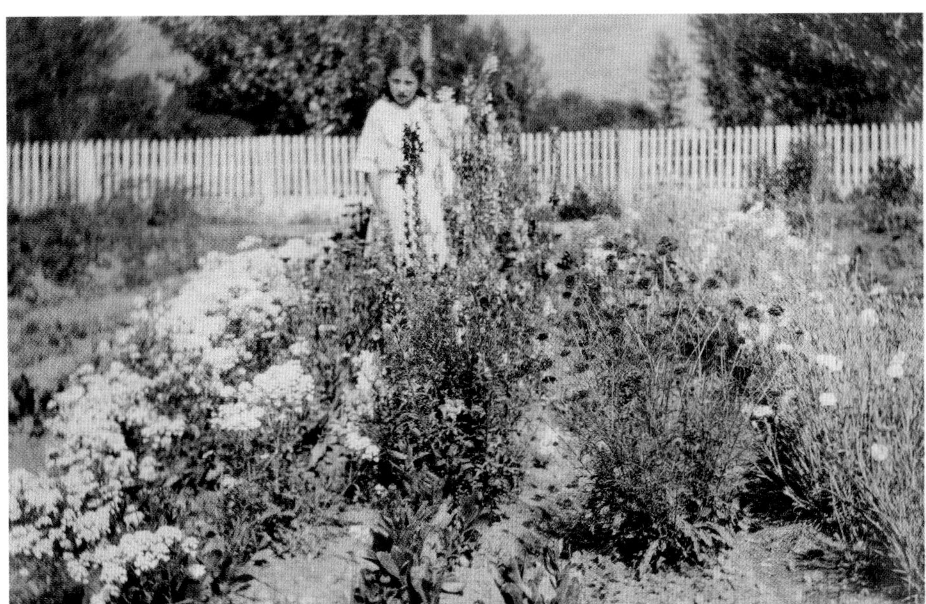

Mabel Wagner in Flower Garden, Matsura postcard, ca. 1903–1913

Matsura's singular body of photography has stirred people's memories, solidified interpersonal bonds, illuminated lost threads of a people's saga, and strengthened their sense of identity. Through his unique gifts as an artist and as a man of tremendous empathy and charm, Matsura has inextricably planted himself in the collective memory of the people of Okanogan County and the Colville reservation.

So, as Frank Matsura's devotees ponder the big mysteries about him—why did he come and why did he stay?—Lynn Palmanteer-Holder offered her answer: "Personally, I believe that there was some purpose for Frank Matsura to come here to the Okanogan and his legacy of creating these images and leaving them behind for future generations. Those [photos] are all really important. Frank Matsura will be [a] link to our past, which is key to who we are today. So, I'm grateful. I'm grateful to Frank Matsura and all of his ancestors for him being here, because future generations will know their place and they'll know their history. So, *Limlimt*. Thank you."[39]

SELECTED PHOTOGRAPHS

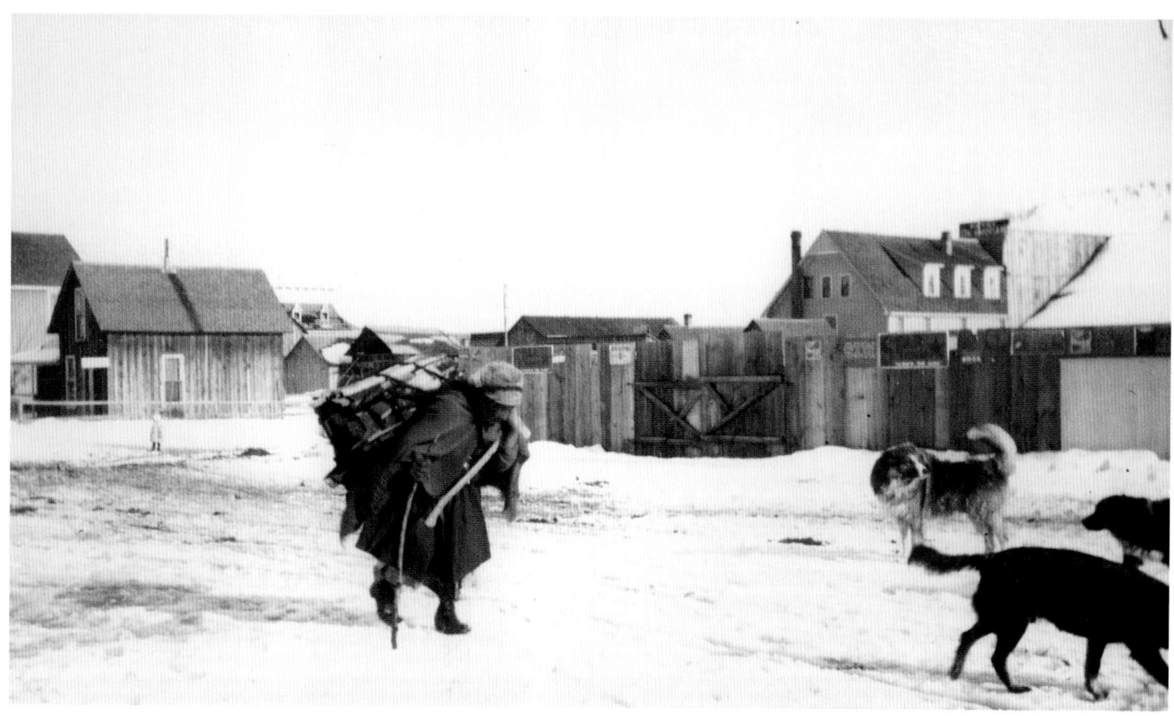

Indian Woman with Wood and Dogs, ca. 1903–1913. Mary Jim
(Ha-mauh) on the street in front of Matsura's studio with her
dogs. She was the wife of Captain Jim, who was once a Native
American scout for the US government.

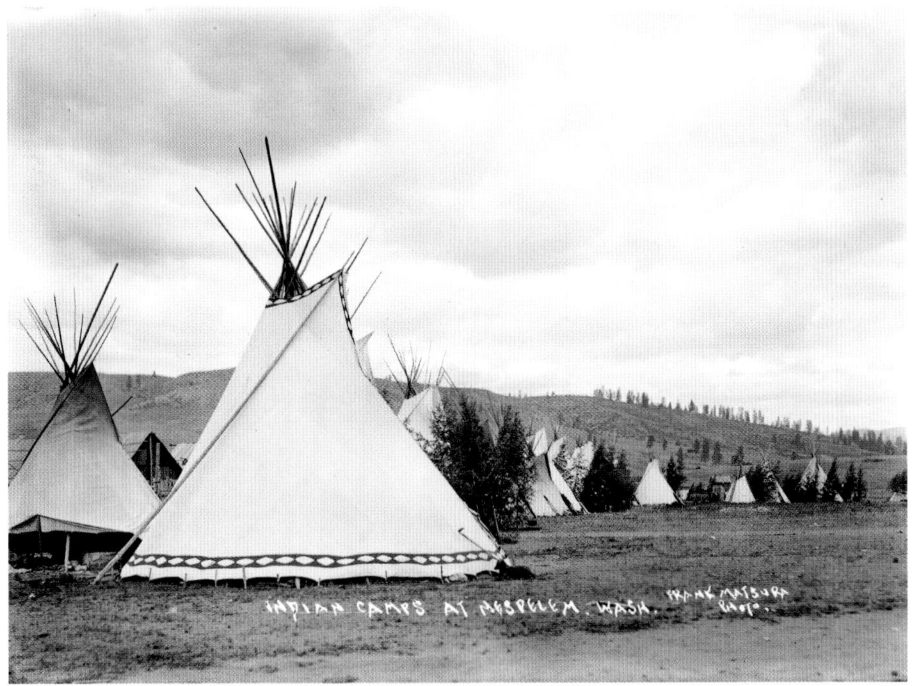

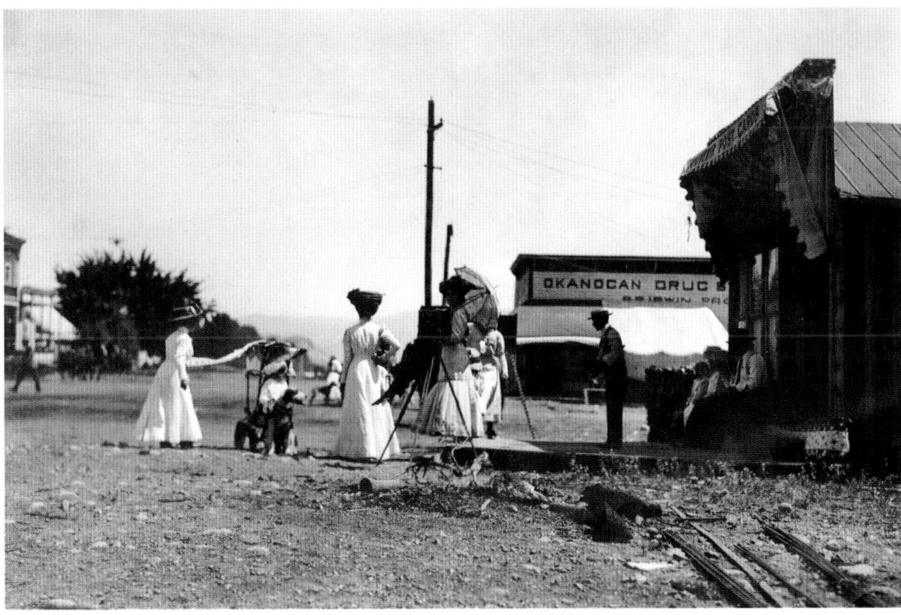

TOP
Indian Camp at Nespelem, ca. 1903–1913

BOTTOM
Okanogan Fourth of July Parade, ca. 1910.
Matsura camera-ready outside his photography studio.

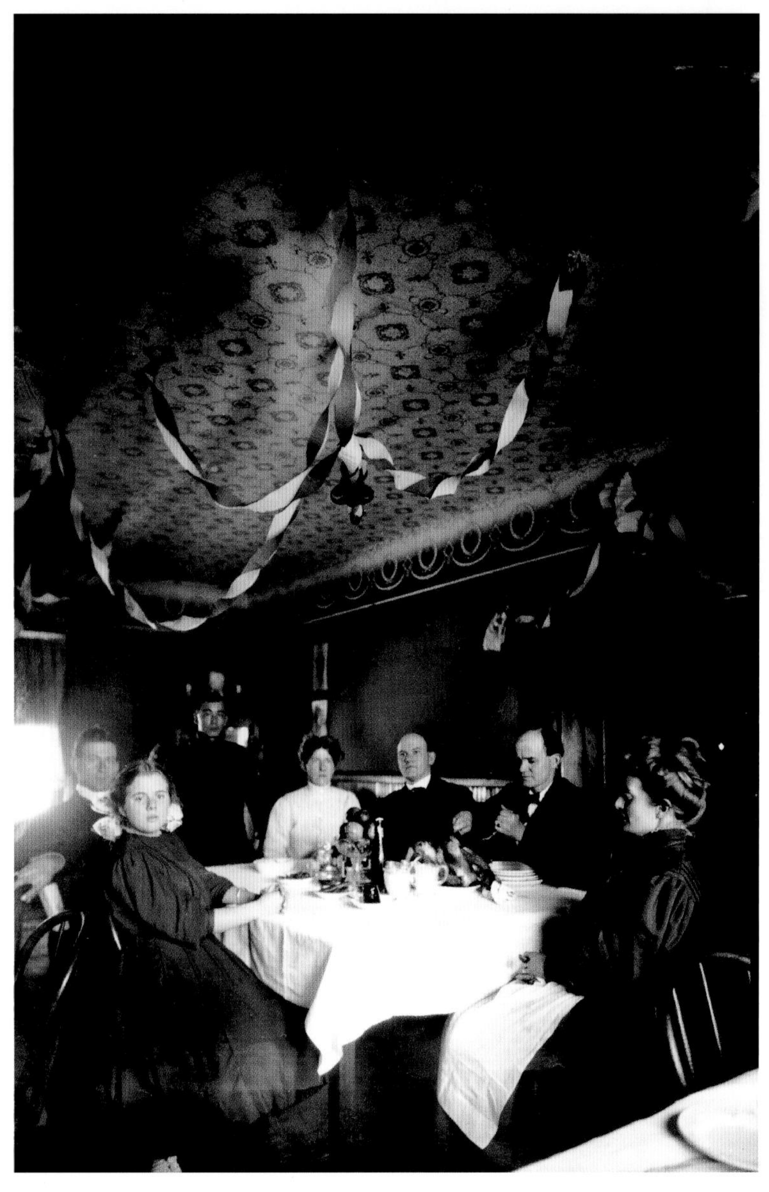

ABOVE
*Mr. and Mrs. Charles Lindsay and Daughter Doll
Share a Meal with Friends,* ca. 1907

OPPOSITE
Portrait of Three Girls, ca. 1903–1913

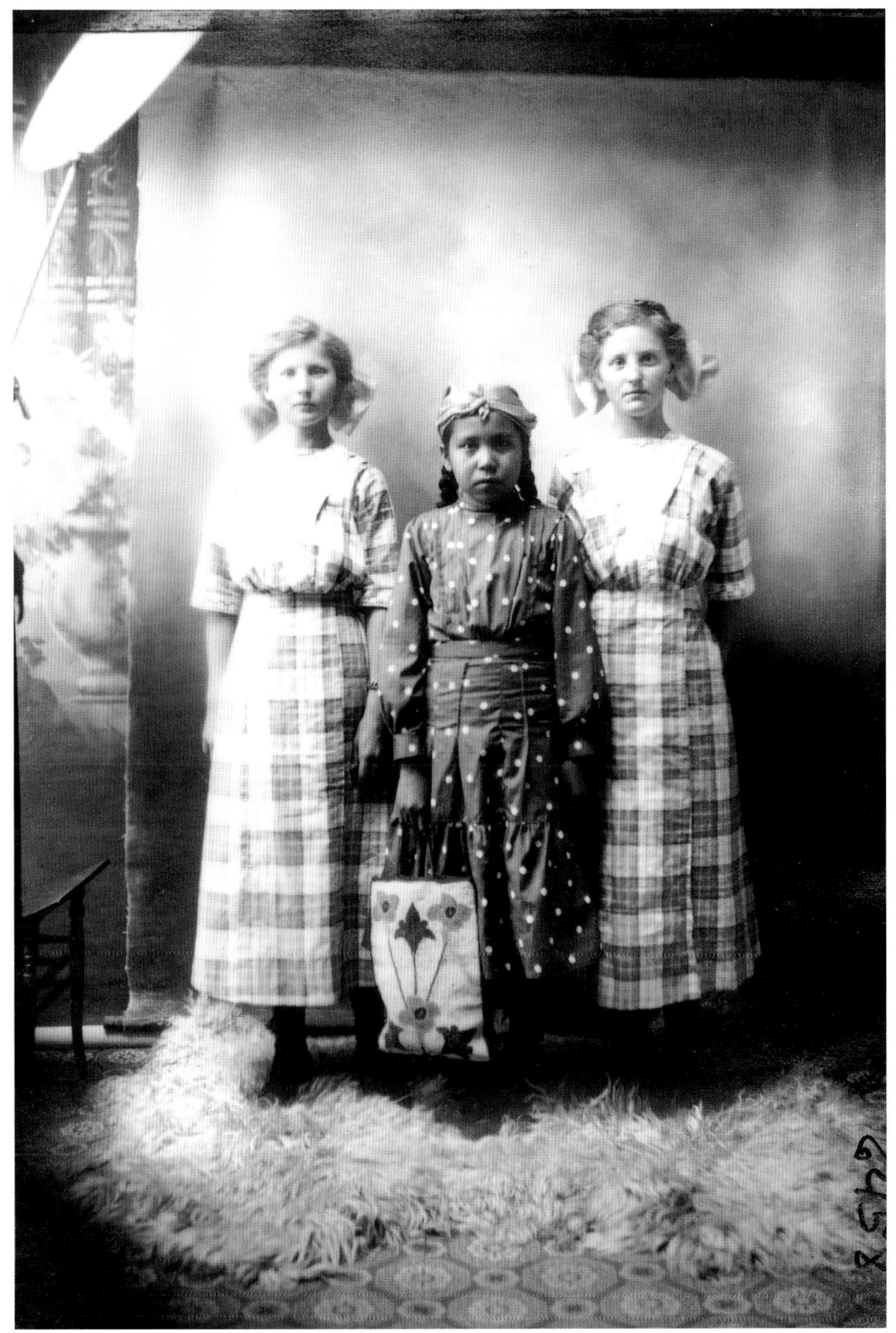

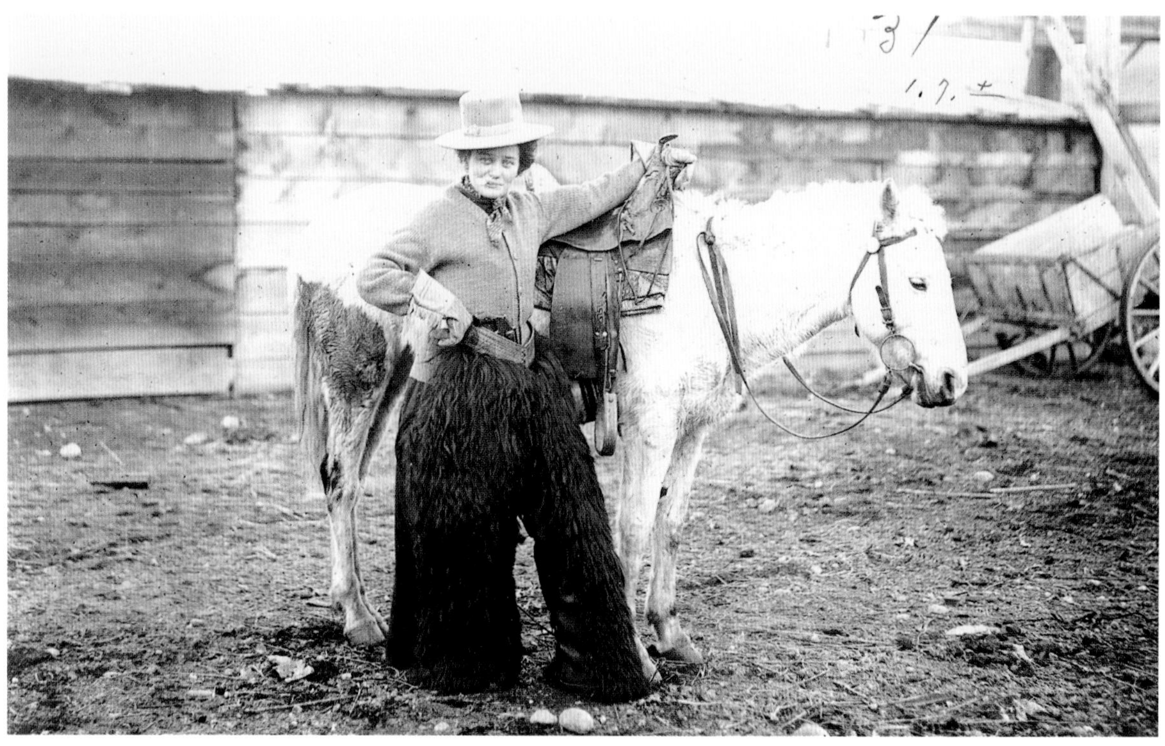

*Cowgirl in Alpaca Chaps Stands Beside
Her Horse*, ca. 1910

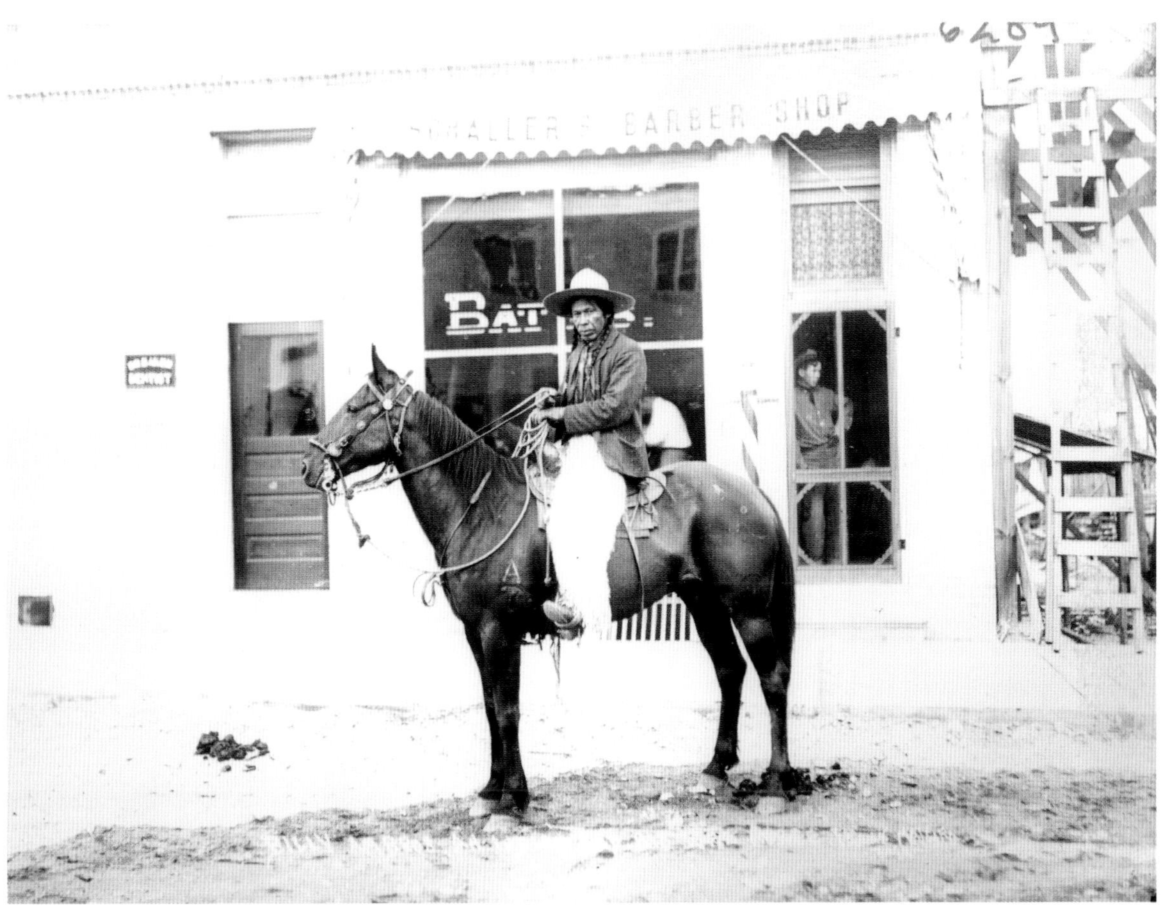

Billy Ambrose and His Horse, ca. 1903–1913

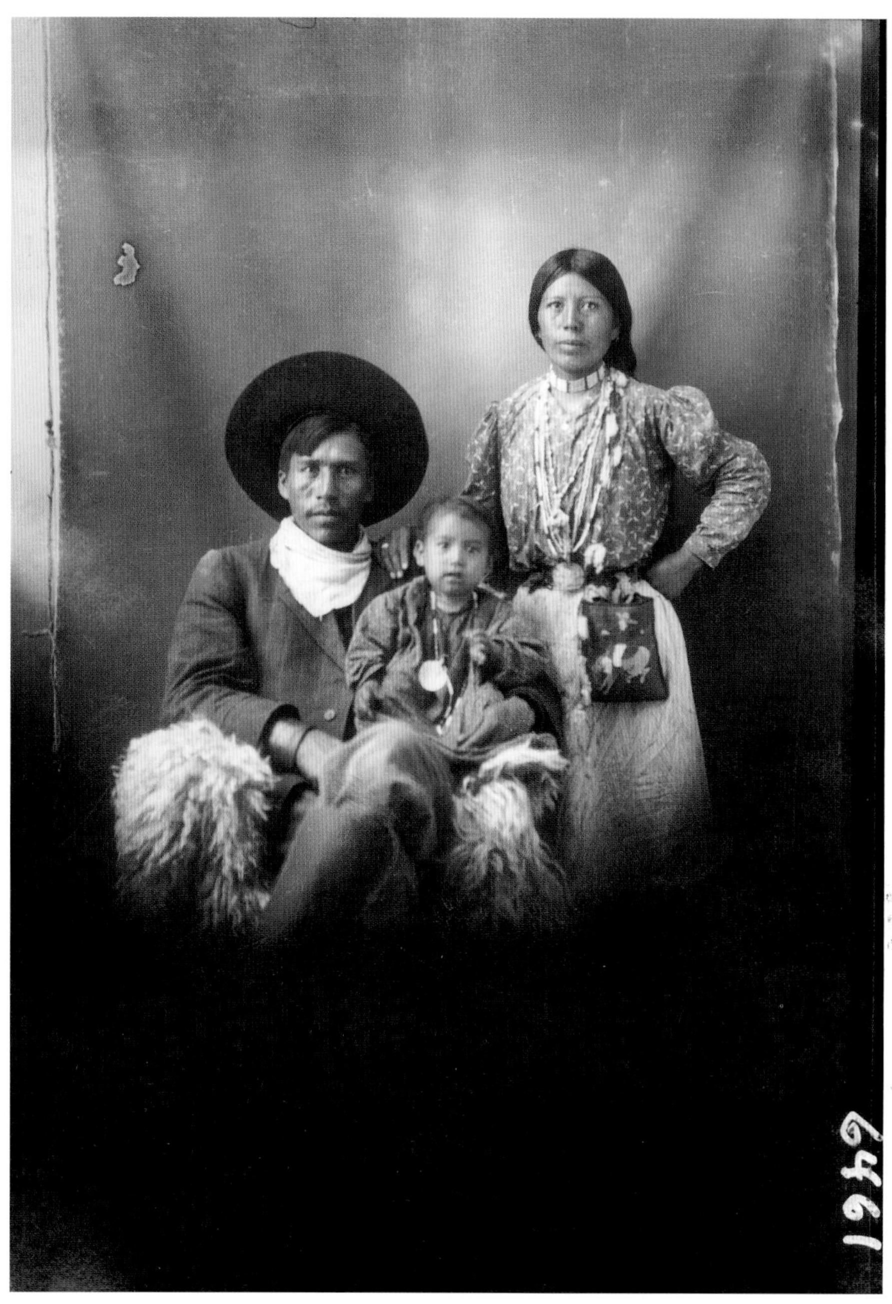

Lucy Jim Timentwa and C. B. Suzen Timentwa, ca. 1903–1913. The baby is Sophia Timentwa Gabouri. They lived in the Malott area.

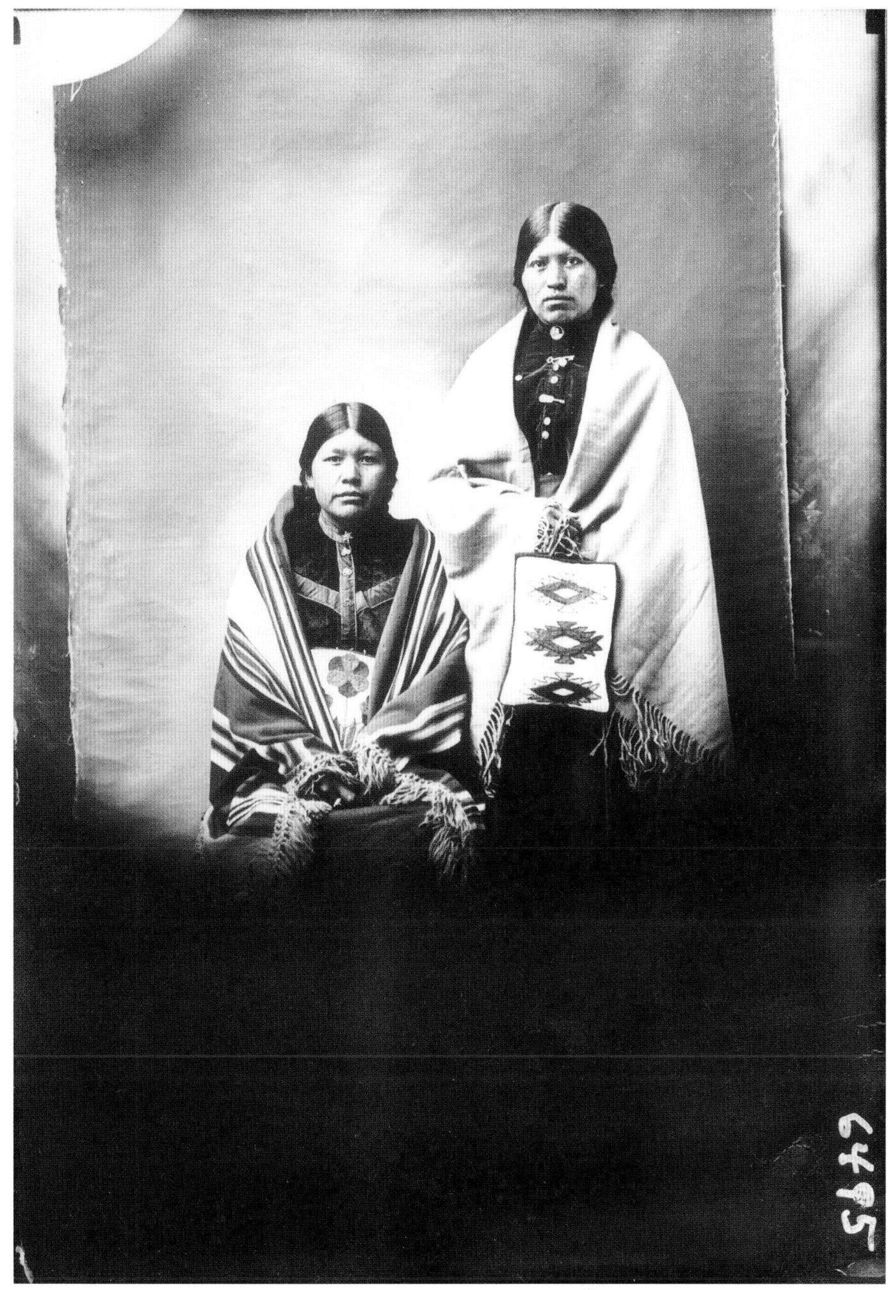

Untitled, Frank Matsura photograph, ca. 1903–1913. Portrait of two Native American women wearing blankets and holding beaded bags. The woman on the left is Moses George's mother, Christine, who was the granddaughter of Chief Seattle.

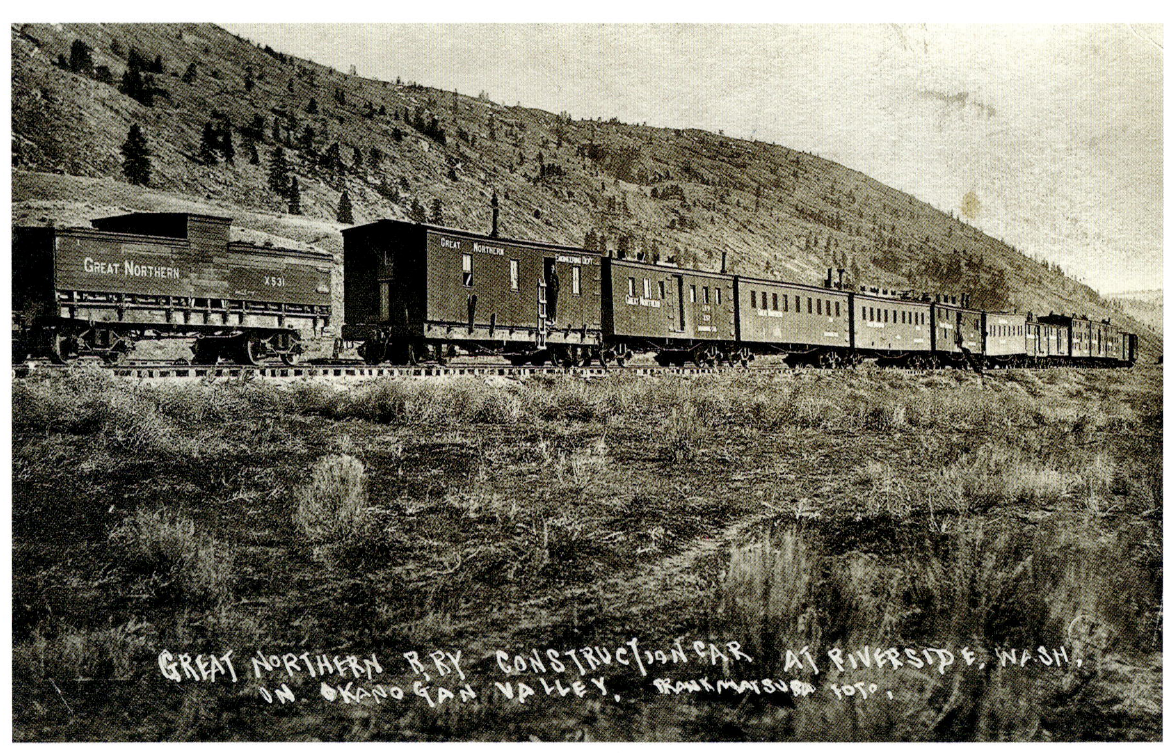

Great Northern Railroad Construction Car at Riverside,
Washington, in Okanogan Valley, ca. 1903–1913

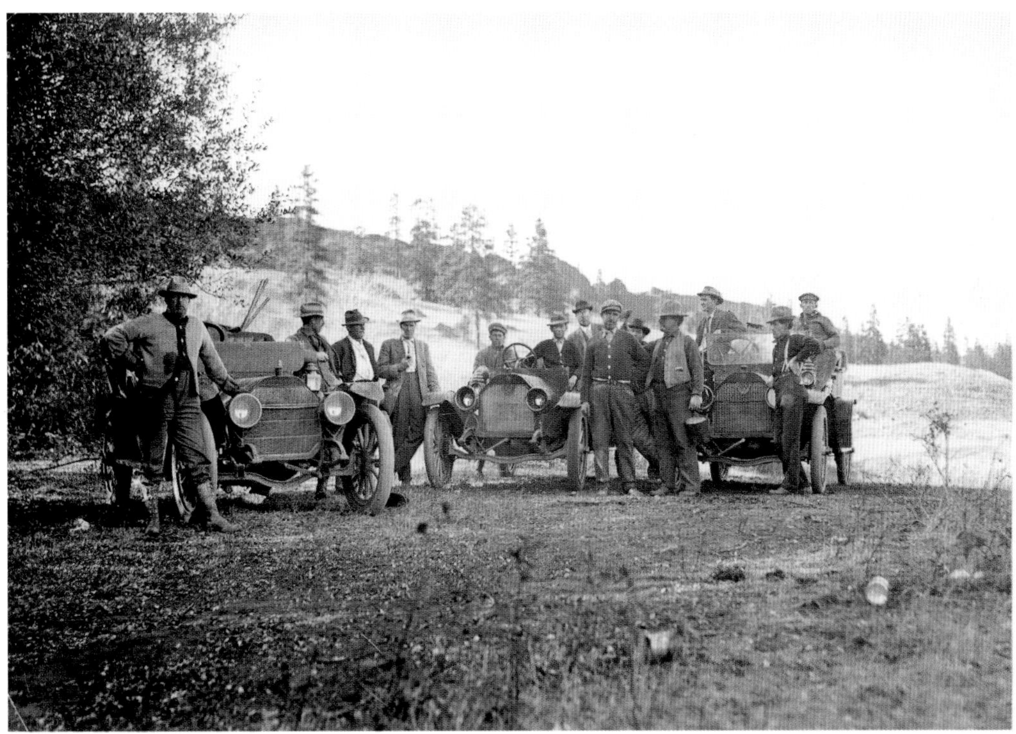

Untitled, Frank Matsura photograph, ca. 1911.
The first automobile to go from the town of Okanogan to
Condon's Ferry. Taken on October 16, 1911.

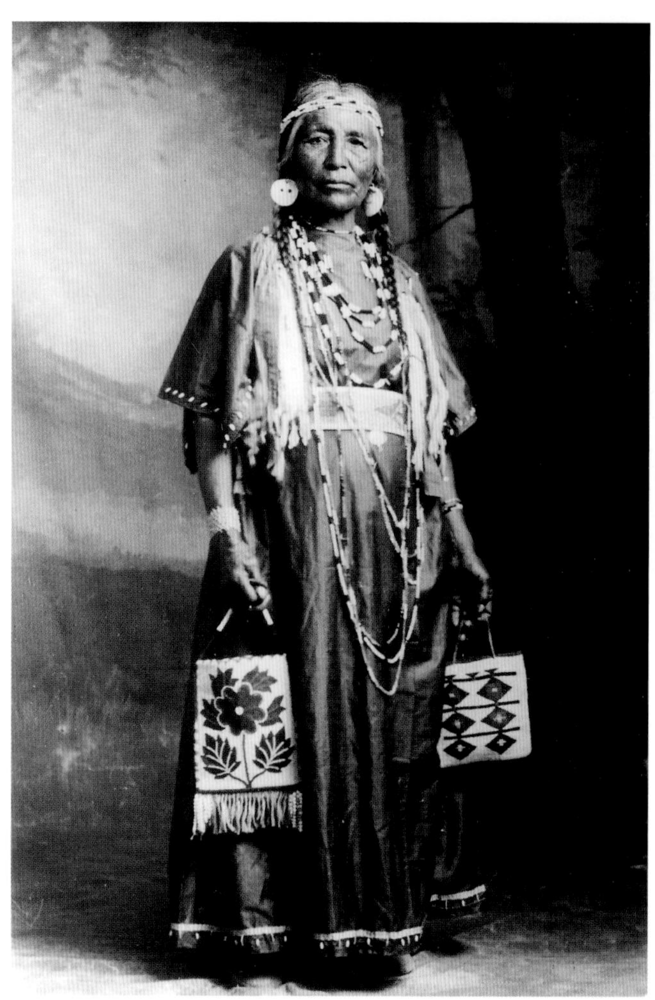

Suzanne George, ca. 1910

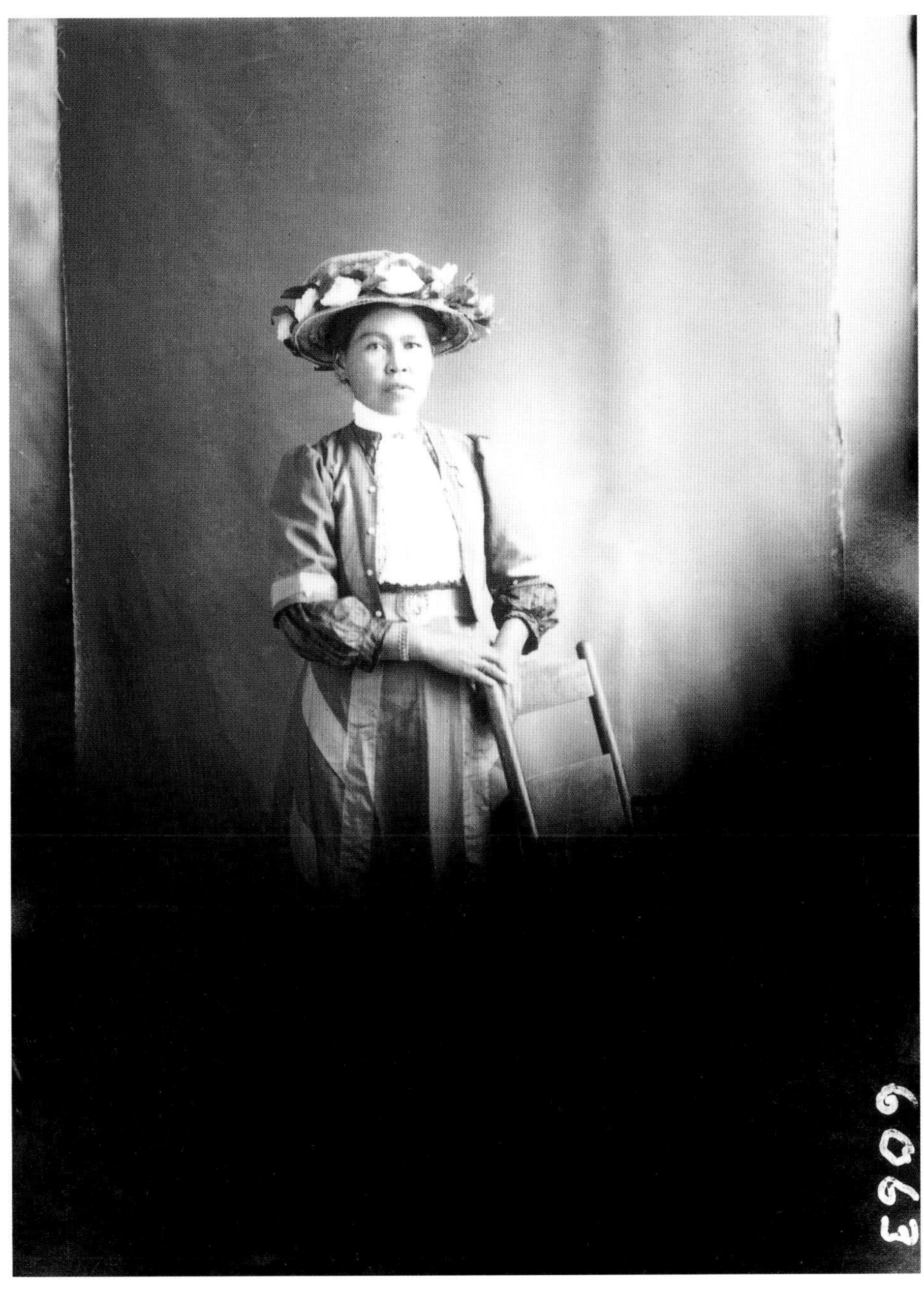

Thesela Paul, June 1911, ca. 1911

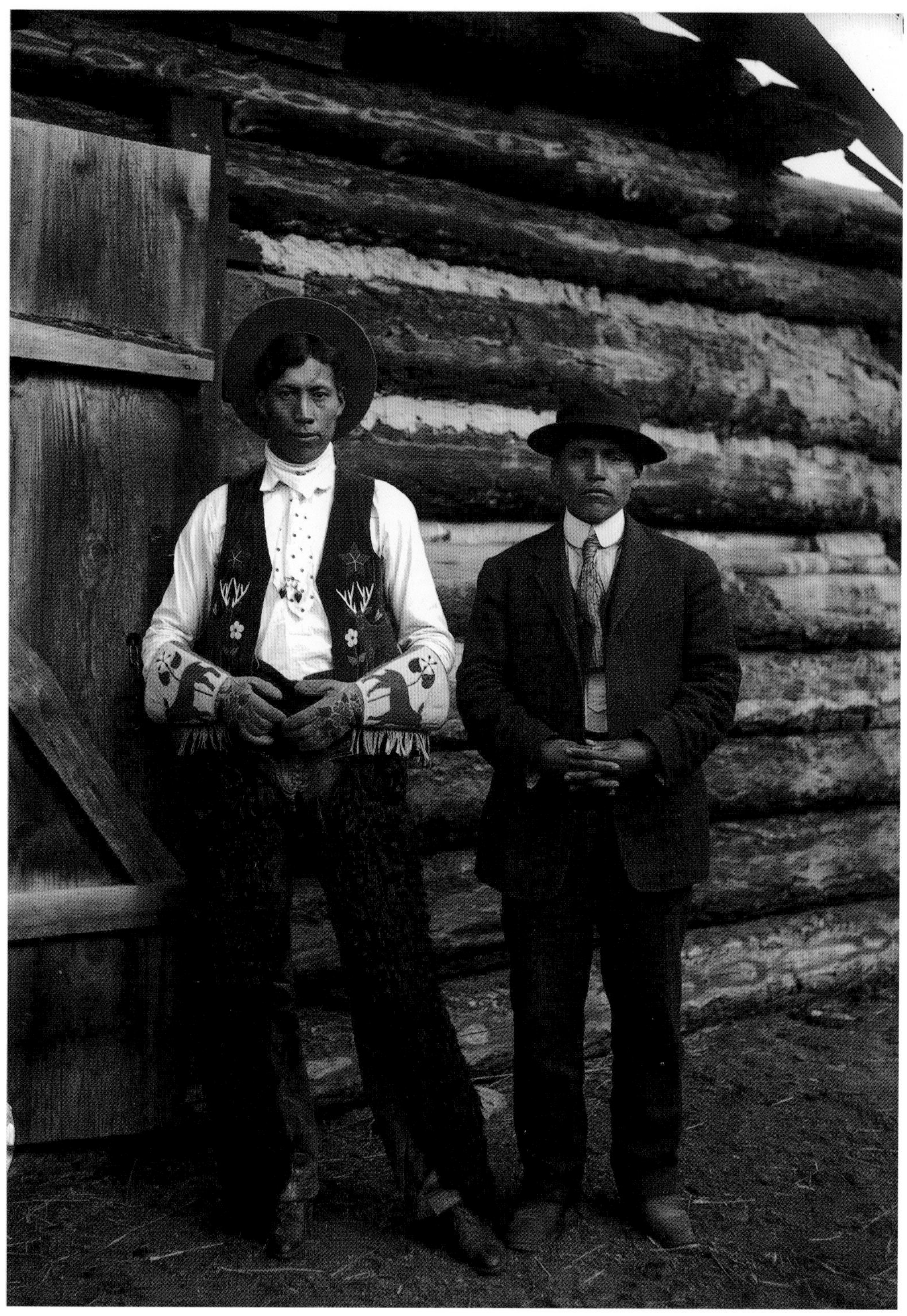

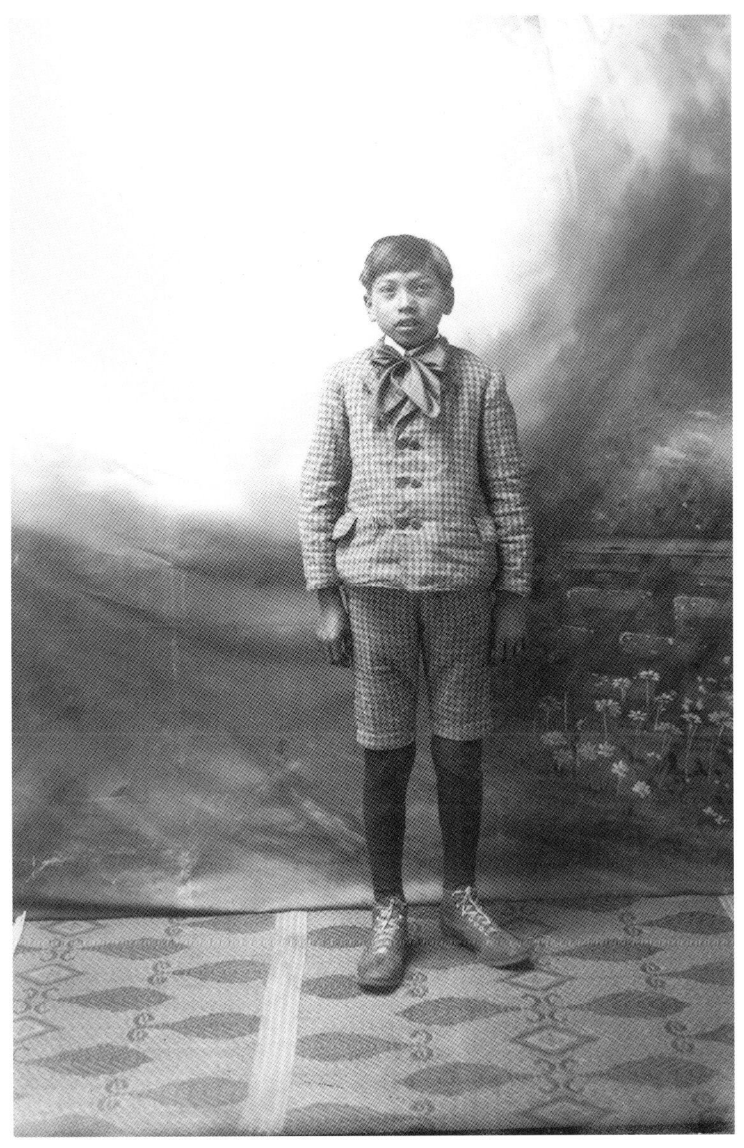

OPPOSITE
Untitled, Frank Matsura photograph, ca. 1903–1913.
Portrait of two men (one with decorated gloves and angora
chaps) in front of a log building. Note on back reads
"L Paul Timentwa."

ABOVE
Smitkin Kid in 1909 Studio Pose (Louis), ca. 1909

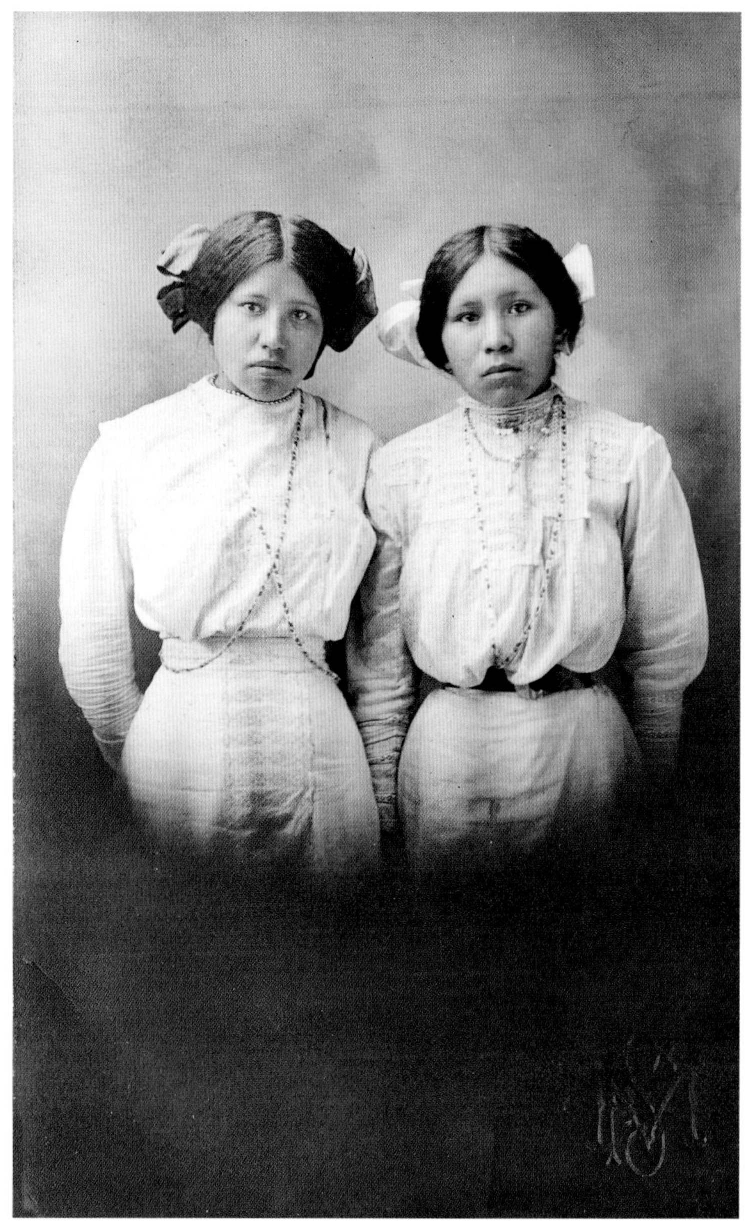

ABOVE
Two Young Women in White Dresses with Necklaces in Studio Portrait, ca. 1903–1913

OPPOSITE
Portrait of Two Young Native American Men, ca. 1903–1913. One of them is John Cleveland of Monse. They were students of St. Mary's Mission under Father DeRouge.

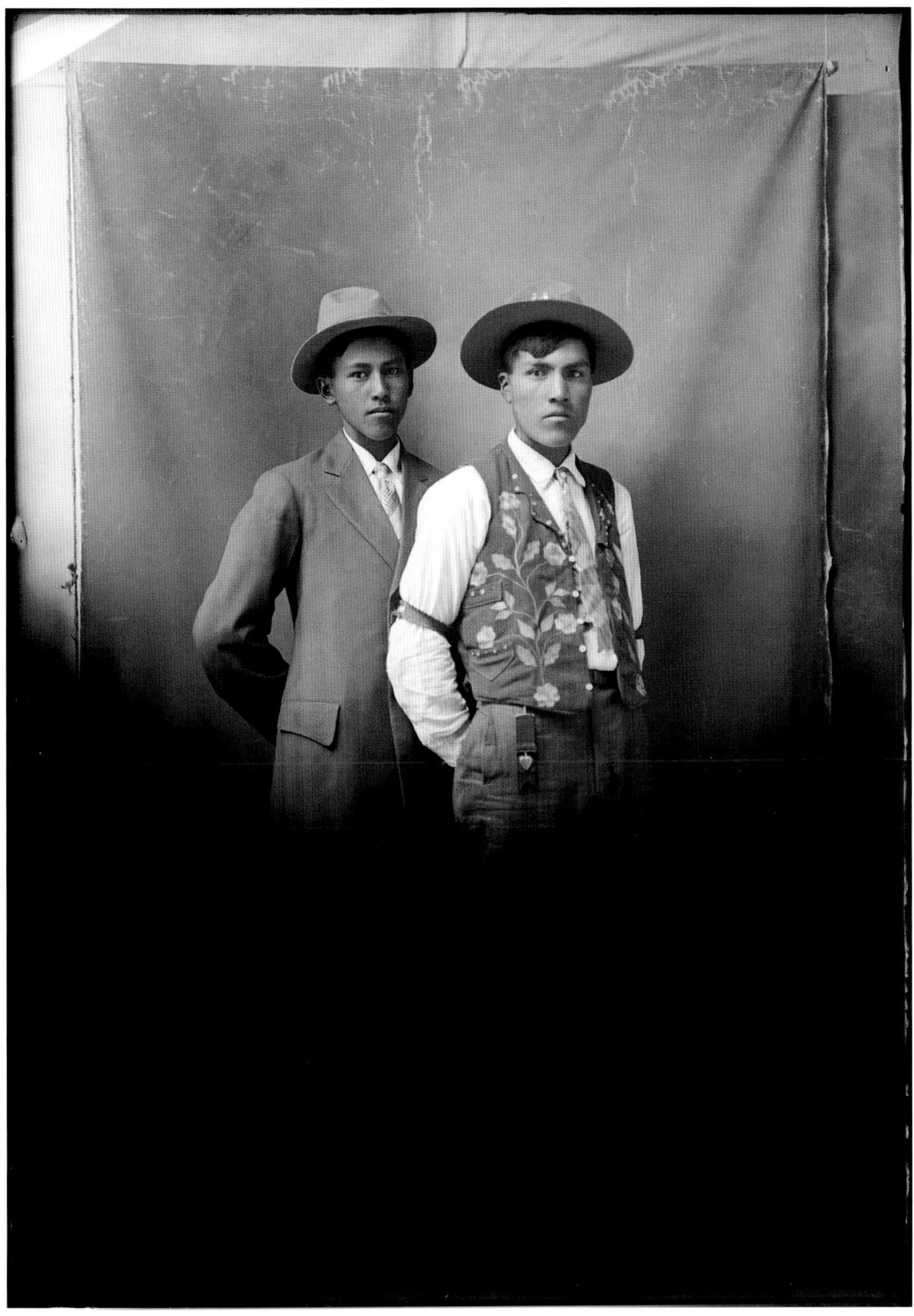

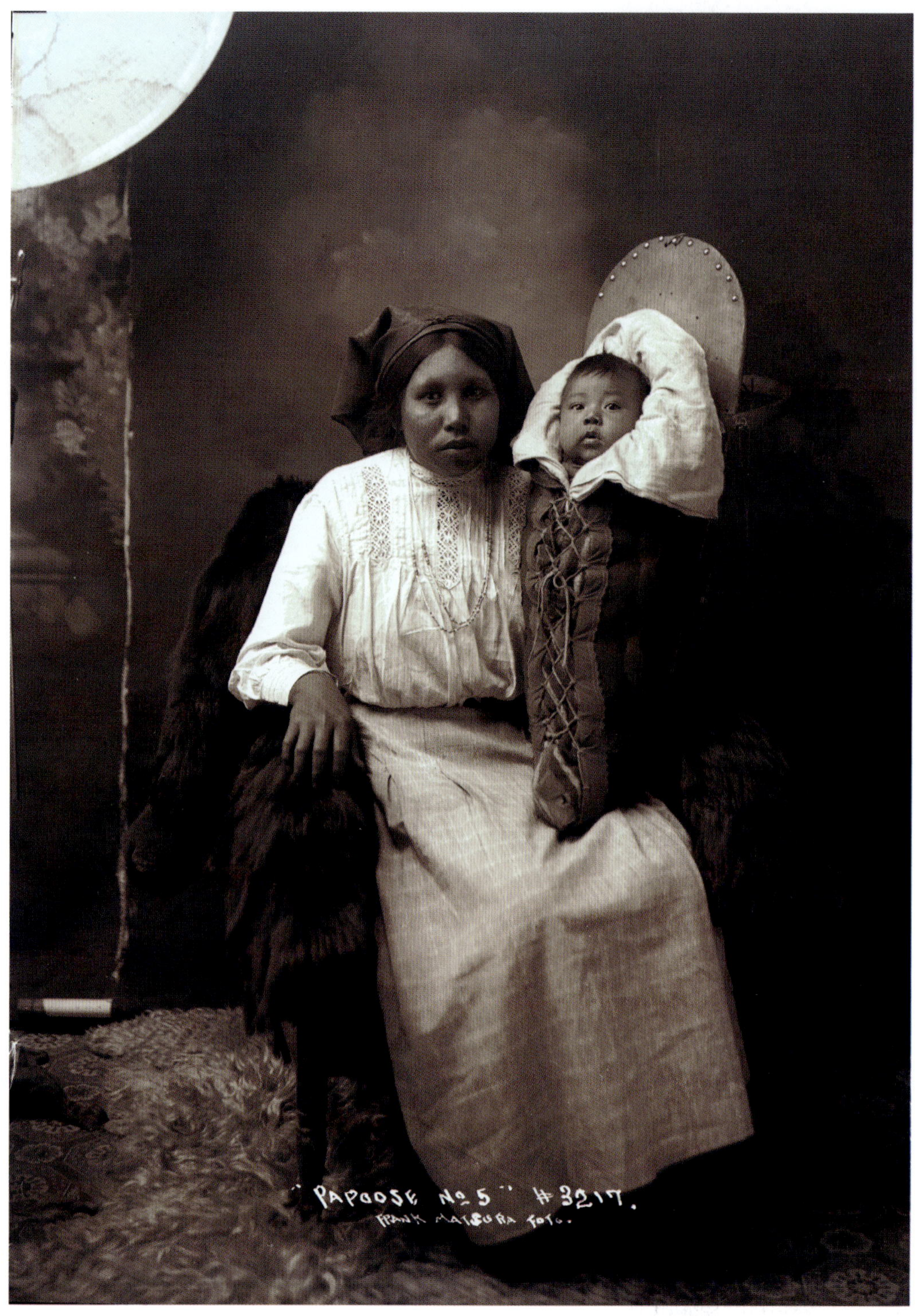
"PAPOOSE No 5" #3217.
FRANK MATSURA FOTO.

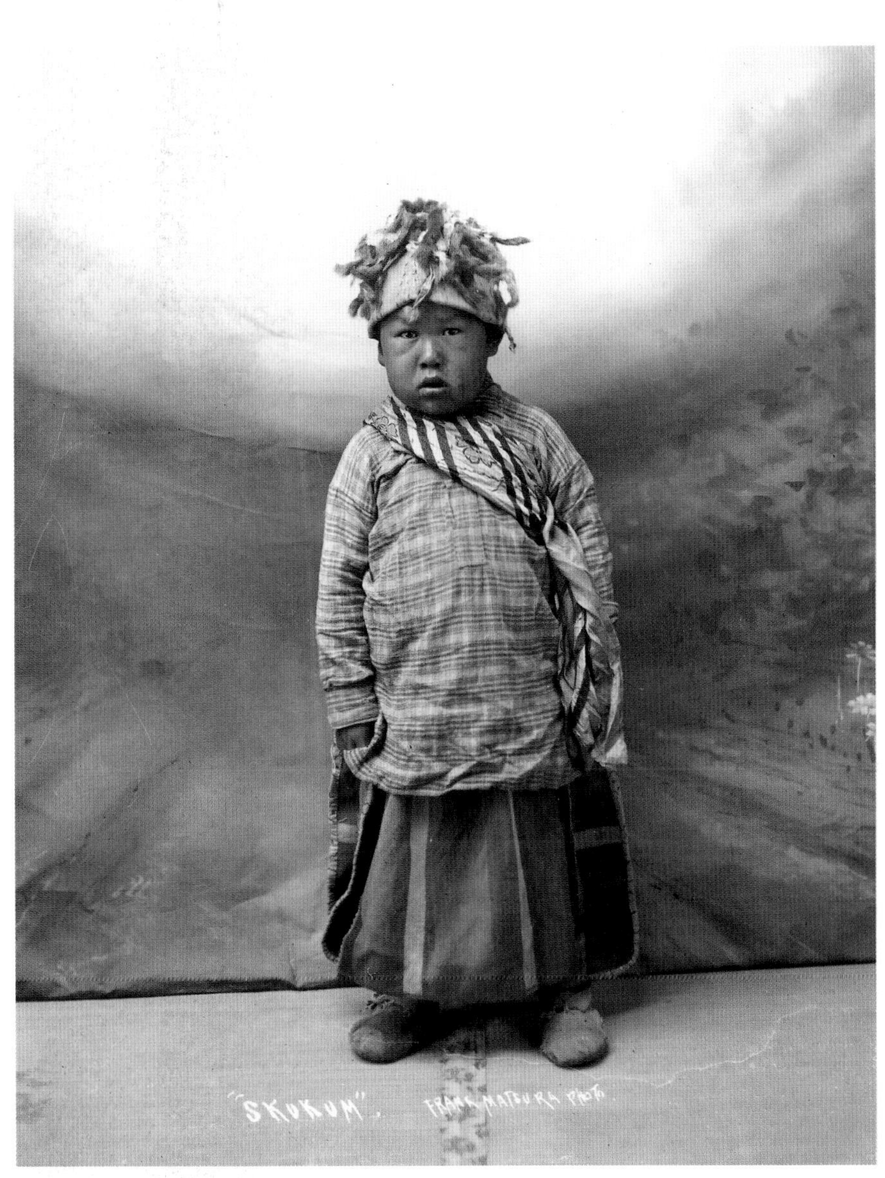

OPPOSITE

Portrait of a Native American Woman Holding a
Baby in a Cradle Board, ca. 1903–1913

ABOVE

"Skookum" Little Indian Boy, ca. 1903–1913. A Chinook
jargon word that means brave or strong.

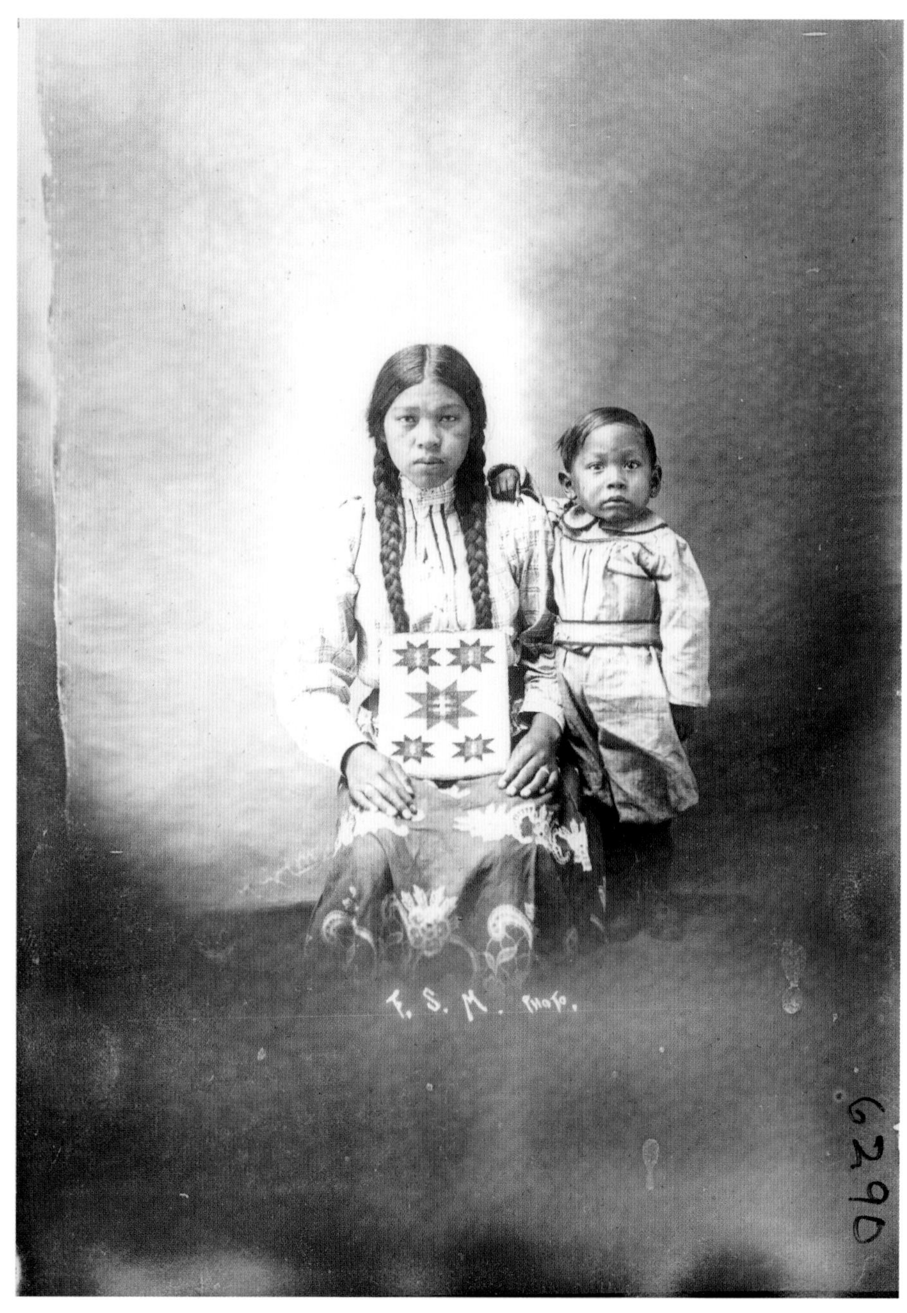

Billy Ambrose's Two Children, ca. 1903–1913

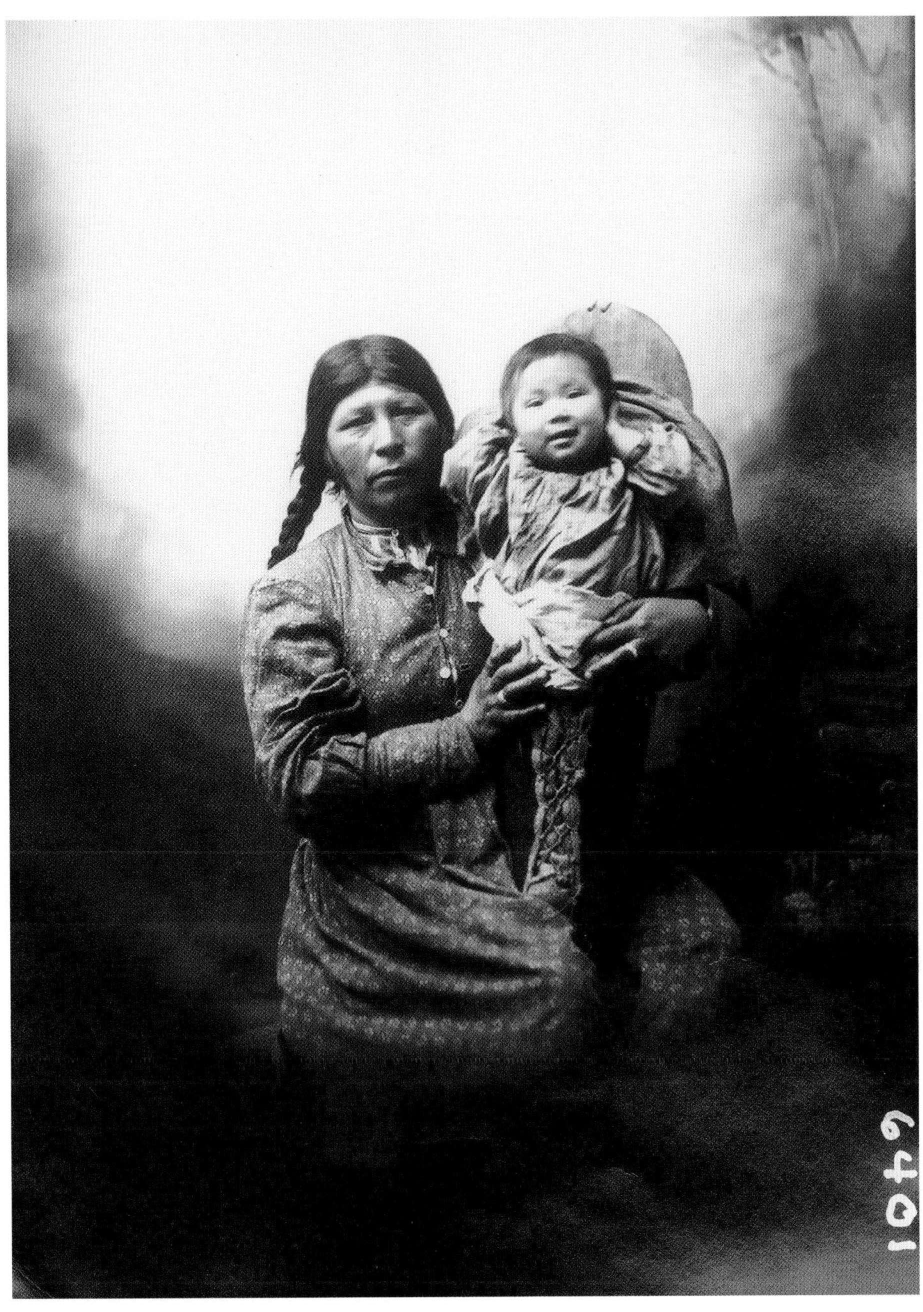

*Portrait of a Native American Woman Holding a
Baby in a Cradleboard*, ca. 1903–1913

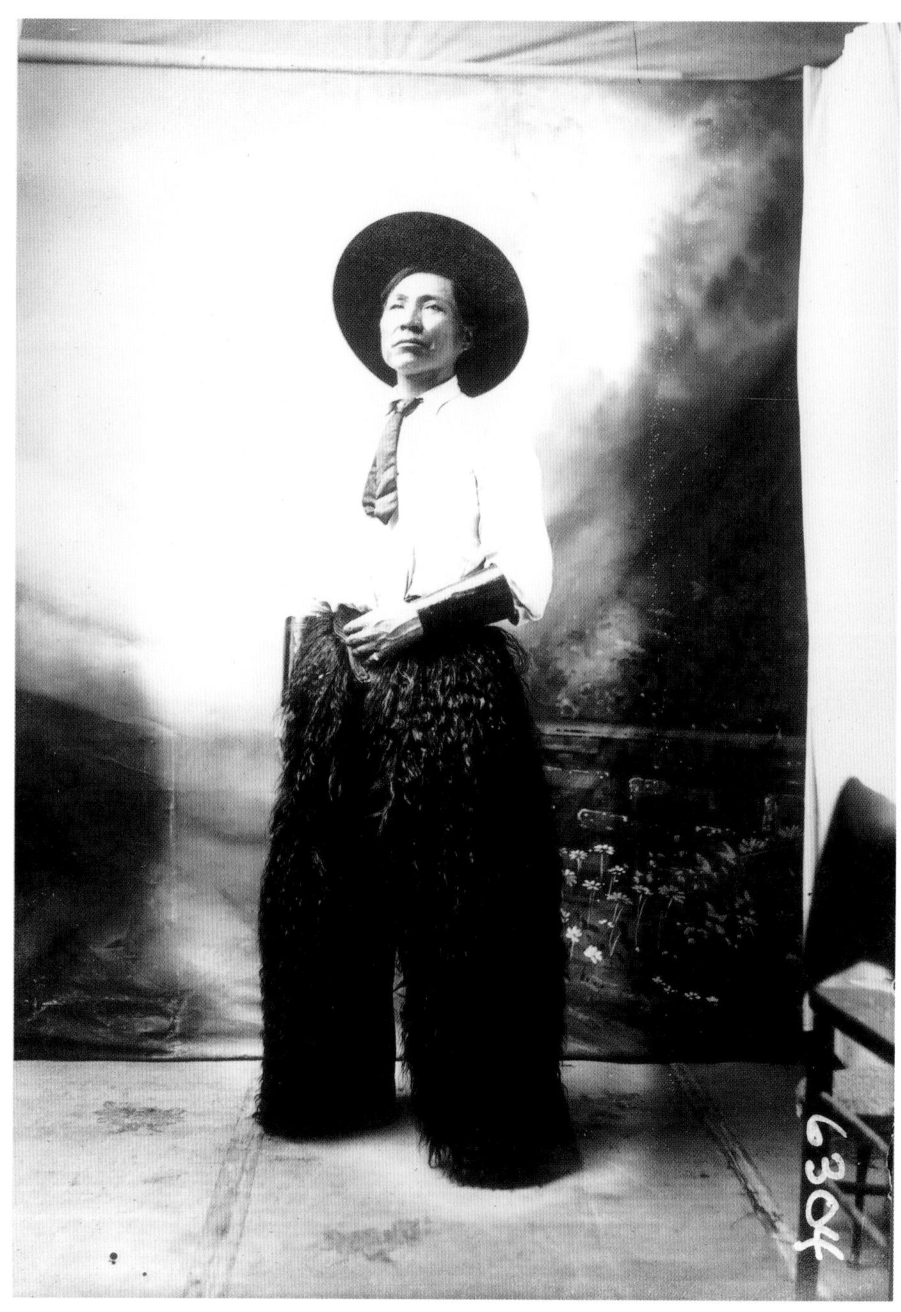

ABOVE
Dick from Riverside, ca. 1910

OPPOSITE
Portrait of a Native American Man and Two Native American Women, ca. 1912. Edward Bessie and daughter Julia Jim.

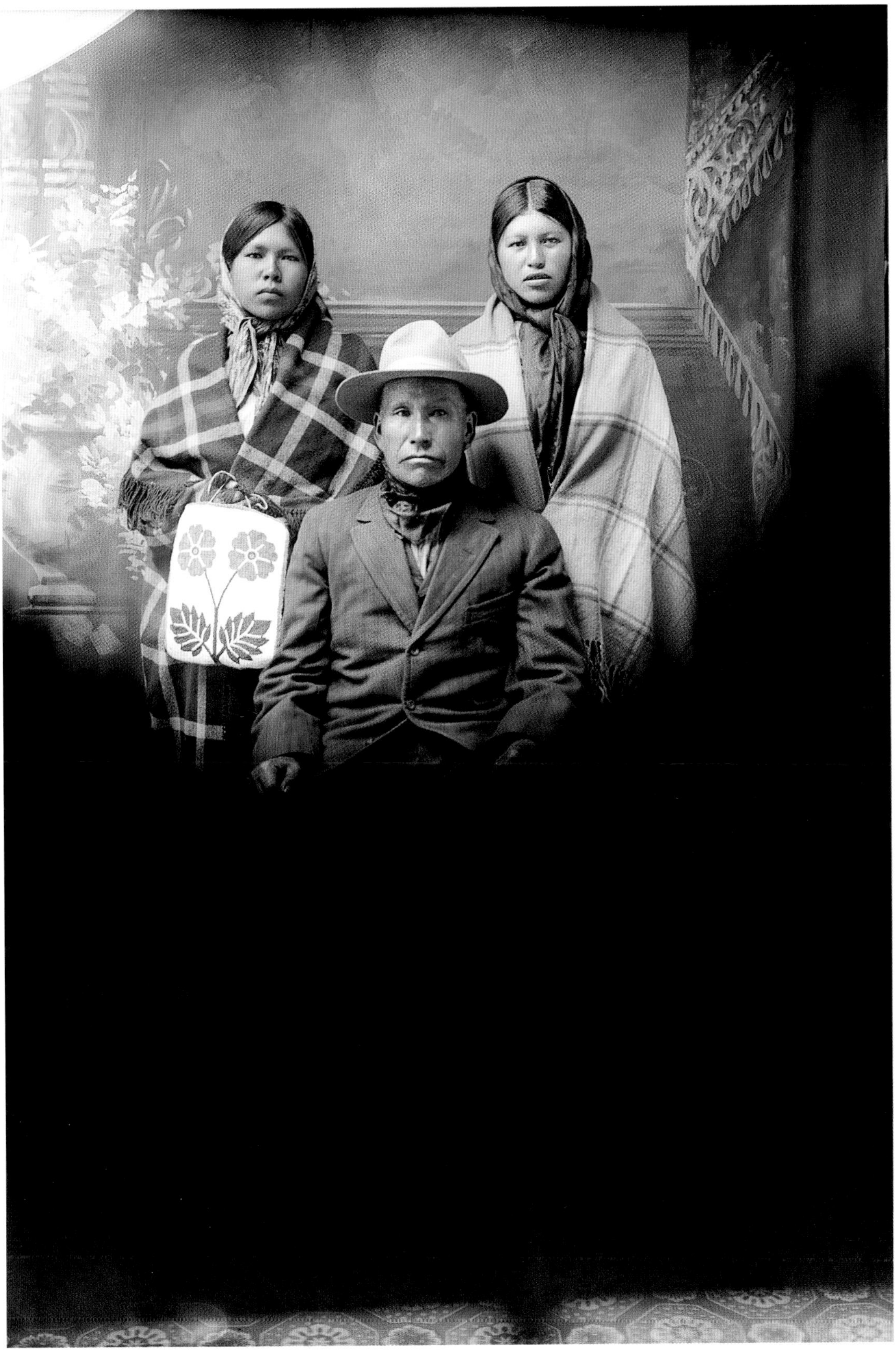

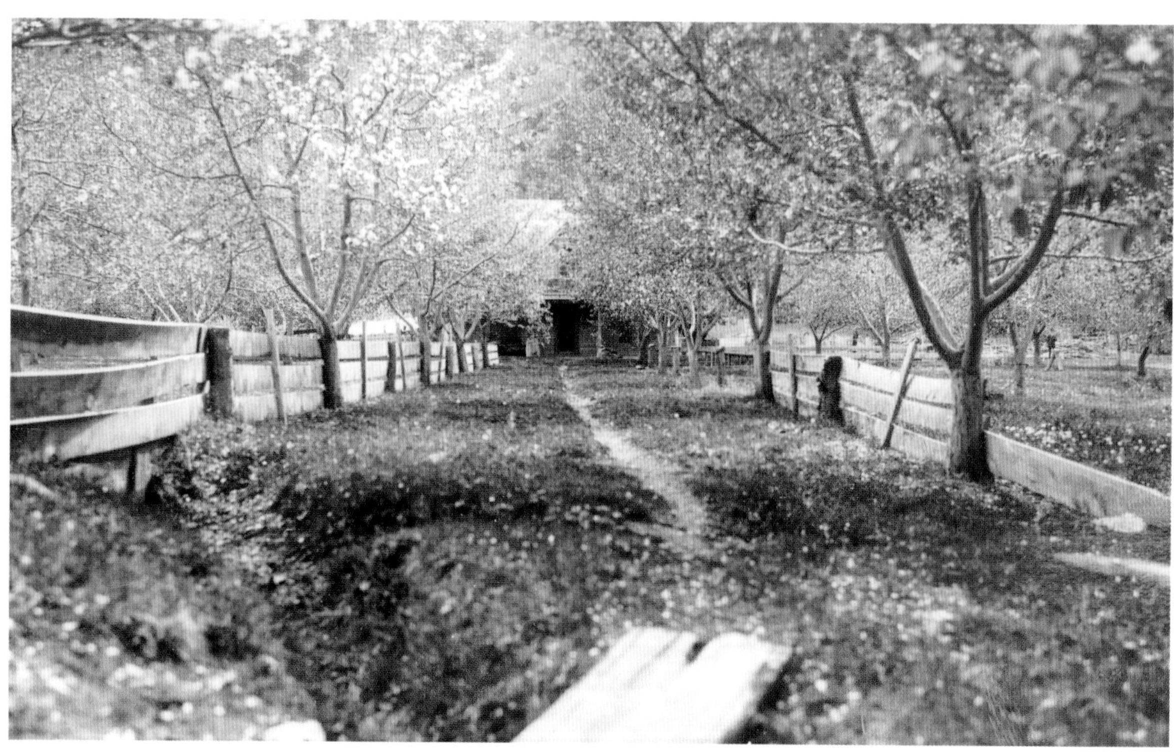

Tree-Lined Lane Leading to House, ca. 1903–1913.
Joseph S. White orchard, Chiliwhist Valley, Washington.

CONCLUSION

Michael Holloman

In 2022 a story hit the national newswire about a couple who had recently purchased a historic commercial building in Okanogan, Washington. Upon their initial renovations they discovered a sixty-foot mural hidden behind a false wall. The 1907 building was first used as a play theater and its date coincided with Frank S. Matsura's presence in the community. Initial reports of the find generated speculation that it could have been a painting done by Matsura himself, who was known to have played there in the theater band. Further research at the Okanogan County Historical Society revealed the painting was done by another individual a couple of years after Matsura had passed. However, what was established was how important this Japanese immigrant photographer has become to the region and the profession.

Beyond the images there is little from Matsura in terms of letters, diaries, and contextual notes to embellish his personal histories, intentions, and reflections, thus leaving much room for pondering and speculation. Like other Japanese immigrant photographers of early twentieth century, such as George Masa and Seiki (Shoki) Kayamori, who photographed local Native populations in Alaska, Matsura's intimate portraitures reflect a fascinating creative commitment that still resonates today. Frequently Matsura's work appears to be one of a singular creative vision, yet a deeper consideration of his known circumstance details a man alone determined to challenge his inexperience as a professional photographer. That any of his work remains after his untimely death is in itself a remarkable story. His friend William Compton Brown (later Judge Brown) thankfully gathered the printed images, postcards, and glass plates as he settled Matsura's estate. However, none of this was edited by Matsura before he passed. In this sense what we get to see is everything: the mundane, the failures, and the seeds of profound artistic expression. Most wonderful are the intimate images of friends together behind closed doors in Matsura's studio engaging in playful posturing and role-playing, adding visual evidence to socially intriguing stories rarely available of the pioneer west.

Peter Selz spoke of the late Nisenan artist Harry Fonseca's popular Coyote character: "He embodies paradox and ambiguity and personifies the Native American as both separate from and a part of the dominant culture."[1] This complexity applies to many of the tribal people Matsura photographed. However, Selz's statement could easily have been describing Matsura's character as the mythic trickster Coyote himself.

The community that Matsura inserted himself into lost one of its most remarkable citizens. The fact that he was not a visual tourist who came, documented, and left is worth emphasizing. It would be too easy to contextualize his story as a fascinating chapter of the American Dream. This is because Matsura was almost forgotten, as dramatic historical events of the twentieth century immediately succeeded him. After two world wars, the Great Depression, the Civil Rights Movement, and numerous federal policies impacting tribal sovereignty, the world that Matsura and his friends inhabited became the antiquated distant past all too quickly. Viewing his images today one might imagine that he lived in an integrated community; however, on a larger social level that was not the case. Yet that didn't stop Matsura, and it hasn't stopped others from heralding Matsura's eternal freshness as an artistic and cultural enigma worthy of his historic acknowledgment.

ACKNOWLEDGMENTS

My closest personal connection to Frank S. Matsura is when a longtime friend of our family, Harley Heath (1880–1967), stepped off a steamboat in 1910 at the Okanogan landing, where across the street stood Frank S. Matsura's popular photography studio. Harley traveled from Indiana to help a friend for a month and stayed for the rest of his life. As he worked for the local newspapers, I am certain Harley knew Frank at least professionally. Harley had a hunting and fishing cabin at Lake Conconully that my father liked to visit. After his service during the Korean War, he returned to the area and married my mother, whose Native family still resides on the Colville reservation, which is located on the east side of the Okanogan River.

I am honored to have met and worked with so many people interested in Frank Matsura from this region and afar. All have been instrumental in bringing the story and photographs of this remarkable adopted citizen of the Okanogan Valley to a larger audience. Thank you to those at the Okanogan County Historical Society; Colville Confederated Tribes; David G. Pollart Center for Arts and Humanities at Washington State University; Northwest Museum of Arts and Culture in Spokane; High Desert Museum in Bend, Oregon; and the following individuals: Richard Reis (you are missed), Hiroko Asakura, Richard Hart, William D. Layman, Karen Beaudette, Emily Anderson, Anne-Claire Mitchell, Elaine Timentwa Emerson, Barry George, Tisa Matheson, Dean Davis, Trevor Bond, John Sirois, Reika Pratt, Anthony Brave, Dan Manwaring, and my peers on this project, Beth, Laurie, Maki, and Glen.

Notes

Introduction

1. JoAnn Roe, *Frank Matsura: Frontier Photographer* (Seattle: Madrona Publishers, 1981).

2. Rayna Green, "Rosebuds of the Plateau: Frank Matsura and the Fainting Couch Aesthetic," in *Partial Recall: With Essays on Photographs of Native North Americans*, ed. Lucy R. Lippard (New York: The New Press, 1992).

3. Richard Avedon, *In the American West, 1979–1984* (New York: Harry N. Abrams, 1985).

4. Walter Benjamin, *The Work of Art in the Age of Mechanical Reproduction*, trans. J. A. Underwood (Harlow: Penguin UK, 2008).

5. Don D. Fowler, *The Western Photographs of John K. Hillers: Myself in the Water* (Washington, DC: Smithsonian Institution Press, 1989), 49.

6. Gerald Vizenor, "Socioacupuncture: Mythic Reversals and the Striptease in Four Scenes," in *Out There: Marginalization and Contemporary Cultures*, ed. Russell Ferguson, Martha Gever, and Trinh T. Minh-Ha (New York: New Museum of Contemporary Art/Boston: MIT Press, 1990), 412.

Indigenous Homelands through a Photographer's Lens

1. Becky Kramer, quoting John Sirois (Colville), "Spawning Hope," *The Spokesman-Review*, July 27, 2014, https://www.spokesman.com/stories/2014/jul/27/spawning -hope/.

2. Kit Oldham, "Columbia Plateau Tribes Rebury the Ancient One (Kennewick Man) on February 18, 2017," History Link, November 21, 2020, accessed March 18, 2014, https://historylink.org/File/21141.

3. Laurie Arnold and Miki'ala Ayau Pescaia, "Considering the Revolution: Indigenous Histories and Memory in Alaska, Hawai'i, and the Indigenous Plateau," *The Public Historian* 43, no. 4 (2021): 7–20.

4. "History of the Confederated Tribes of the Colville Reservation," Colville Confederated Tribes, accessed March 22, 2024, https://www.cct-fnw.com/ct-fish-history.

5. Christine Quintasket to Lucullus McWhorter, December 23, 1929, cage 55, box 46, folder 444, Lucullus Virgil McWhorter Papers, Manuscripts, Archives, and Special Collections, Washington State University Libraries (hereafter McWhorter Papers).

6. "The Sons of Beaver and Coyote," story 19, original copy of casting of Mourning Dove's Legends, 1914–1922, n.d., cage 55, box 45, folder 433, McWhorter Papers, 1.

7. Quintasket to McWhorter, November 30, 1918, cage 55, box 46, folder 444, McWhorter Papers.

8. Quintasket to McWhorter, June 8, 1930, cage 55, box 46, folder 444, McWhorter Papers.

9. "A Song for the Horse Nation," American Indian, accessed April 15, 2024, https://americanindian.si.edu /exhibitions/horsenation/index.html.

10. *Horse Race*, ca. 1910, Frank S. Matsura Image Collection, Manuscripts, Archives, and Special Collections, Washington State University Libraries, accessed April 1, 2024, https://content.libraries.wsu.edu/digital/collection /matsura/id/388/rec/1.

11. Eve Darian-Smith, *New Capitalists: Law, Politics, and Identity Surrounding Casino Gaming on Native American Land* (Boston: Cengage Learning, 2003), 57.

12. LeAnne Howe, *Miko Kings: An Indian Baseball Story* (San Francisco: Aunt Lute Books, 2007), 40–41, 43.

13. Charlie Vascellaro, "The Real Indians of Baseball," *American Indian* 13, no. 2 (Summer 2012), accessed April 10, 2024, https://www.americanindianmagazine.org/story /real-indians-baseball.

14. Cary Rosenbaum, "The Ghost: How the Epic Story of One Colville Indian Died with Him," *Tribal Tribune*, September 16, 2016, accessed April 15, 2024, https://www .tribaltribune.com/sports/article_e9574a56-7c3c-11e6-8596 -abe87f39c595.html

15. Chad S. Hamill, *Songs of Power and Prayer in the Columbia Plateau: The Jesuit, the Medicine Man, and the Indian Hymn Singer* (Corvallis: Oregon State University Press, 2012).

16. Anishinaabe writer and scholar Gerald Vizenor reframed this term to represent Native American ways of survival and resistance of colonialism. See *Survivance: Narratives of Native Presence* (Lincoln: University of Nebraska Press, 2008) and *Manifest Manners: Narratives on Postindian Survivance* (Lincoln: Bison Books/University of Nebraska Press, 1999).

17. John Troutman, *Indian Blues: American Indians and the Politics of Music, 1879–1934* (Norman: University of Oklahoma Press, 2012); "Musicians," The United States

World War One Centennial Commission, accessed April 18, 2024, https://www.worldwar1centennial.org/index.php /american-indians-in-ww1-branches-of-service/american -indians-in-ww1-branch-musicians.html.

18. Laurie Arnold and Paul G. Wapato, "Paschal Sherman: Blue Jay, Ph.D," in *"Our Cause Will Ultimately Triumph": Profiles in American Indian Sovereignty*, ed. Tim Alan Garrison (Durham, NC: Carolina Academic Press, 2014), 65–75.

Frank Matsura's Coyote Photography: Between Settler Colonialism and Native Survivance

1. The Syilx/Okanagan people of the province of British Columbia and the Okanogan Band of the Confederated Tribes of the Colville Reservation in Washington State historically were one larger nation that is now separated by the 49th parallel between Canada and the United States.

2. On Matsura's radical difference from American West photography and studio portraiture, respectively, see Glen Mimura, "A Dying West? Reimagining the Frontier in Frank Matsura's Photography, 1903–1913," *American Quarterly* 62, no. 3 (2010): 687–716; and ShiPu Wang, "Going 'Native' in an American Borderland: Frank S. Matsura's Photographic Miscegenation," in *The Other American Moderns: Matsura, Ishigaki, Noda, Hayakawa* (University Park: Pennsylvania State University Press, 2017).

3. Wang, *The Other American Moderns*, 4.

4. Mimura, "A Dying West?," 692–96.

5. Zane Grey, *The Vanishing American* (New York: Harper and Brothers Publishers, 1925), 308.

6. Michael Holloman, Curator's Introduction, *Frank S. Matsura: Portraits from the Borderland* exhibition at the Northwest Museum of Arts and Culture, Spokane, WA, April 29, 2023–June 9, 2024.

7. Gerald Vizenor, *Manifest Manners: Narratives on Postindian Survivance* (Lincoln: Bison Books/University of Nebraska Press, 1999), vii.

8. "Our Mr. Matsura: A Japanese Immigrant Photographer in the Borderlands," panel event at Northwest Museum of Arts and Culture, Spokane, WA, March 14, 2024.

9. Mourning Dove (Humishuma), *Coyote Stories* (Caldwell, ID: The Caxton Printers, Ltd., 1933), 7.

10. Wendell George, *Coyote Finishes the People*, 2nd ed. (Scotts Valley, CA: self-published, 2012), 4.

11. Wang, *The Other American Moderns*.

12. The stamp camera is a subset of multiplying cameras, according to expert Rob Niederman and the California Museum of Photography in Riverside.

13. Masao Adachi, interview by Jasper Sharp, *Midnight Eye: Visions of Japanese Cinema*, August 21, 2007, http:// www.midnighteye.com/interviews/masao-adachi.

14. Joseph Bruchac, *The Dreams of Jesse Brown* (Austin, TX: Cold Mountain Press, 1978).

15. George, *Coyote Finishes the People*.

16. George, *Coyote Finishes the People*, 30.

Photography, Play, and Dissonant Seeing

1. The original Japanese pronunciation of his family name in Hirado is Matsura, distinct and unique from the more common pronunciation of the same name that uses a long vowel of *u*, spelled in the Roman alphabet as Matsuura. In this respect, he had a modified Anglophone spelling to capture the regionally distinct sound by dropping the double *u*.

2. Printed on Matsura's business card, reproduced in *Frank S. Matsura: A Scrapbook*, ed. Georgene Fitzgerald (Okanogan, WA: Okanogan County Historical Society, 2007), 55.

3. It is worth highlighting because Kimura Kunaji, who baptized Frank, had been a student of Shimooka, learning photography. This is one of the associative links between Matsura and photography that have been suggested.

4. Maki Fukuoka, "Selling Portrait Photographs: Early Photographic Business in Asakusa, Japan," *History of Photography* 35, no. 4 (November 2011): 355–73, and "'The Fluidity of Representation: Early Photographs, Asakusa, and Kabuki," in *Portraiture and Early Studio Photography in China and Japan*, ed. Luke Gartlan and Roberta Wue (London: Routledge, 2017), 159–72.

5. Diary of Frank Sakae Matsura, in private collection.

6. Fukushima Kanako, "Meiji kokkakyōiku wo meguru shikaku media riyō: 'Shūshin' gentō no henkan wo chūshin ni," in *Eizōgaku* 107 (2022): 60–83. See also Lewis Bremner, "The Transformation of Magic Lantern Technology in Nineteenth Century Japan," in *Reopening the Opening of Japan*, ed. Lewis Bremner, Manimporok Dotulong, and

Sho Konishi (Leiden, The Netherlands: Brill, 2023), doi: https://doi.org/10.1163/9789004685208_008.

7. Diary of Frank Sakae Matsura, in private collection.

8. Richard M. Reitan, *Making a Moral Society: Ethics and the State in Meiji Japan* (Honolulu: University of Hawai'i Press, 2010).

9. Frank Matsura, "Education of the Japanese Women," *Okanogan Record*, March 31, 1905.

10. For a close reading of the significance of the blanket/robe Matsura is wearing, see ShiPu Wang, "Going 'Native' in an American Borderland: Frank S. Matsura's Photographic Miscegenation," *Trans Asia Photography* 5, no. 1 (Fall 2014), https://quod.lib.umich.edu/t/tap/7977573 .0005.103?view=text;rgn=main.

11. The origin of Kabuki theater is attributed to Okuni, a woman dancer in the early seventeenth century. In 1629, the feudal authority banned all women from acting in this theater, which led to men performing the roles of women.

12. Both of them feature as one of Matsura's many frequent sitters. According to the information provided on the WSU database, they traveled to Chicago often for educational purposes.

13. Indeed, although I do not have space to expand on this relationship here, it is worth noting that film historian Tom Gunning's conceptualization of early cinema through "cinema of attraction" provides a way to understand quality with Matsura's staged images. See Tom Gunning, "The Cinema of Attractions: Early Film, Its Spectator and the Avant-Garde," in *Early Cinema: Space, Frame, Narrative,* ed. Thomas Elsaesser (London: British Film Institute, 1990), 56–63; and "Attractions: How They Came into the World," in *The Cinema of Attractions Reloaded,* ed. Wanda Strauven (Amsterdam: Amsterdam University Press, 2006), 31–39.

14. I am indebted to Barry George, a volunteer at Okanogan County Historical Society, for his generosity in sharing materials and knowledge; Barry George, "Uncovering Our Past: From a Harness Shop to Theater," *Okanogan County Heritage* 60, no. 2 (2022): 2–8.

"Matsura Did Them Right"

1. Edward S. Curtis, *The North American Indian* (Boston: Charles E. Lauriat, 1935).

2. Rod Slemmons, *Shadowy Evidence: The Photography of Edward S. Curtis and His Contemporaries* (Seattle: Seattle Art Museum, 1989).

3. Georgene Fitzgerald, interview by Beth Harrington, at Davis Ranch, Brewster, WA, October 2022, video, *Our Mr. Matsura* film archives. Beth Harrington Productions, Vancouver, WA.

4. O. H. Woody, "A Saga of Old Conconully in Her Heyday," *Okanogan Independent,* August 13, 1944, 2.

5. Georgene Fitzgerald, ed., *Frank S. Matsura: A Scrapbook* (Okanogan, WA: Okanogan County Historical Society, 2007).

6. Fitzgerald interview.

7. Randy Lewis, interview by Beth Harrington, at Paschal Sherman Indian School, Omak, WA, October 22, 2022, video, *Our Mr. Matsura* film archives. Beth Harrington Productions, Vancouver, WA.

8. Lewis interview.

9. Lewis interview.

10. Lewis interview.

11. Lewis interview.

12. Lewis interview.

13. Lewis interview.

14. Lewis interview.

15. Lewis interview.

16. Lewis interview.

17. Lynn Palmanteer-Holder, interview by Beth Harrington, at Okanogan County Historical Society, Okanogan, WA, October 13, 2023, video, *Our Mr. Matsura* film archives. Beth Harrington Productions, Vancouver, WA.

18. Palmanteer-Holder interview.

19. Palmanteer-Holder interview.

20. Palmanteer-Holder interview.

21. Palmanteer-Holder interview.

22. Palmanteer-Holder interview.

23. Wendell George, interview by Beth Harrington, at Okanogan County Historical Society, Okanogan, WA, December 17, 2021, video, *Our Mr. Matsura* film archives Beth Harrington Productions, Vancouver, WA.

24. Wendell George, *Last Chief Standing: A Tale of Two Cultures* (self-published, 2012), 73.

25. George interview.

26. George interview.

27. George interview.

28. George interview.

29. Julia Dolan, interview by Beth Harrington, at Video Is the Future Studio, Portland, OR, October 28, 2021, video, *Our Mr. Matsura* film archives Beth Harrington Productions, Vancouver, WA.

30. Dolan interview.

31. Michael Maslan, interview by Beth Harrington, at Michael Maslan Vintage Posters Photographs Postcards & Ephemera, Seattle, WA, September 11, 2023, video, *Our Mr. Matsura* film archives Beth Harrington Productions, Vancouver, WA.

32. Jason Benjamin, interview by Beth Harrington, at Benjamin home, Lake Tapps, WA, September 10, 2023, video, *Our Mr. Matsura* film archives Beth Harrington Productions, Vancouver, WA..

33. Benjamin interview.

34. Benjamin interview.

35. Mabel Wagner Schurle, "A Small History of My Family," *Okanogan County Heritage* 38, no. 3 (June 2000): 19.

36. Schurle, "A Small History of My Family."

37. Schurle, "A Small History of My Family."

38. Schurle, "A Small History of My Family."

39. Lynn Palmanteer-Holder, interview by Beth Harrington, at Okanogan County Historical Society, Okanogan, WA, October 13, 2023, video, *Our Mr. Matsura* film archives. Beth Harrington Productions, Vancouver, WA.

Conclusion

1. Peter Selz, *Art of Engagement: Visual Politics in California and Beyond* (Los Angeles: University of California Press, 2006), 164.

Credits

All images are by Frank S. Matsura unless otherwise noted.

Okanogan County Historical Society (OCHS): pages 2, 6, 11, 17, 21, 23, 26, 28 top and bottom, 31 top and bottom, 33, 36, 38, 39 top (courtesy Frank DeVos, Gresham, Oregon), 43, 46, 47, 68, 79 bottom, 89 left and right, 92 top and middle, 101 left and right, 103 all, 105, 106, 110, 114 top and bottom, 119, 120, 121 left and right, 123 top and bottom, 124, 126, 127, 128, 136, 137 top, 139, 141, 142, 143, 144, 145, 146, 147, 148, 149, 150, 151, 152, 153, 154, 155, 156, 157, 158, 168. Captions have been adapted from the Frank S. Matsura glass plate; film and print collection at the Okanogan County Historical Society, where information was recorded on storage sleeves of the images.

Frank S. Matsura Collection (FMC) at Washington State University Libraries' Manuscripts, Archives, and Special Collections (MASC): pages 8, 12, 15 bottom, 18, 20, 25 top and bottom, 29 top and bottom, 39 bottom, 40, 48, 51, 53, 54, 55, 57, 58, 59, 61, 62 left and right, 63, 65, 66 top and bottom, 69, 70 top and bottom, 72 left and right, 73, 74 top and bottom, 75, 76 all, 79 top, 81, 82, 87, 90, 92 bottom, 96, 97, 98, 102, 108, 109, 116, 137 bottom, 138, 140. Captions have been adapted from the Frank Matsura digital collection at the Washington State University Libraries' Manuscripts, Archives, and Special Collections (MASC), where they were originally researched and created by Mari Hillestad.

Library of Congress Prints and Photographs Division: page 15 top left

Wisconsin Historical Society: page 15 top right

James Earl Fraser and Laura Gardin Fraser Studio Papers, Dickinson Research Center, National Cowboy & Western Heritage Museum, 68.001: page 16

Nora Cole, photographer: page 125

Matsura postcard: pages 130, 133

Beth Harrington, photographer: page 131

CONTRIBUTOR BIOGRAPHIES

Michael Holloman is an enrolled member of the Colville Confederated Tribes and an associate professor in the Department of Art at Washington State University (WSU). He teaches undergraduate and graduate courses in Native American art history and the studio arts, while maintaining duties for the department as the drawing coordinator. In 2010 he arrived at WSU as the director of the Plateau Center for American Indian Studies. Previously, he was the director of American Indian exhibitions, collection management, and educational programming at the Northwest Museum of Arts and Culture in Spokane. He began his professional career at Seattle University as an assistant professor in the fine arts department. He continues to paint and exhibit his artwork.

Laurie Arnold is an enrolled citizen of the Sinixt Band of the Colville Confederated Tribes. She is a professor of history, director of Native American Studies, and a former Robert K. and Ann J. Powers Chair of the Humanities at Gonzaga University. Her book, *Bartering with the Bones of Their Dead: The Colville Confederated Tribes and Termination*, was published by the University of Washington Press in 2012. Her scholarship includes Colville author Mourning Dove, the Indigenous Columbia Plateau, and Indian gaming; her current research considers how contemporary Native American playwrights are using theater to tell Native narratives of the past and present.

Glen Mimura is an associate professor of film and media studies and affiliated professor of Asian American studies at the University of California, Irvine. He is the author of *Ghostlife of Third Cinema: Asian American Film and Video* (University of Minnesota Press, 2009), and he is currently writing a book on the films and martial arts career of Bruce Lee.

Maki Fukuoka first moved to a farm in Pryor, Oklahoma, as a high school exchange student. She then moved to Tucson and finished her BA at the University of Arizona. She completed her MA and PhD in art history at the University of Chicago. She then taught at the University of Michigan until she relocated to Leeds, UK, in 2012. Having moved almost every three years throughout childhood, often challenged by dialects, foreign languages, and customs, she has grown familiar with finding a way around an unfamiliar place through experiment, trial, and error. She continues to explore such modes of knowledge production in research and teaching activities.

Beth Harrington is an Emmy-winning, Grammy-nominated filmmaker whose work most often focuses on American history, music, art, and culture. Harrington has worked with public television stations WGBH Boston and Oregon Public Broadcasting Portland producing, directing, and developing shows for national and local air on series such as *Nova*, *Frontline*, *History Detectives*, *Oregon Art Beat*, and *Oregon Experience*. She holds a BA in public communications from Syracuse University and an MA in American studies from University of Massachusetts Boston. She is the producer and director of the feature documentary *Our Mr. Matsura*.

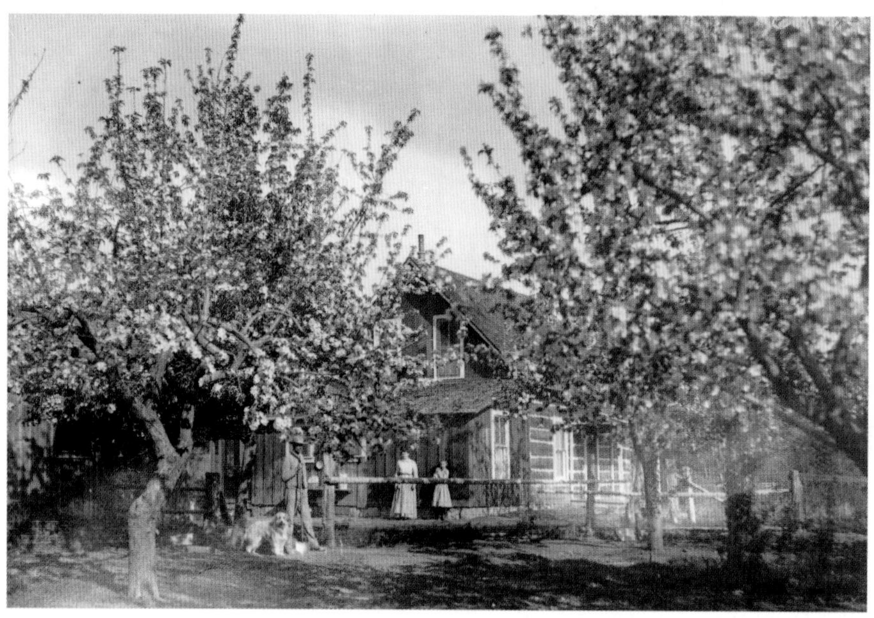

The J. S. White Home Surrounded by a Mature Orchard Blooming, ca. 1909

Published by
Princeton Architectural Press
A division of Chronicle Books LLC
70 West 36th Street, New York, NY 10018
papress.com

Editor: Lynn Grady
Designer: Paul Wagner

Library of Congress Cataloging-in-Publication Data
Names: Holloman, Michael, 1961- editor.
Title: Frank S. Matsura : iconoclast photographer of the American West / edited by Michael Holloman.
Description: First edition. | New York : Princeton Architectural Press, [2025] | Summary: "The compelling Native American portraiture and works of Frank S. Matsura, with a look into his unique personal life"—Provided by publisher.
Identifiers: LCCN 2024047834 | ISBN 9781797232812 | ISBN 9781797232829 (ebook)
Subjects: LCSH: Matsura, Frank, 1873-1913. | Colville Indians—Biography—20th century—Portraits. | Japanese Americans—Washington (State)—Okanogan County—Biography. | Photographers—Washington (State)—Okanogan County—Biography. | Okanogan County (Wash.)—Portraits.
Classification: LCC TR140.M37 F73 2025 | DDC 779/.9979728041 [B]—dc23/eng/20241227
LC record available at https://lccn.loc.gov/2024047834